R. Gupta's®

POPULAR

English Grammar *for* Competitions

by
Sanjay Kumar
M.A., LL.B., PGDPM & I.R.

&

RPH EDITORIAL BOARD

Ramesh Publishing House, New Delhi

Published by
O.P. Gupta *for* Ramesh Publishing House

Admin. Office
12-H, New Daryaganj Road, Opp. Officers' Mess,
New Delhi-110002 ℐ 23261567, 23275224, 23275124

E-mail: info@rameshpublishinghouse.com
Website: www.rameshpublishinghouse.com

Showroom
● Balaji Market, Nai Sarak, Delhi-6 ℐ 23253720, 23282525
● 4457, Nai Sarak, Delhi-6, ℐ 23918938

Book Code: R-938

19th Edition: Printed in February, 2020

ISBN: 978-93-86298-70-6

HSN Code: 49011010

CONTENTS

ENGLISH GRAMMAR
for COMPETITIONS

BASIC RULES WITH ILLUSTRATIONS

NOUN

- **Singular in form but plural in use :** Some nouns are singular in form but they are used as plurals.
  Poultry, Peasantry, People, Clergy, Cattle, Gentry, Infantry, Nobility, etc.

  Illustration: | People | | are | gathering in a meeting.

- **Plural in form but singular in use :** Some nouns are plural in form but they are used as singulars.
  Politics, News, Summons, Gallows, Innings, etc.

  Illustration: This | news | | is | not true (✓)

- **A list of such nouns which remain plural all the time :** Athletics, Alms, Archives, Amends, Ashes, Auspices, Annals, Arrears, Billards, Binoculars, Bellows, Braces, Bowels, Cards, Curds, Customs, Congratulations, Earnings Embers, Funds, Fireworks, Glasses, Guts, Lees, Mumps, Measles, Odds, Out skirts, Pioneers, Particulars, Regards, Seals, Scissors, Spectacles, Stairs, Troops, Trousers, Tactics, Victuals, Wages, etc.

- **Nouns in the same form in both Numbers :** Such nouns are used in both numbers i.e., singular number and plural number.
  Deer, Sheep, Yoke, Gross, Public, Japanese, Means, etc.

- **A list of such nouns which remain singular all the time :** Scenery, Offspring, Furniture, Information.

All About Noun and Number

Formation of Plural Noun from Singular Noun

- A noun
  (i) ending with 'y'
  (ii) preceded by a consonant.

  Illustration: C I (T) (Y) = Noun.

  [Here 'T' is consonant.]

Rule of Transformation

(i) Change 'Y' into 'i' → CIT(I)

(ii) Add 'es' ———→ CITI(ES)

(Hence Plural of city is cities.)

- A noun ending with 's'/'ch'/'sh'/'x'.
  Illustration: GLAS(S) = Noun
  Rule of Transformation : Add 'es' only. → GLASS +(ES)= GLASS(ES).
- A noun ending with 'f'/'fe'
  Illustration: WI(FE) = Noun
  Rule of Transformation :

  (i) Omit 'f'/'fe' → WI

  (ii) Insert 'ves' → WI(VES)
- A noun ending with 'o'
  Illustration: HER(O) = Noun
  Rule of Transformation : Add 'es' only → HERO +(ES) = HERO(ES).
- **Nouns having different meaning in singular and plural forms :** While transforming a noun from singular number to plural number, its meaning also changes.
  Illustration: Advice (Sing. No.) means counsel.

  Advice (S) (Pl. No.) means information.
- However, the general conception is to make a noun in Plural number from Singular number we have to add 's' only.
  Illustration: Orange [Noun is singular number]
  Rule of Transformation : Add 's' only → ORANGE (+S)= ORANGES.

All About Noun and Gender

Formation of Feminine Gender from Masculine Gender

- By adding 'ess'/'trix'/'a'/'sne' etc.

SI. No.	Masculine gender	Feminine gender
1.	Lion	Lioness
2.	Poet	Poetess
3.	Host	Hostess
4.	Author	Authoress
5.	Patron	Patroness
6.	Heir	Heiress

Note: A word which is considered as noun may be in the form of either masculine gender or feminine gender. So, the nature of noun can be shown in the form of gender.

- **Placement of a word before or after Noun**

SI. No.	Masculine gender	Feminine gender
1.	Servant	Maid-servant
2.	He-goat	She-goat
3.	Cock-sparrow	Hen-sparrow
4.	Milkman	Milkmaid
5.	Washerman	Washerwoman
6.	Landlord	Landlady

- **A masculine noun containing vowel**

Illustration: A C T O R
→ VOWEL

Rule of Transformation :

(i)   Omission of vowel → ACTR

(ii) Add 'ess' → ACTR (+ ESS)

(Hence feminine gender of Actor is Actress.)

- While changing into feminine gender of a noun no specific rule will be applied in some nouns.

SI. No.	Masculine gender	Feminine gender
1.	Father	Mother
2.	Horse	Mare
3.	Wizard	Witch
4.	Bachelor	Maid
5.	Dog	Bitch
6.	Monk	Nun
7.	Brother	Sister
8.	Drone	Bee
9.	Drake	Duck
10.	Buck	Doe

JUDGE YOURSELF

In the following questions choose the correct option to fill the blank.

1. There are not many .... in your town.
   (*a*) gentries (*b*) gentry
   (*c*) (*a*) and (*b*) (*d*) any of these

2. Don't write ....
   (*a*) 3's like 8's (*b*) 3s like 8s
   (*c*) (*a*) and (*b*) (*d*) any of these

3. I gave him ....
   (*a*) three and a half rupees
   (*b*) three rupees and a half
   (*c*) (*a*) and (*b*)
   (*d*) any of these

4. What are the .... of this place doing?
   (*a*) people (*b*) peoples
   (*c*) pupils (*d*) any of these

5. Whose .... are these?
   (*a*) poultries
   (*b*) poultry
   (*c*) (*a*) or (*b*)
   (*d*) (*a*) and (*b*) both

6. Is it a .... college?
   (*a*) girls'
   (*b*) girl's
   (*c*) (*a*) or (*b*)
   (*d*) (*a*) and (*b*) both

7. It is ....
   (*a*) nice poetry
   (*b*) a nice poem
   (*c*) a nice poetry
   (*d*) (*a*) and (*b*) both

8. Rishav is looking for a good ....
   (*a*) job

   (*b*) employment
   (*c*) either (*a*) or (*b*)
   (*d*) both (*a*) and (*b*)

9. Slow and steady .... the race.
   (*a*) wins
   (*b*) win
   (*c*) either (*a*) or (*b*)
   (*d*) both (*a*) and (*b*)

10. The road is under ....
    (*a*) repairs
    (*b*) repair
    (*c*) either (*a*) or (*b*)
    (*d*) both (*a*) and (*d*)

11. I do no like the .... of cricket.
    (*a*) game
    (*b*) play
    (*c*) either (*a*) or (*b*)
    (*d*) both (*a*) and (*b*)

12. The earthquake caused ....
    (*a*) many damages
    (*b*) much damage
    (*c*) only (*a*)
    (*d*) all

13. One of my .... is mad.
    (*a*) friend
    (*b*) friends
    (*c*) either (*a*) or (*b*)
    (*d*) both (*a*) and (*b*)

14. Please put your .... there.
    (*a*) signature
    (*b*) sign
    (*c*) any of these
    (*d*) both (*a*) and (*b*)

15. No news .... good news.
    (*a*) were
    (*b*) was

(*c*) both (*a*) and (*b*)
(*d*) any of these

(*a*) thiefs   (*b*) theifs
(*c*) thieves   (*d*) theives

16. My .... black.
(*a*) hairs are   (*b*) hair is
(*c*) hairs shall (*d*) hair will

17. She saw two .... on the last Sunday.

18. My sister is a ....
(*a*) bacheloress
(*b*) bachelor
(*c*) unmaried
(*d*) spinster

ANSWERS

1	2	3	4	5	6	7	8	9	10
(*b*)	(*a*)	(*b*)	(*a*)	(*b*)	(*a*)	(*d*)	(*a*)	(*a*)	(*b*)

11	12	13	14	15	16	17	18
(*a*)	(*b*)	(*b*)	(*a*)	(*b*)	(*b*)	(*c*)	(*d*)

PRONOUN

- Pronoun ——agrees with——→ Antecedent **[In terms of person, number and gender.]**

Illustration: One must do one's duty (✓)

One must do his duty (×)

- **Position of Pronoun in a sentence**

(i) For good purpose

[Remember the *magic formula* 231]

Illustration: You,   he   and   I are going to Mumbai. (✓)

(2nd-P.) (3rd P.) (1st P.)   (Here, P. = Person)

② ③ ①

I, You and he are going to Mumbai. (×)

(ii) For bad purpose

[Remember the *magic formula* 123]

Illustration: I,   You   and he should beat him. (✓)

(1st P.) (2nd P.) (3rd P.)   (Here, P. = Person)

① ② ③

You, he and I should beat him. (×)

- **Use of Personal Pronoun**

  I, we, myself etc. (Who is speaking)

  You, thou, theyself etc. (Who are spoken)

  He, she, it himself, herself etc. (Persons spoken of)

- **Use of Interrogative pronoun**

  What — in general meaning + in exclamatory sentence.

  Who, which — in special meaning.

  Illustration: What novel is that?

  Which novel do you want to purchase?

- **'Let' is used with pronoun in nominative case.**

  Illustration:

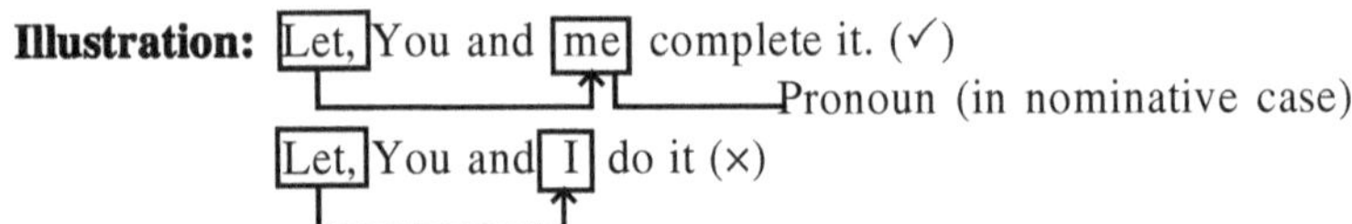

- **Use of Reflexive Pronoun**

  (a) To reveal that the person does something to himself.

  (b) For emphasising on Pronoun.

  Illustration:

  (a) I admire my own story.

  (b) I myself saw the disastrous scene.

- **Some other use of Pronoun** : My, her, his, its, your, our, their (Pronoun as well as possessive adjective)

  Position of the above said pronouns : Before the nouns with these are joined.

  Illustration:

JUDGE YOURSELF

In the following questions choose the correct option to fill the blank.

1. One is supposed to do ....
   - (a) our duty
   - (b) their duty
   - (c) one's duty
   - (d) his duty

2. Take anything .... you want.
   - (a) that
   - (b) which
   - (c) than
   - (d) then

3. I cannot tolerate ....
   - (a) separated you
   - (b) your separation
   - (c) separation from you
   - (d) you separated

4. He is .... faithful partner.
   - (a) Yours
   - (b) You
   - (c) Your
   - (d) Your's

5. Ajay is more smart than ....
   - (a) her
   - (b) hers
   - (c) herself
   - (d) she

6. Vivek works harder than ....
   - (a) me
   - (b) I
   - (c) her
   - (d) his

7. They should help ....
   (*a*) the poor people
   (*b*) the poor
   (*c*) the poor persons
   (*d*) the poor peoples

8. .... are mad.
   (*a*) All his sons (*b*) His all sons
   (*c*) Sons all his (*d*) All sons his

9. The poor fellow .... to fate.
   (*a*) resigned
   (*b*) resigned himself
   (*c*) resigned itself
   (*d*) either (*a*) or (*c*)

10. No body will help you but ....
   (*a*) I   (*b*) me
   (*c*) ours   (*d*) his

11. It is a good chance, You must avail .... this opportunity.
   (*a*) of
   (*b*) yourself of
   (*c*) for
   (*d*) from

12. The person who is elected .... my relative.
   (*a*) is   (*b*) he is
   (*c*) his   (*d*) him

13. He made ....
   (*a*) yours mention
   (*b*) mention of you
   (*c*) mention for you
   (*d*) mention about you

14. .... I know, he is quite faithful.

   (*a*) As far as   (*b*) So far as
   (*c*) So far this (*d*) So far so

15. It is a duty of a person to take .... for his family.
   (*a*) pain
   (*b*) pains
   (*c*) either (*a*) or (*b*)
   (*d*) pained

16. She does not love .... husband.
   (*a*) his   (*b*) her
   (*c*) its   (*d*) (*a*) or (*c*)

17. Let, ... work together.
   (*a*) him and me
   (*b*) he and I
   (*c*) (*a*) and (*b*) both
   (*d*) I and me

18. Copper, Silver and Gold ....
   (*a*) each will do
   (*b*) either will do
   (*c*) any one will do
   (*d*) (*a*) and (*b*) both

19. Jessica and Roma are very irregular .... habits.
   (*a*) in her   (*b*) in their
   (*c*) in its   (*d*) (*a*) or (*c*)

20. One likes to enjoy .... who was a great poet.
   (*a*) The sonnets of Shakespeare
   (*b*) Shakespeare's sonnets
   (*c*) Either (*a*) or (*b*)
   (*d*) (*a*) and (*b*)

ANSWERS

1	2	3	4	5	6	7	8	9	10
(*c*)	(*a*)	(*c*)	(*c*)	(*d*)	(*b*)	(*b*)	(*a*)	(*b*)	(*b*)

11	12	13	14	15	16	17	18	19	20
(*b*)	(*a*)	(*b*)	(*a*)	(*b*)	(*b*)	(*a*)	(*c*)	(*b*)	(*a*)

ADJECTIVE

- **In a sentence, the position of 'adjective' is before the noun.**

  Illustration: I saw a | beautiful | | picture.

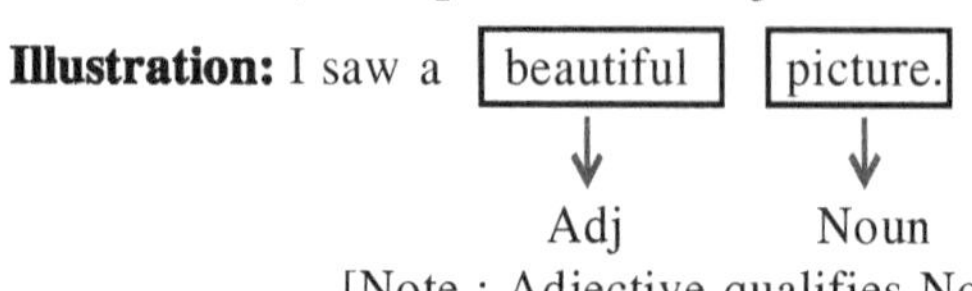

  [Note : Adjective qualifies Noun]

- **Adjective** ——denotes—→ **a group of people** then, ('the' + 1st form of Adjective) will be followed.

  Illustration: The English ——refers—→ English people.

  English ——refers—→ English language.

- **Superlative Adjective takes definite article.**

  The + Superlative Adjective

  Illustration: He is | the || best | player in Team India.

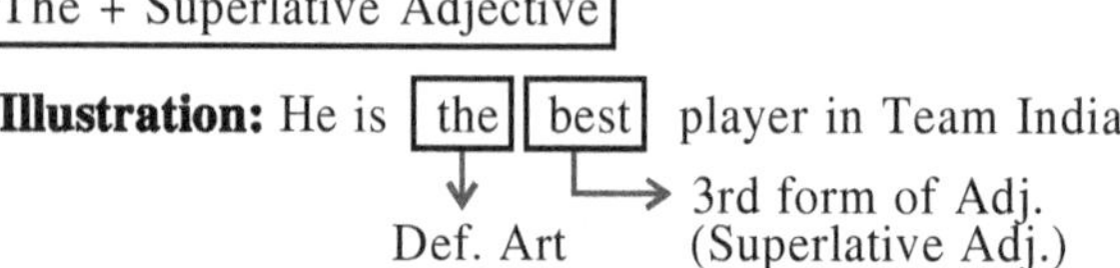

  3rd form of Adj.

  Def. Art (Superlative Adj.)

- **An Adjective which shows quality, always comes after the verb.**

  Illustration: She looked charming.

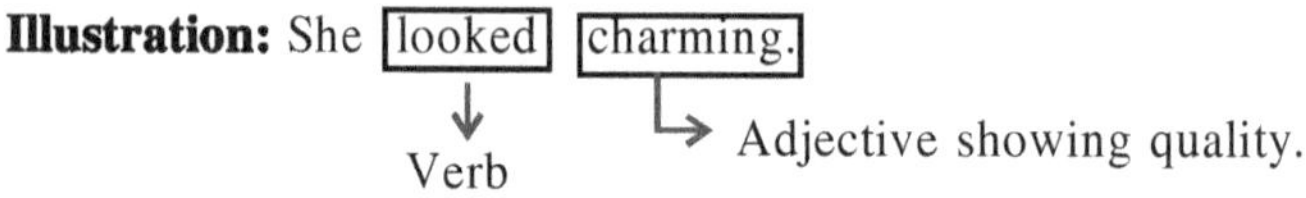

  Verb → Adjective showing quality.

- **'as...........as' ....**
  (a) Affirmative sentence, and
  (b) Positive degree of Adjective

  will be used.

  Illustration: Her sister is as clever as she is. (Aff. sent.)

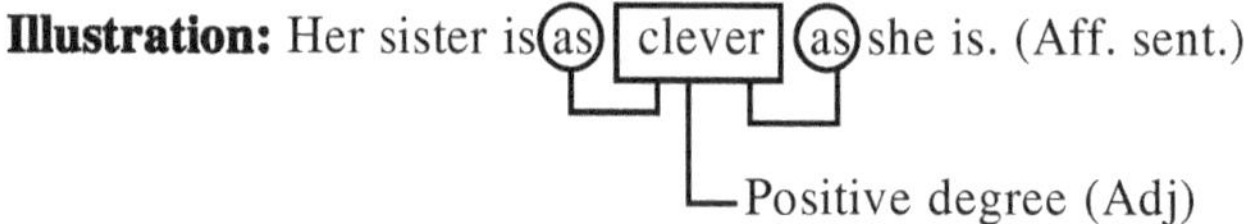

  Positive degree (Adj)

- **'not so...........as' ....**
  (a) Negative sentence, and
  (b) Positive degree of Adjective

  will be used.

  Illustration: Your curd is not so cold as mine is. (Neg. sent.)

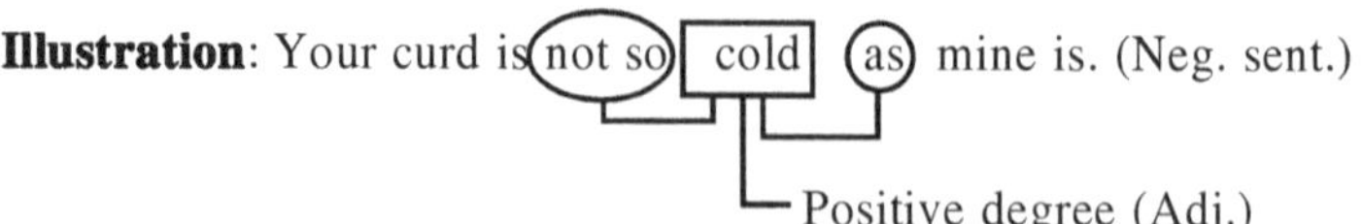

  Positive degree (Adj.)

- **In a Sentence, use of double superlative or double comparative is a blunder.**

  Illustration: The Sun is (more) (brighter) than the moon. (×)

  both are in comparative degree.

  The Sun is brighter than the moon. (✓)

- **A general conception regarding the formation of Adjective**
  (a) Adjective having one syllable can be changed in to comparative/superlative by adding 'er'/'es'.

  Illustration:

Adjective	Positive degree	Comparative degree	Superlative degree
1. Tall	Tall	Taller	Tallest
2. Short	Short	Shorter	Shortest

  (b) Adjective having three or more syllables can be changed into comparative/superlative by placing 'more'/'must' before the said adjective.

Adjective	Positive degree	Comparative degree	Superlative degree
1. Beautiful	Beautiful	More beautiful	Most beautiful
2. Brightening	Brightening	More brightening	Most brightening

- **For the purpose of comparison having different sense.**

Comparative degree	Superlative degree	Sense
elder	eldest	comparison in respect of relation
older	oldest	comparison in respect of age

  Illustration: Yashwant is my elder brother.

  I am older than you.

- **Repeatation of verb is essential when 'as'/'than' will be followed by pronoun (IIIrd-person)**

  Illustration: Kalpana (is) not *as* clever *as* (her) sister (is)

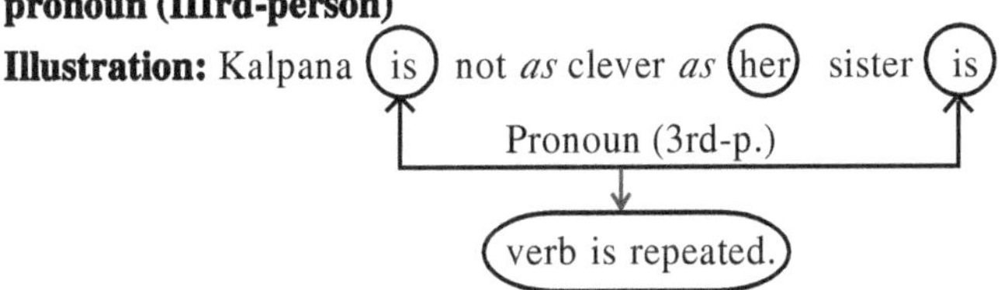

- **Omission of verb is essential when 'as'/'than' will be followed by Ist/ IInd person.**

  Illustration: She is more beautiful than (I). (✓)
  └——Ist person

  She is more beautiful than I am (×)

JUDGE YOURSELF

In the following questions choose the correct option to fill the blank.

1. The girl whom you met is the .... sister of Ravi Tanti.
(*a*) eldest   (*b*) elder
(*c*) older   (*d*) oldest

2. The historical place is ....
(*a*) seeing worth
(*b*) worthy of seeing
(*c*) worth seeing
(*d*) either (*a*) or (*b*)

3. These flowers smell ....
(*a*) sweet
(*b*) sweetly
(*c*) more sweetly
(*d*) either (*b*) or (*c*)

4. .... aspirant can not pass the UPSC examination.
(*a*) Each   (*b*) Every
(*c*) All   (*d*) No.

5. Harivansh Rai .... second Shakespeare.
(*a*) is a
(*b*) is
(*c*) the
(*d*) either (*b*) or (*c*)

6. .... student in the class got prizes.
(*a*) Each and every
(*b*) Every and each
(*c*) Every
(*d*) Never

7. It is .... picture than the one we saw last Monday.
(*a*) interesting
(*b*) much interesting
(*c*) more interesting
(*d*) either (*a*) or (*b*)

8. She is clever ....
(*a*) that her mother is
(*b*) as her mother is
(*c*) so her mother is
(*d*) none

9. They will get ....
(*a*) Red, green and black paper
(*b*) Red, green black paper
(*c*) Red and green and black paper
(*d*) Either (*b*) or (*c*)

10. Health is .... wealth.
(*a*) preferable to
(*b*) more preferable than
(*c*) more preferable to
(*d*) most preferable then

11. .... water that was in the jug evaporated.
(*a*) Little   (*b*) The little
(*c*) Small   (*d*) A small

12. He has not sung .... songs.
(*a*) much   (*b*) most
(*c*) more   (*d*) many

13. Srishti has searched .... office.
    (*a*) whole the (*b*) the whole
    (*c*) a whole (*d*) some whole
14. K.R. Dhiraj was .... best and
    .... famous writer.
    (*a*) a, the most (*b*) the, a most
    (*c*) the, more (*d*) the, the most
15. Willam Shakespeare is famous as
    ....
    (*a*) a poet and a dramatist
    (*b*) a poet and dramatist
    (*c*) the poet and the dramatist
    (*d*) either (*a*) or (*c*)
16. What does .... leader suggest?
    (*a*) other (*b*) another
    (*c*) others (*d*) anothers
17. He .... money
    (*a*) has, few (*b*) have, few
    (*c*) has, little (*d*) have, little
18. The .... boys are rewarded.
    (*a*) first two (*b*) two first
    (*c*) firsts two (*d*) two's first
19. He is .... brave.
    (*a*) stronger than
    (*b*) stronger then
    (*c*) more strong then
    (*d*) more strong than

ANSWERS

1	2	3	4	5	6	7	8	9	10
(*a*)	(*c*)	(*a*)	(*b*)	(*a*)	(*c*)	(*c*)	(*c*)	(*a*)	(*a*)

11	12	13	14	15	16	17	18	19
(*b*)	(*d*)	(*b*)	(*d*)	(*b*)	(*b*)	(*c*)	(*a*)	(*d*)

AGREEMENT BETWEEN SUBJECT & VERB

- **There is a close relation between subject and verb of a sentence.**
- **Showing the relationship between the two, we have a general conception**

$$S - S : P - P$$

i.e. (a) Singular subject requires singular verb.
    (b) Plural subject requires plural verb.

Illustration:

(a) He performs well in examination.

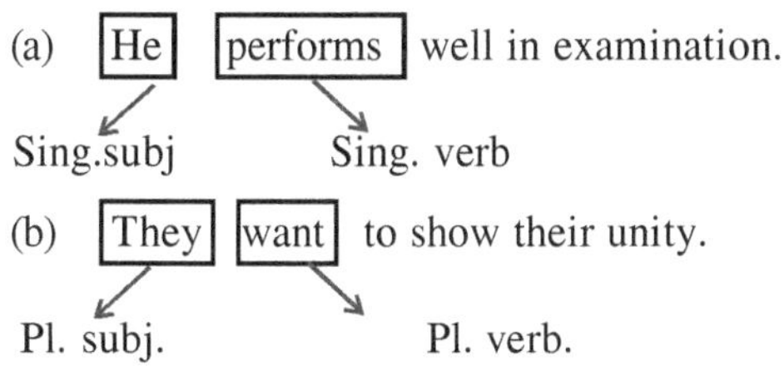

Sing.subj   Sing. verb

(b) They want to show their unity.

Pl. subj.   Pl. verb.

Here, Sing. = Singular
      Pl.   = Plural

Note : Sing. Subj. means a subject in its original form without containing s/es, while sing verb means a verb which contains s/es in its original form.

I, he, she, it, name of any thing (Cow, Apple, Boy, ...)— Sing. subj. want + s = **wants**, perform + s = **performs** — sing. verb.

- Pl. subject means a subject which contains s/es in its original form while Pl. verb means a verb in its original form without containing s/es.
  They, we, name of anything (Cow+s = Cows, Apple+s = Apples,....)
  └─Pl. subj.

want, perform, go, think — Pl. verb.

Exceptions to Common Conception

- **If a sentence reveals condition/wish/supposition then plural verb is used for singular subject.**

  Illustration: I wish | I | were | a top writer.

  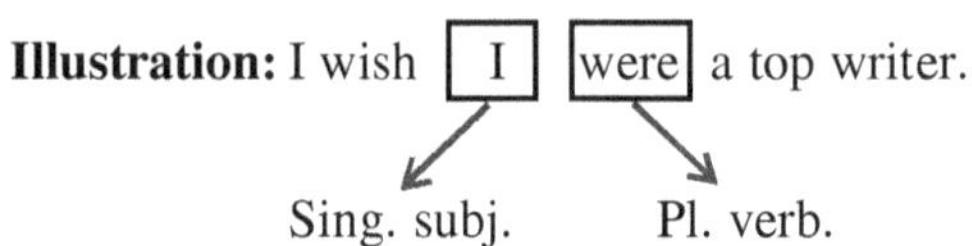

- **'Dare not'/'Need not' takes singular subject, however those are in plural form.**
  Illustration: He dare not oppose me.

Some Keys

Singular Collective Noun + of + Plural Noun

This type of structure in a sentence take singular verb.

Illustration: A group of students has been   selected

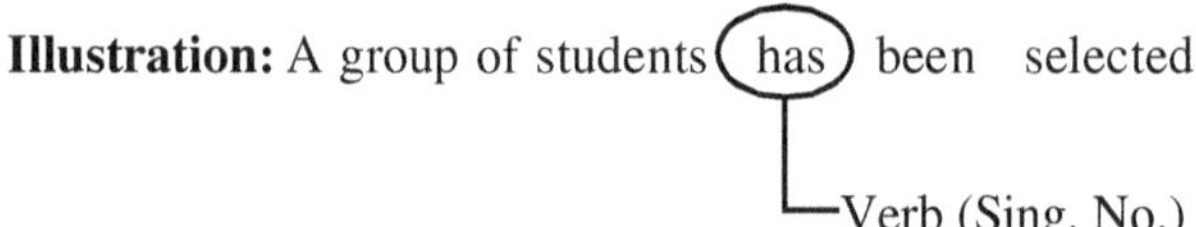

- **If weight/measure/distance/amount is shown by a subject then singular verb will be used. However, subject may be in plural form.**

  Illustration: Ten miles is   a long distance to walk.

  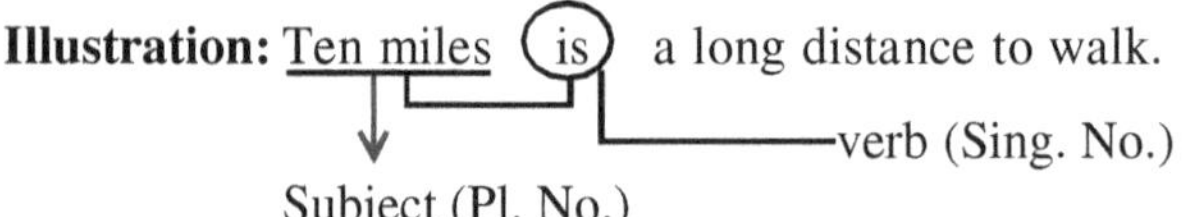

- **Singular Verb with Names/Titles**
  Illustration: The United states of America is a powerful country.

- **In modern age, names of sports/country/state etc. used in plural sense. So, use of plural verb is not wrong.**
  Illustration: India have won the match.

JUDGE YOURSELF

In the following questions choose the correct option to fill the blank.

1. The bus with all its passengers .... lost.
(*a*) were
(*b*) was
(*c*) are
(*d*) either (*a*) or (*c*)

2. You as well as I .... responsible for this work.
(*a*) am
(*b*) are
(*c*) was
(*d*) either (*a*) or (*c*)

3. Raghava like all his companions .... a spoiled child.
(*a*) are
(*b*) were
(*c*) is
(*d*) either (*a*) or (*b*)

4. Pen and ink .... required for me.
(*a*) are
(*b*) were
(*c*) is
(*d*) either (*a*) or (*b*)

5. Every girl and every boy .... attended the seminar.
(*a*) have   (*b*) has
(*c*) is   (*d*) are

6. Not only she but all her sisters .... been married.
(*a*) has   (*b*) have
(*c*) is   (*d*) are

7. There .... nothing but miseries in life.
(*a*) is
(*b*) are
(*c*) were
(*d*) either (*b*) or (*c*)

8. Neither prose nor poem .... given.
(*a*) were
(*b*) was
(*c*) not required any word
(*d*) either (*a*) or (*b*)

9. Either he or I .... wrong.
(*a*) is
(*b*) are
(*c*) am
(*d*) Either (*a*) or (*b*)

10. Either Sulekha or Rekha .... coming here.
(*a*) are
(*b*) is
(*c*) were
(*d*) either (*a*) or (*c*)

11. .... the child or his parents to blame?
(*a*) Is
(*b*) Are
(*c*) Were
(*d*) Either (*b*) or (*c*)

12. You and I .... neighbours.
(*a*) am
(*b*) are
(*c*) was
(*d*) either (a) or (*c*)

13. The house with all its belongings .... sold away.
(*a*) were   (*b*) are
(*c*) was   (*d*) no word

14. Either water or juice .... required.
    (*a*) is
    (*b*) are
    (*c*) were
    (*d*) no word

15. There were not as many tables as .... required.
    (*a*) was
    (*b*) were
    (*c*) is
    (*d*) either (*a*) or (*c*)

16. They each .... a book.
    (*a*) have   (*b*) are
    (*c*) has   (*d*) is

17. He and I .... class friends.
    (*a*) is   (*b*) am
    (*c*) was   (*d*) are

18. She as well as I .... guilty.
    (*a*) is
    (*b*) are
    (*c*) am
    (*d*) either (*b*) or (*c*)

19. Purushottam .... not read more on this chaper.
    (*a*) needs
    (*b*) has been need
    (*c*) need
    (*d*) had been need

ANSWERS

1	2	3	4	5	6	7	8	9	10
(*b*)	(*b*)	(*c*)	(*c*)	(*b*)	(*b*)	(*a*)	(*b*)	(*c*)	(*b*)

11	12	13	14	15	16	17	18	19
(*a*)	(*b*)	(*c*)	(*a*)	(*b*)	(*a*)	(*d*)	(*a*)	(*c*)

ADVERB

- **Probably and Perhaps :** Probably means most likely.
  Perhaps means possibly.

Illustration:

Where is Aishwarya? Probably she is not at class (✓)

Where is Aishwarya? Perhaps she is not at class (✗)

- **Hardly and Scarcely :** Hardly or scarcely is followed by When

Illustration:

Scarcely had they reached the station when she saw them.

- **Too :** Meaning of this word is 'more than enough' and it is used in the process of comparison.

  Illustration: She is too hungry to eat.

- **Not :** This adverb will not be used with a word having negative sense.

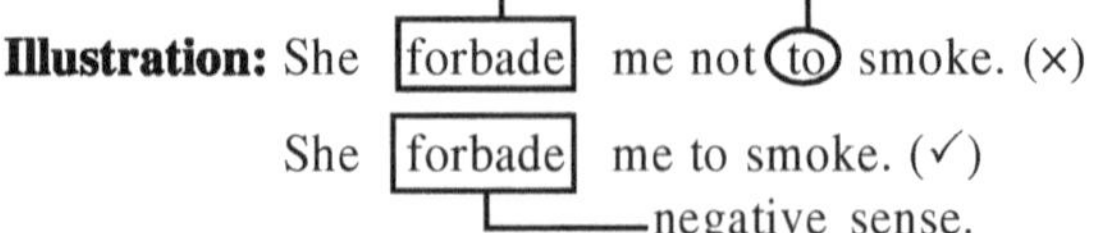

Illustration: She | forbade | me not to smoke. (✗)

She | forbade | me to smoke. (✓)

negative sense.

- **Else :** It is followed by 'but' only.

  Illustration: It is nothing else but a joke ($\checkmark$)

  It is nothing else than a joke. ($\times$)

- **Some words are used before the qualifying verb :** i.e. never, often, ever, seldom, always and generally etc.

  Illustration: Srishti never gazed at him ($\checkmark$)

  Srishti gazed at him never. ($\times$)

- **Since :** It is an adverb represents the meaning of 'ago'.

  Illustration: I have been feeling guilty ever since. ($\checkmark$)

  Ever since I felt sorry. ($\times$)

- **Fast :** It is a confusing word which comes as an adverb and adjective also.

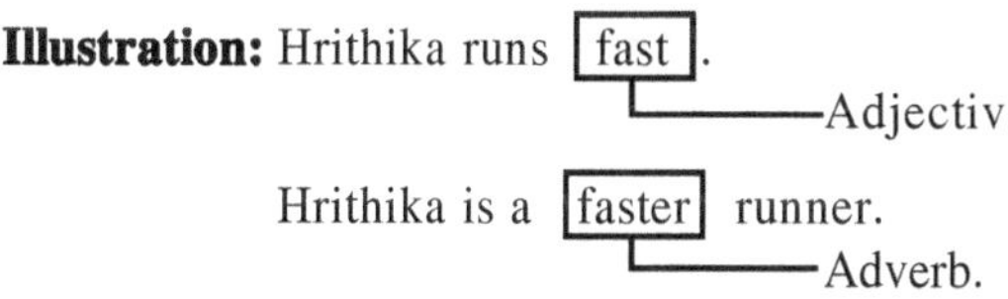

  Illustration: Hrithika runs ⎡fast⎤.

  ⎣————Adjective

  Hrithika is a ⎡faster⎤ runner.

  ⎣————Adverb.

  [Note : Mark the difference.]

- **Only :** It is an adverb which is used before the qualifying words. But sometimes it comes as an adjective also.

  Illustration: Only he said to her. (nobody else)

  He said to her only. (to none else)

  He only said to her (did nothing else)

- **Some words are used as adjectives and adverbs**

  Very :

  (i) qualifies past participle, which is used an adjective.

  (ii) used in the positive degree.

  (iii) normally, it qualifies present participle.

  Much :

  (i) Used in comparative degree.

  (ii) Normally, it qualifies past participle.

  Illustration:

  1. Raghav was ⎡much⎤ astonished at the occurrence.

  ⎣——qualifies past participle

  2. He is ⎡very⎤ disgusted.

  ⎣——(used as adjective)

18

3. Your farmhouse is much bigger than the other one.
                                               → (used in comparative degree)

4. She purchased the car very easily.
                                               → (used in positive degree)

- **No sooner is followed by 'than' showing comparison.**

  Illustration: No sooner did I see her than I trembled with fear. (✓)

  No sooner I saw her I trembled with fear. (×)

- **Transformation process**

  From Adjective to Adverb

  (a) by adding ly

SI. No.	Adjective	Adverb
1.	Wise	Wisely
2.	Kind	Kindly
3.	Quick	Quickly
4.	Clever	Cleverly

  (b) An adjective ends with le/e, will be changed into 'y'.

SI. No.	Adjective	Adverb
1.	Double	Doubly
2.	Single	Singly
3.	Triple	Triply

- **Degree of Adverbs**

  (a) Adverb having one Syllable in Positive degree then we should add 'er' to change into comparative degree. Likewise by adding 'est' in positive degree it will become superlative degree.

SI. No.	Positive Degree	Comparative Degree	Superlative Degree
1.	Hard	Harder	Hardest
2.	Fast	Faster	Fastest
3.	Long	Longer	Longest

  (b) Adverb ending with 'ly' will be transformed into comparative degree by using 'more' before it and while transforming into superlative degree we have to use 'most'.

SI. No.	Positive Degree	Emparative Degree	Superlative Degree
1.	Swiftly	<u>more</u> swiftly	<u>most</u> swiftly
2.	Skilfully	<u>more</u> skilfully	<u>most</u> skilfully

(c) Some adverbs do not follow any rule while transforming into one degree to another.

SI. No. Degree	Positive Degree	Comparative Degree	Superlative Degree
1.	For	Farther	Farthest
2.	Much	More	Most
3.	Late	Later	Last
4.	Little	Less	Least
5.	Near	Nearer	Next

JUDGE YOURSELF

In the following questions choose the correct option to fill the blank.

1. No sooner said ....
(*a*) so done   (*b*) and done
(*c*) then done (*d*) but done

2. She returned .... than I had thought.
(*a*) quickly
(*b*) more quicker
(*c*) more quickly
(*d*) quicker

3. I an .... foolish person.
(*a*) rather the   (*b*) a rather
(*c*) rather a   (*d*) rather

4. This pen .... rupees.
(*a*) costs twenty
(*b*) twenty costs only
(*c*) costs only twenty
(*d*) only costs twenty

5. It is .... pride.
(*a*) nothing else but
(*b*) nothing else than
(*c*) else nothing than
(*d*) but

6. This tea is .... to drink.
(*a*) too hot
(*b*) very hot
(*c*) enough hot
(*d*) much hot

7. She can read this novel .... than I.
(*a*) more quick
(*b*) more quickly
(*c*) quick
(*d*) quickly

8. He has gone .... to the airport.
(*a*) directly
(*b*) direct
(*c*) very directly
(*d*) a direct

9. Every body should worship
....
- (*a*) only God
- (*b*) God only
- (*c*) God only one
- (*d*) only one God

10. I was .... pleased to see my brother.
- (*a*) too
- (*b*) very
- (*c*) some
- (*d*) few

11. He was .... by his father.
- (*a*) hated even
- (*b*) hated even after
- (*c*) hated well
- (*d*) even hated

12. They advised me ....
- (*a*) walk quick
- (*b*) to walk quickly
- (*c*) walk quickly
- (*d*) to walk quick

13. She .... refuses to help her brother.
- (*a*) seldom or ever
- (*b*) seldom or always
- (*c*) seldom or never
- (*d*) seldom or generally

14. I shall be .... obliged to you.
- (*a*) much
- (*b*) most
- (*c*) very
- (*d*) either (*b*) or (*c*)

15. It was .... hot yesterday.
- (*a*) very
- (*b*) too
- (*c*) to
- (*d*) either (*b*) or (*c*)

16. All must work very ....
- (*a*) hardly
- (*b*) hard
- (*c*) harden
- (*d*) hardlly

17. It was .... hot yesterday.
- (*a*) too
- (*b*) to
- (*c*) so
- (*d*) very

18. The Indian crocodile can swim
....
- (*a*) very fastly
- (*b*) more fastly
- (*c*) very fast
- (*d*) more fast

19. This movie is .... good.
- (*a*) very
- (*b*) too
- (*c*) much
- (*d*) most

20. Priya is .... intelligent.
- (*a*) very much
- (*b*) much
- (*c*) more
- (*d*) very

21. She resembles .... her father.
- (*a*) with
- (*b*) to
- (*c*) for
- (*d*) no word required

ANSWERS

1	2	3	4	5	6	7	8	9	10
(*c*)	(*c*)	(*c*)	(*c*)	(*a*)	(*a*)	(*b*)	(*b*)	(*b*)	(*b*)

11	12	13	14	15	16	17	18	19	20
(*a*)	(*b*)	(*c*)	(*a*)	(*a*)	(*b*)	(*d*)	(*c*)	(*a*)	(*a*)

21
(*d*)

PREPOSITION

- **Preposition of Place**
1. *Among*   More than two persons/things
   Example: You have to select *among* five options.
2. *Above*   Higher than
   Example: The kite is flying *above* the buildings.
3. *At*   With festivals
   Example: I will come to you *at* Diwali.
4. *Below*   Lower than
   Example: My house is *below* the hill.
5. *Between*   For two persons/things
   Example: The property will be shared *between* Rajesh and his brother.
6. *Beneath*   In a lower position but figuratively.
   Example: It is *beneath* my dignity.
7. *In*   For a larger area
   Example: I live *in* Delhi at Rohini.
8. *Over*   Vertically above
   Example: My book is *over* the table.

- **Preposition of Time**
1. *At*   Exact point/time/place
   Example: He will be there *at* 5 O' Clock.
2. *By*   Latest time
   Example: The show will be over *by* 9 p.m.
3. *For*   Period of action, used with pref. cont. tense.
   Example: I have been working her *for* the last six years.
4. *From*   Beginning point of action of the past
   Example: I was a collector at Bhagalpur *from* 1986 to 1988.
5. *In*   Parts of the year/month/day etc.
   In future tense related to time
   Example: India won World Cup *in* 1975.
   I will come back *in* a weak.
6. *On*   General point of time like Monday, Independence day etc.
   Example: The office will be inaugurated *on* coming Monday.
7. *Since*   Point of time (Perfect continuous)
   Example: I have been playing cricket *since* 2004.

- **Preposition of Direction.**
1. *Against*   For pressure
   Example: She stands *against* the pillar.

2. *At*   Denotes aim
  Example: The police aimed *at* the criminal.
3. *From* For the point of departure.
  Example: She brought the money *from* the A.T.M.
4. *For*   Refers direction
  Example: I shall leave *for* Bhagalpur tomorrow.
5. *Into*   Refers motion towards the interior
  Example: The teacher entered *into* the classroom.
6. *Off*   Reflects Separation
  Example: He jumped *off* the roof of his house.
7. *To*   Shows destination
  Example: I will go *to* your office.
8. *Towards* Shows direction
  Example: He is going towards railway station.

JUDGE YOURSELF

Pick out the most effective word(s) from the given options to fill the blank to make the sentence meaningfully complete.

1. He was charged .... murder.
 (*a*) about (*b*) of
 (*c*) from (*d*) for

2. You gained an advantage .... me.
 (*a*) over (*b*) on
 (*c*) upon (*d*) from

3. He rested .... the shade of mango tree.
 (*a*) below (*b*) beneath
 (*c*) under (*d*) in

4. The storehouse was infested .... rats.
 (*a*) of (*b*) with
 (*c*) about (*d*) from

5. My father deals .... iron.
 (*a*) with (*b*) in
 (*c*) within (*d*) for

6. Her nature is quite different .... her sister.
 (*a*) with (*b*) in
 (*c*) on (*d*) from

7. Pratap Singh is devoid .... any common sense.
 (*a*) of (*b*) from
 (*c*) with (*d*) for

8. She devotes seven hours .... her studies daily.
 (*a*) on (*b*) for
 (*c*) to (*d*) with

9. Ramesh died .... cholera last year.
 (*a*) with (*b*) of
 (*c*) in (*d*) from

10. Our neighbour died .... over work.
 (*a*) of (*b*) in
 (*c*) for (*d*) from

11. He has disposed .... his house.
 (*a*) of (*b*) in
 (*c*) at (*d*) from

12. He was never entitled .... this high post.
(*a*) of   (*b*) to
(*c*) for   (*d*) over

13. Suraj is fit .... joining her duty.
(*a*) to   (*b*) in
(*c*) for   (*d*) from

14. We have full faith .... our leaders.
(*a*) in   (*b*) with
(*c*) of   (*d*) over

15. My friend promised to come but never turned ....
(*a*) on   (*b*) over
(*c*) up   (*d*) with

16. The stranger turned .... be a thief.
(*a*) to   (*b*) in
(*c*) on   (*d*) with

17. I shall look .... the matter.
(*a*) in   (*b*) about
(*c*) into   (*d*) after

18. He invited me .... tea.
(*a*) on   (*b*) for
(*c*) to   (*d*) at

19. He is blind .... one eye.
(*a*) in   (*b*) of
(*c*) to   (*d*) on

20. He looked .... his watch everywhere.
(*a*) after   (*b*) into
(*c*) to   (*d*) for

21. He is blind .... his defects.
(*a*) to   (*b*) of
(*c*) from   (*d*) about

22. My friend willingly complied .... my request.
(*a*) of   (*b*) to
(*c*) with   (*d*) upon

23. The robbers set .... the passengers.
(*a*) in   (*b*) on
(*c*) for   (*d*) with

24. For several days he kept .... from the school.
(*a*) from   (*b*) off
(*c*) away   (*d*) on

25. The discussion was held .... till the next meeting.
(*a*) on   (*b*) over
(*c*) with   (*d*) in

26. Go on .... you see a church on your right.
(*a*) until   (*b*) of
(*c*) on   (*d*) out

27. The police drew .... the truth from the thief.
(*u*) on   (*b*) with
(*c*) over   (*d*) out

28. Ritu has deposited five thousands rupees .... the Bank of India.
(*a*) in   (*b*) with
(*c*) for   (*d*) against

29. He is envious .... his brother's success.
(*a*) of   (*b*) from
(*c*) to   (*d*) for

30. We should not hanker .... money.
(*a*) with   (*b*) in
(*c*) after   (*d*) for

31. Ignorance .... law is no excuse.
    (*a*) from   (*b*) in
    (*c*) for   (*d*) of

32. The forest is infested ....
beasts.
    (*a*) with   (*b*) from
    (*c*) for   (*d*) on

33. We must lay .... something for
the rainy day.
    (*a*) by   (*b*) for
    (*c*) in   (*d*) at

34. Do not believe .... love at first
sight.
    (*a*) in   (*b*) at
    (*c*) for   (*d*) to

35. He lives .... honest labour.
    (*a*) with   (*b*) at
    (*c*) for   (*d*) by

36. This dish is not .... my taste.
    (*a*) for   (*b*) to
    (*c*) in   (*d*) with

37. He persisted .... accusing me.
    (*a*) in   (*b*) for
    (*c*) on   (*d*) at

38. Mohan was married ....
Sheela.
    (*a*) to   (*b*) in
    (*c*) with   (*d*) at

39. Which hand do you write ....?
    (*a*) in   (*b*) at
    (*c*) with   (*d*) of

40. He reached .... the station in
time.
    (*a*) at   (*b*) to
    (*c*) no word (*d*) on

41. A pedestrian was run .... by
the car.
    (*a*) by   (*b*) down
    (*c*) over   (*d*) in

42. Under this heavy load the bridge
will give ....
    (*a*) way   (*b*) in
    (*c*) out   (*d*) away

43. With great difficulty I brought
him ....
    (*a*) about   (*b*) in
    (*c*) round   (*d*) up

44. Without thinking he turned
.... the proposal.
    (*a*) out   (*b*) up
    (*c*) down   (*d*) in

45. Please pay attention .... what
I say.
    (*a*) in   (*b*) on
    (*c*) to   (*d*) for

46. I assured him .... my full help.
    (*a*) above   (*b*) for
    (*c*) with   (*d*) of

47. You should not associate ....
bad boys.
    (*a*) with   (*b*) in
    (*c*) on   (*d*) over

48. The criminal begged ....
mercy.
    (*a*) on   (*b*) against
    (*c*) for   (*d*) with

49. The house belongs .... my
father.
    (*a*) with   (*b*) to
    (*c*) for   (*d*) of

50. We kept .... with the times.
    (*a*) of   (*b*) with
    (*c*) up   (*d*) on

51. He does not care .... his family.
  (a) in   (b) for
  (c) from   (d) over

52. He borrowed a book .... me.
  (a) with   (b) for
  (c) from   (d) over

53. The function began .... a song.
  (a) with   (b) in
  (c) for   (d) on

54. She blushed .... his remark.
  (a) in   (b) over
  (c) at   (d) on

55. We are confident .... our ultimate victory.
  (a) about   (b) in
  (c) on   (d) of

56. He confided his secrets .... me.
  (a) about   (b) in
  (c) on   (d) of

57. Nowadays nobody cares .... a poor man.
  (a) for   (b) to
  (c) with   (d) of

58. The Principal advised the students to desist .... the acts of violence.
  (a) in   (b) for
  (c) from   (d) on

59. He has no right to encroach .... my land.
  (a) in   (b) an
  (c) for   (d) upon

60. Mr. Bhardwaj presided .... the meeting.
  (a) over   (b) in
  (c) on   (d) for

61. I presented him .... a beautiful watch.
  (a) in   (b) for
  (c) with   (d) on

62. They prohibited him .... entering the house.
  (a) for   (b) in
  (c) on   (d) from

63. He takes pride .... his knowledge of grammar.
  (a) on   (b) in
  (c) over   (d) with

64. Our teacher is not partial .... any boy.
  (a) to   (b) on
  (c) with   (d) in

65. This blanket will protect you .... cold.
  (a) against   (b) for
  (c) with   (d) from

66. It is our birth right to protest .... an injustice.
  (a) for   (b) on
  (c) against   (d) from

67. The transistor fell .... the shelf.
  (a) off   (b) of
  (c) on   (d) at

68. None .... the brave deserve the fair.
  (a) of   (b) but
  (c) from   (d) at

69. He revenged himself .... his enemy.
  (a) of   (b) from
  (c) upon   (d) on

70. He came and sat ……… his mother.
   (*a*) besides   (*b*) beside
   (*c*) after   (*d*) off

71. He has no taste ……… music.
   (*a*) of   (*b*) in
   (*c*) at   (*d*) for

72. He placed the thing ……… the curtain.
   (*a*) beneath   (*b*) under
   (*c*) below   (*d*) behind

73. He will abide ……… the rules.
   (*a*) by   (*b*) up
   (*c*) in   (*d*) at

74. She came to the club neatly turned ……… .
   (*a*) down   (*b*) in
   (*c*) up   (*d*) at

75. You must keep ……… the reputation of the family.
   (*a*) down   (*b*) in
   (*c*) at   (*d*) up

76. You must go ……this book
   (*a*) in for   (*b*) in
   (*c*) for   (*d*) at

77. The thief broke ……… the house.
   (*a*) in   (*b*) into
   (*c*) up   (*d*) open

78. He turned ……… to be a cheat.
   (*a*) out   (*b*) up
   (*c*) in   (*d*) round

79. The police deals ……… the criminals.
   (*a*) out   (*b*) in
   (*c*) with   (*d*) up

80. Why do you boast ……… your wealth?
   (*a*) in   (*b*) about
   (*c*) of   (*d*) for

81. The Rajputs always fought ……… the last man.
   (*a*) upto   (*b*) till
   (*c*) to   (*d*) for

82. Do you know how to look ……… a word in the dictionary?
   (*a*) about   (*b*) for
   (*c*) into   (*d*) on

83. Mala tied the cow with a rope ……… a tree.
   (*a*) to   (*b*) with
   (*c*) from   (*d*) on

84. I have learnt this lesson word ……… word.
   (*a*) by   (*b*) to
   (*c*) for   (*d*) upon

85. His services have been dispensed ……… .
   (*a*) of
   (*b*) with
   (*c*) off
   (*d*) no Preposition is needed.

86. We should always stick to our decisions otherwise the people will mock ……… us.
   (*a*) on   (*b*) at
   (*c*) upon   (*d*) over

87. I cannot put up ……… this insult.
   (*a*) on   (*b*) upon
   (*c*) with   (*d*) at

88. His appeal ……… mercy has been turned down.
   (*a*) of   (*b*) about
   (*c*) on   (*d*) for

89. It is ……… my dignity to talk to her.

(*a*) beneath   (*b*) under
(*c*) below   (*d*) off

90. He introduced me .... his boss.
(*a*) from   (*b*) to
(*c*) for   (*d*) in

91. We must not jeer .... others.
(*a*) on   (*b*) with
(*c*) at   (*d*) in

92. He is jealous .... my promotion.
(*a*) in   (*b*) with
(*c*) for   (*d*) of

93. I have very intimate relations .... his brother.
(*a*) to   (*b*) from
(*c*) with   (*d*) for

94. This pen is inferior .... that.
(*a*) from   (*b*) to
(*c*) with   (*d*) for

95. She is knocking .... our door.
(*a*) on   (*b*) in
(*c*) at   (*d*) with

96. We must be loyal .... our country.
(*a*) in   (*b*) to
(*c*) at   (*d*) with

97. He has a great lust .... wealth.
(*a*) in   (*b*) of
(*c*) on   (*d*) for

98. There is a limit .... everything in life.
(*a*) to   (*b*) on
(*c*) in   (*d*) with

99. He is not living .... his means.
(*a*) in   (*b*) for
(*c*) within   (*d*) from

100. He parted .... all his possessions happily.
(*a*) for   (*b*) with
(*c*) on   (*d*) from

101. I prefer death .... dishonour.
(*a*) to   (*b*) than
(*c*) from   (*d*) in

102. His father prevailed .... him to join the government service.
(*a*) upon   (*b*) on
(*c*) in   (*d*) from

103. The students protested .... the ill-treatment of their leaders.
(*a*) for   (*b*) to
(*c*) against   (*d*) over

104. The old man brought .... a reconciliation between the two brothers.
(*a*) in   (*b*) through
(*c*) of   (*d*) about

105. The teacher should not be partial .... any student.
(*a*) for   (*b*) to
(*c*) against   (*d*) over

106. He is fully prepared .... the examination.
(*a*) in   (*b*) to
(*c*) of   (*d*) for

107. He is in the habit of reasoning .... everybody on trifles.
(*a*) to   (*b*) for
(*c*) on   (*d*) with

108. The matter has been referred .... the minister for decision.
(*a*) to   (*b*) with
(*c*) for   (*d*) over

109. Please remind Gopal .... his promise.
(*a*) about (*b*) for
(*c*) with (*d*) of

110. One must stand .... one's relative in times of difficulty.
(*a*) by (*b*) with
(*c*) over (*d*) against

111. He has no ambition .... earning wealth.
(*a*) to (*b*) in
(*c*) for (*d*) on

112. Cigarette smoking is injurious .... health.
(*a*) for (*b*) to
(*c*) about (*d*) on

113. In the dark, he knocked .... the wall.
(*a*) at (*b*) on
(*c*) against (*d*) over

114. He jumped .... my offer.
(*a*) at (*b*) on
(*c*) to (*d*) over

115. He was unjustified in accusing us ....theft.
(*a*) for (*b*) of
(*c*) with (*d*) upon

116. His comments were almost irrelevant .... topic of the evening.
(*a*) for (*b*) about
(*c*) to (*d*) on

117. He was exempted .... the payment of the tax.
(*a*) of (*b*) from
(*c*) on (*d*) in

118. He hastily jumped .... the conclusion that I was to blame for all his losses.
(*a*) at (*b*) on
(*c*) to (*d*) over

119. I congratulated him .... his success.
(*a*) for (*b*) about
(*c*) of (*d*) on

120. She resembles .... her mother.
(*a*) with
(*b*) no need of Preposition
(*c*) from
(*d*) for

121. She accused the servant .... stealing.
(*a*) of (*b*) with
(*c*) in (*d*) at

122. I am quite .... home in this subject.
(*a*) in (*b*) to
(*c*) of (*d*) at

123. I am posted .... your case.
(*a*) with (*b*) at
(*c*) for (*d*) in

124. He resembles .... his father.
(*a*) with (*b*) in
(*c*) no word (*d*) at

125. The group comprises .... four persons.
(*a*) no word (*b*) of
(*c*) with (*d*) at

126. I am not getting .... well with him.
(*a*) on (*b*) at
(*c*) in (*d*) with

127. This tea is too hot .... take.
(*a*) to (*b*) for
(*c*) no word (*d*) in

128. He is always boasting .... his talents.
   (*a*) of   (*b*) at
   (*c*) in   (*d*) to

129. The principal called .... the names of the winners.
   (*a*) on   (*b*) at
   (*c*) out   (*d*) for

130. He has taken .... going for long walks.
   (*a*) in   (*b*) for
   (*c*) to   (*d*) at

131. We looked forward .... seeing you.
   (*a*) to   (*b*) in
   (*c*) at   (*d*) for

132. We are accountable .... God for our actions.
   (*a*) at   (*b*) for
   (*c*) to   (*d*) in

133. He is not familiar .... this locality.
   (*a*) to   (*b*) from
   (*c*) for   (*d*) with

134. His face is not familiar .... me.
   (*a*) to   (*b*) with
   (*c*) of   (*d*) about

135. I found him leaning .... the wall.
   (*a*) to   (*b*) over
   (*c*) about   (*d*) against

136. The strain is telling .... his health.
   (*a*) upon   (*b*) of
   (*c*) in   (*d*) from

137. I saw .... trick.
   (*a*) into   (*b*) from
   (*c*) through   (*d*) to

138. He is .... head and ears in debt.
   (*a*) in   (*b*) of
   (*c*) upon   (*d*) over

139. We are .... war with them.
   (*a*) at   (*b*) in
   (*c*) through   (*d*) of

140. He carried .... his performance.
   (*a*) on   (*b*) through
   (*c*) out   (*d*) with

141. The thunder was accompanied .... a heavy rain.
   (*a*) with   (*b*) by
   (*c*) up   (*d*) through

142. I do not believe .... what he says.
   (*a*) in   (*b*) of
   (*c*) at   (*d*) with

143. The teacher frowned .... the students.
   (*a*) at   (*b*) on
   (*c*) in   (*d*) with

144. He feels .... the well being of the poor pcoplc.
   (*a*) in   (*b*) on
   (*c*) for   (*d*) by

145. She is enraged .... me.
   (*a*) with   (*b*) on
   (*c*) in   (*d*) over

146. Ram was engrossed .... his studies.
   (*a*) on   (*b*) with
   (*c*) in   (*d*) over

147. He was excluded .... the team.
   (*a*) on   (*b*) from
   (*c*) by   (*d*) for

148. There is an exception .... every rule.

(a) to (b) in
(c) for (d) with

149. He is very grateful .... me.
(a) for (b) to
(c) from (d) with

150. He has copied this letter word .... word.
(a) by (b) in
(c) for (d) from

151. The water supply at last gave ....
(a) out (b) off
(c) of (d) about

152. Sabina has invited her friends .... dinner.
(a) for (b) to
(c) with (d) over

153. He prevented me .... going to the school.
(a) from (b) for
(c) with (d) on

154. Her mother was very angry .... her.
(a) on (b) in
(c) with (d) by

155. My mother-in-law is blind .... one eye.
(a) from (b) in
(c) on (d) of

156. Janardhan was appointed .... the post of section officer.
(a) to (b) on
(c) with (d) for

157. Compare Gandhi .... Karl Marx.
(a) to (b) with
(c) over (d) in

158. The terrorist shot the policeman .... his gun.
(a) by (b) for
(c) with (d) in

159. The land was devided .... the two sisters.
(a) among (b) between
(c) with (d) for

160. He has not met his mother .... long.
(a) for (b) with
(c) since (d) by

161. The players have gone .... the playground.
(a) in (b) over
(c) with (d) to

162. Sheela burst .... the room when Mohini as writing a letter.
(a) on (b) in
(c) of (d) out

163. She is gifted .... common sense.
(a) on (b) by
(c) with (d) over

164. I am fond .... reading novel.
(a) of (b) by
(c) on (d) with

165. Beware .... back-biters.
(a) from (b) to
(c) of (d) with

166. The principal will preside .... the function.
(a) on (b) upon
(c) with (d) over

167. A bad workman quarrels .... his tools.
(a) for (b) of
(c) with (d) beside

168. We should be prepared to make sacrifice .... our motherland.
(*a*) to   (*b*) on
(*c*) for   (*d*) at

169. I told him .... his face that he was a liar.
(*a*) in   (*b*) on
(*c*) with   (*d*) at

170. This chair is much inferior .... that.
(*a*) than   (*b*) to
(*c*) of   (*d*) from

171. The old man was deprived .... his only son.
(*a*) from   (*b*) for
(*c*) at   (*d*) of

172. Ram was charged with murder but the magistrate acquitted him .... the crime.
(*a*) from   (*b*) of
(*c*) on   (*d*) about

173. The money must be dealt .... fairly and justly.
(*a*) in   (*b*) with
(*c*) out   (*d*) off

174. He is prepared .... the worst.
(*a*) for   (*b*) in
(*c*) to   (*d*) with

175. He persisted .... disobeying the order.
(*a*) on   (*b*) in
(*c*) to   (*d*) for

176. You must adhere .... some principles in life.
(*a*) to   (*b*) on
(*c*) in   (*d*) with

177. He is not amenable .... any kind of discipline.
(*a*) in   (*b*) for
(*c*) to   (*d*) with

178. The minister enjoys full authority .... his department.
(*a*) in   (*b*) on
(*c*) over   (*d*) with

179. My friend has been absolved .... the charge of forgery.
(*a*) of   (*b*) on
(*c*) in   (*d*) over

180. The people are clamouring .... lower prices of essential goods.
(*a*) with   (*b*) in
(*c*) for   (*d*) to

181. His views are identical .... mine.
(*a*) on   (*b*) in
(*c*) for   (*d*) with

182. The students should not take .... drugs.
(*a*) to   (*b*) in
(*c*) out   (*d*) with

183. Please listen ....what I say.
(*a*) in   (*b*) for
(*c*) to   (*d*) with

184. She took offence .... my remarks.
(*a*) in   (*b*) at
(*c*) on   (*d*) with

185. He opposed .... my plans.
(*a*) with   (*b*) in
(*c*) for   (*d*) to

186. He is neglectful .... his duties.
(*a*) with   (*b*) on
(*c*) of   (*d*) in

187. Exercise is necessary .... health.
   (*a*) with   (*b*) for
   (*c*) in   (*d*) over

188. The beautiful earnings set .... the maiden' beauty.
   (*a*) off   (*b*) on
   (*c*) in   (*d*) out

189. She is no match .... you.
   (*a*) from   (*b*) over
   (*c*) on   (*d*) for

190. Do not meddle .... the affairs of others.
   (*a*) on   (*b*) from
   (*c*) with   (*d*) by

191. I bear no malice .... any body.
   (*a*) on   (*b*) against
   (*c*) in   (*d*) over

192. He is very lavish .... his expenditure.
   (*a*) in   (*b*) on
   (*c*) with   (*d*) from

193. Let us seize .... the opportunity offered to us.
   (*a*) on   (*b*) with
   (*c*) upon   (*d*) against

194. They have set out .... a journey to a hill station.
   (*a*) in   (*b*) on
   (*c*) of   (*d*) with

195. Please stick .... the point and do not beat about the bush.
   (*a*) in   (*b*) on
   (*c*) over   (*d*) to

196. He is ineligible .... this post.
   (*a*) to   (*b*) of
   (*c*) for   (*d*) at

197. A steady mind triumphs .... difficulties.
   (*a*) in   (*b*) over
   (*c*) at   (*d*) with

198. Ruin stared him .... his face.
   (*a*) in   (*b*) at
   (*c*) of   (*d*) on

199. I was disgusted .... their treatment.
   (*a*) with   (*b*) at
   (*c*) in   (*d*) on

200. Artists like Kalidas belong .... all ages and all countries.
   (*a*) with   (*b*) for
   (*c*) to   (*d*) about

201. Please pay .... your bill.
   (*a*) for
   (*b*) in
   (*c*) off
   (*d*) no need of Preposition

202. Be .... good cheer.
   (*a*) at   (*b*) in
   (*c*) of   (*d*) on

203. Hope .... the best and prepare .... the worst.
   (*a*) at, at   (*b*) for, for
   (*c*) in, in   (*d*) of, of

204. You are sure to run .... difficulties.
   (*a*) in   (*b*) into
   (*c*) at   (*d*) of

205. Let ne acquaint him .... the facts.
   (*a*) in   (*b*) of
   (*c*) with   (*d*) for

206. I do not agree .... you on this point.

(*a*) to   (*b*) with
(*c*) in   (*d*) at

207. The rains have set ....
(*a*) of   (*b*) out
(*c*) on   (*d*) in

208. He has servants to attend ....
him.
(*a*) in   (*b*) over
(*c*) upon   (*d*) to

209. He is averse .... hard work.
(*a*) on   (*b*) to
(*c*) upon   (*d*) with

210. The dog barked .... the passer-
by.
(*a*) at   (*b*) on
(*c*) over   (*d*) in

211. I am aware .... my shortcomings.
(*a*) at   (*b*) over
(*c*) of   (*d*) with

212. He is lax .... morals.
(*a*) in   (*b*) on
(*c*) with   (*d*) of

213. We marvelled .... the tricks of
the magician.
(*a*) in   (*b*) on
(*c*) at   (*d*) with

214. The patient has lapsed .... a
coma.
(*a*) over   (*b*) in
(*c*) to   (*d*) into

215. I am sorry for having intruded
.... your privacy.
(*a*) in   (*b*) on
(*c*) with   (*d*) for

216. One must have some incentive
.... work.

(*a*) to   (*b*) in
(*c*) over   (*d*) for

217. Your views are identical ....
mine.
(*a*) to   (*b*) for
(*c*) from   (*d*) in

218. You should guard .... bad
habits.
(*a*) with   (*b*) against
(*c*) for   (*d*) in

219. The principal has exonerated
him .... the blame.
(*a*) from   (*b*) in
(*c*) of   (*d*) with

220. Do not expose yourself ....
danger for nothing.
(*a*) from   (*b*) in
(*c*) to   (*d*) for

221. I entrusted my brother .... my
property.
(*a*) of   (*b*) with
(*c*) in   (*d*) for

222. She has been endowed .... a
sweet voice.
(*a*) in   (*b*) on
(*c*) with   (*d*) for

223. He is not eligible .... this
post.
(*a*) for   (*b*) to
(*c*) in   (*d*) on

224. You should divest your mind
.... fear.
(*a*) in   (*b*) of
(*c*) with   (*d*) from

225. The examination will commence
.... the 7th September.

(*a*) on   (*b*) from
(*c*) in   (*d*) at

226. The officer deals well .... his subordinates.
(*a*) on   (*b*) in
(*c*) of   (*d*) with

227. My son is desirous .... joining the Army.
(*a*) in   (*b*) on
(*c*) of   (*d*) for

228. We owe a duty .... our motherland.
(*a*) for   (*b*) to
(*c*) on   (*d*) with

229. Have you thought .... the matter?
(*a*) of   (*b*) about
(*c*) over   (*d*) in

230. He leaned .... the tree.
(*a*) to   (*b*) over
(*c*) about   (*d*) against

231. When I parted .... my sister, there were tears in my eyes.
(*a*) with   (*b*) about
(*c*) from   (*d*) to

232. A miser cannot part .... his gold.
(*a*) with   (*b*) about
(*c*) from   (*d*) to

233. She takes pride .... her beauty.
(*a*) of   (*b*) in
(*c*) about   (*d*) for

234. He is proud .... his powers.
(*a*) about   (*b*) over
(*c*) in   (*d*) of

235. He should be held responsible ....this act.

236. Mala is engaged .... Chander.
(*a*) with   (*b*) in
(*c*) to   (*d*) for

237. I prefer coffee .... tea.
(*a*) from   (*b*) over
(*c*) on   (*d*) to

238. No one has yet discovered a cure .... the common cold.
(*a*) of   (*b*) for
(*c*) from   (*d*) about

239. He was congratulated .... his success.
(*a*) on   (*b*) by
(*c*) for   (*d*) with

240. The invigilator connived .... the unfair means.
(*a*) with   (*b*) at
(*c*) in   (*d*) for

241. I tried to dissuade him .... joining army.
(*a*) in   (*b*) at
(*c*) from   (*d*) with

242. Have you pondered .... my case?
(*a*) over   (*b*) on
(*c*) about   (*d*) with

243. The peon seems to have lost the confidence .... his boss.
(*a*) over   (*b*) of
(*c*) about   (*d*) with

244. He is capable .... doing anything.
(*a*) in   (*b*) about
(*c*) for   (*d*) of

245. He is fully contented .... his life.
(*a*) to   (*b*) of
(*c*) with   (*d*) in

246. She has been fully cured .... the chronic pain in her legs.
(*a*) of   (*b*) in
(*c*) from   (*d*) with

247. The culprit has been charged .... murder.
(*a*) of   (*b*) with
(*c*) into   (*d*) after

248. The shopkeeper has charged me ten rupees .... this book.
(*a*) for   (*b*) on
(*c*) of   (*d*) in

249. We can compare life .... a drama.
(*a*) in   (*b*) for
(*c*) from   (*d*) to

250. Om Prakash can always count .... my help.
(*a*) for   (*b*) in
(*c*) on   (*d*) from

251. Yesterday a truck collided .... a bus.
(*a*) to   (*b*) in
(*c*) over   (*d*) with

252. All the students have committed this lesson .... memory.
(*a*) to   (*b*) for
(*c*) in   (*d*) with

253. The servant always complies .... the wishes of his master.
(*a*) to   (*b*) for
(*c*) in   (*d*) with

254. I called .... his house yesterday.

(*a*) on   (*b*) at
(*c*) over   (*d*) into

255. He got .... the examination with good marks.
(*a*) of   (*b*) through
(*c*) on   (*d*) for

256. He is proud .... his honour.
(*a*) to   (*b*) with
(*c*) of   (*d*) for

257. I was amazed .... his misbehavior.
(*a*) with   (*b*) in
(*c*) for   (*d*) at

258. Sharma amused us .... jokes.
(*a*) with   (*b*) in
(*c*) of   (*d*) for

259. Renu has special aptitude .... music.
(*a*) to   (*b*) in
(*c*) for   (*d*) on

260. She has not applied .... this post.
(*a*) for   (*b*) to
(*c*) in   (*d*) with

261. The train has arrived .... the station.
(*a*) in   (*b*) on
(*c*) at   (*d*) over

262. You should be ashamed .... your bad conduct.
(*a*) at   (*b*) of
(*c*) with   (*d*) over

263. I was astonished .... his failure.
(*a*) at   (*b*) in
(*c*) on   (*d*) for

264. The letter was written .... red ink.
   (*a*) with   (*b*) by
   (*c*) in   (*d*) into

265. My brother went .... abroad last year.
   (*a*) to   (*b*) from
   (*c*) at   (*d*) for

266. This economist will discuss .... the unemployment problem in India.
   (*a*) about
   (*b*) no need of Preposition
   (*c*) for
   (*d*) in

267. I wonder if I shall get .... my history examination.
   (*a*) at   (*b*) from
   (*c*) on   (*d*) through

268. The party comprises .... Ram, Mohan, Sita and myself.
   (*a*) of   (*b*) about
   (*c*) off   (*d*) in

269. Please continue this exercise where you had left ....
   (*a*) no need of Preposition
   (*b*) at
   (*c*) on
   (*d*) about

270. I am tired .... walking.
   (*a*) of   (*b*) off
   (*c*) with   (*d*) from

271. We discussed .... the matter for over an hour.
   (*a*) about
   (*b*) on
   (*c*) no Preposition is needed
   (*d*) for

272. Many people have died .... malaria.
   (*a*) of   (*b*) from
   (*c*) with   (*d*) for

273. He ordered .... the dinner when we had finished work.
   (*a*) for   (*b*) to
   (*c*) about   (*d*) off

274. That young man is very keen .... cycling.
   (*a*) on   (*b*) about
   (*c*) of   (*d*) for

275. The lion sprang .... the cow.
   (*a*) on   (*b*) at
   (*c*) over   (*d*) upon

276. His idleness accounts .... his poverty.
   (*a*) for   (*b*) to
   (*c*) in   (*d*) into

277. I have no belief .... his honesty.
   (*a*) for   (*b*) into
   (*c*) in   (*d*) about

278. I am writing this essay .... blue ink.
   (*a*) in   (*b*) with
   (*c*) from   (*d*) on

279. He congratulated you .... your promotion.
   (*a*) in   (*b*) of
   (*c*) on   (*d*) for

280. I met Anita .... the way to my office.
   (*a*) in   (*b*) on
   (*c*) upon   (*d*) with

281. She jumped .... the river.
   (*a*) on   (*b*) in
   (*c*) into   (*d*) to

282. The jug is full .... milk.
    (*a*) of   (*b*) with
    (*c*) in   (*d*) upon

283. Bacon had a thirst .... knowledge.
    (*a*) of   (*b*) about
    (*c*) for   (*d*) to

284. The Hindu religion has been in existence .... times immemorial.
    (*a*) since   (*b*) for
    (*c*) on   (*d*) from

285. It has been raining .... Monday.
    (*a*) since   (*b*) for
    (*c*) from   (*d*) of

286. There was no heir .... the throne.
    (*a*) to   (*b*) in
    (*c*) on   (*d*) over

287. He got .... his illness in two weeks
    (*a*) on   (*b*) by
    (*c*) with   (*d*) over

288. I could not guess .... the answer to this question.
    (*a*) in   (*b*) for
    (*c*) at   (*d*) on

289. I am very grateful .... Mr. Nair for his timely help.
    (*a*) for   (*b*) to
    (*c*) by   (*d*) with

290. This is the book I was telling you ....
    (*a*) about   (*b*) of
    (*c*) on   (*d*) for

291. Do not despair .... failures in life.
    (*a*) on   (*b*) in
    (*c*) over   (*d*) of

292. The watch has run ....
    (*a*) out   (*b*) about
    (*c*) down   (*d*) of

293. A cat differs .... a dog.
    (*a*) with   (*b*) from
    (*c*) for   (*d*) in

294. He is completely involved .... his family affairs.
    (*a*) in   (*b*) on
    (*c*) with   (*d*) over

295. I am indebted .... you for this kind favour.
    (*a*) with   (*b*) for
    (*c*) to   (*d*) in

296. You should not indulge .... idle talks.
    (*a*) on   (*b*) over
    (*c*) about   (*d*) in

297. She is hopeful .... her success in the I.A.S. examination.
    (*a*) in   (*b*) by
    (*c*) of   (*d*) on

298. Rich men are greedy .... money.
    (*a*) for   (*b*) of
    (*c*) in   (*d*) with

299. We could not help .... it.
    (*a*) to
    (*b*) no need of Preposition
    (*c*) about
    (*d*) through

300. I warned him .... the pick pockets.

(a) about   (b) in
(c) from   (d) against

301. He fell a victim .... plague.
(a) on   (b) to
(c) in   (d) for

302. Trust .... God and do the right.
(a) in   (b) on
(c) with   (d) by

303. Good triumphs .... evil in the long run.
(a) on   (b) over
(c) with   (d) against

304. You should not trifle .... his feelings.
(a) on   (b) after
(c) over   (d) with

305. Translate the following passage .... a modern Indian language.
(a) in   (b) from
(c) of   (d) into

306. He turned .... my request.
(a) down   (b) out
(c) about   (d) off

307. He is .... his study table.
(a) on   (b) over
(c) about   (d) at

308. Ram has been blessed .... a son.
(a) of   (b) for
(c) with   (d) upon

309. He is always boasting .... his wealth.
(a) with   (b) for
(c) upon   (d) of

310. She is always busy .... her work.
(a) upon   (b) on
(c) with   (d) of

311. This train is bound .... Patna.
(a) on   (b) with
(c) to   (d) for

312. I have made a complaint .... him to the police.
(a) to   (b) against
(c) in   (d) for

313. Mala was married .... Chander.
(a) with   (b) to
(c) for   (d) of

314. He was destined .... the bar.
(a) to   (b) for
(c) about   (d) beside

315. I am writing this letter in pursuance .... my previous letter dated 10-7-1988.
(a) on   (b) in
(c) of   (d) with

316. You should purge your mind .... false notions.
(a) in   (b) of
(c) with   (d) into

317. You should not try to pry .... her secrets.
(a) to   (b) in
(c) over   (d) into

318. He was overwhelmed .... grief when he came to know about the news of his father's death.
(a) in   (b) with
(c) of   (d) into

319. She look offence .... the abusive language used by him.
(a) in   (b) of
(c) with   (d) at

320. My father lives .... Sonepat.
(a) in   (b) into
(c) within   (d) at

321. Students do have a claim .... their teachers.
(*a*) at   (*b*) on
(*c*) upon   (*d*) of

322. You must get rid .... unnecessary things.
(*a*) of   (*b*) about
(*c*) off   (*d*) over

323. Their country has no mineral resources to speak ....
(*a*) of   (*b*) in
(*c*) on   (*d*) with

324. The roof of this house gave .... and the inmates of the house received serious injuries.
(*a*) in   (*b*) for
(*c*) out   (*d*) way

325. Seema takes .... her father.
(*a*) on   (*b*) with
(*c*) after   (*d*) from

326. We are sick .... him.
(*a*) of   (*b*) by
(*c*) with   (*d*) on

327. Please send .... the doctor at once.
(*a*) on   (*b*) by
(*c*) for   (*d*) with

328. He delights .... teasing me.
(*a*) to   (*b*) on
(*c*) in   (*d*) at

329. I was delighted .... your success.
(*a*) at   (*b*) to
(*c*) in   (*d*) on

330. The hunter aimed .... the tiger.
(*a*) to   (*b*) at
(*c*) in   (*d*) for

331. I am alive .... my duties.
(*a*) to   (*b*) of
(*c*) in   (*d*) for

332. The principal was very angry .... the students.
(*a*) in   (*b*) for
(*c*) after   (*d*) with

333. The Government is fully aware .... the situation.
(*a*) after   (*b*) of
(*c*) with   (*d*) in

334. Many young men were drawn .... the freedom struggle by Mahatma Gandhi.
(*a*) on   (*b*) against
(*c*) into   (*d*) with

335. The bandits fell .... the lonely traveller.
(*a*) on   (*b*) upon
(*c*) with   (*d*) for

336. The Vice-President was invited to give .... prizes to the winners.
(*a*) on   (*b*) of
(*c*) upon   (*d*) away

337. Radha parted .... her parents in tears.
(*a*) from   (*b*) of
(*c*) with   (*d*) by

338. I took strong objection .... the proposal.
(*a*) on   (*b*) to
(*c*) against   (*d*) with

339. She was mistaken .... a switch.
(*a*) with   (*b*) as
(*c*) for   (*d*) from

340. I am badly in need .... money.
    (*a*) of   (*b*) for
    (*c*) with   (*d*) on

341. Rama was married .... Sita.
    (*a*) by   (*b*) to
    (*c*) with   (*d*) on

342. One should live .... honest labours.
    (*a*) by   (*b*) with
    (*c*) on   (*d*) for

343. I long .... a quiet life in a hill station.
    (*a*) in   (*b*) by
    (*c*) for   (*d*) with

344. He is not known .... my brother.
    (*a*) with   (*b*) about
    (*c*) for   (*d*) to

345. You should not jest .... his poverty.
    (*a*) in   (*b*) at
    (*c*) for   (*d*) with

346. We should never laugh .... the poor.
    (*a*) on   (*b*) upon
    (*c*) over   (*d*) at

347. I will stand by you .... thick and thin.
    (*a*) by   (*b*) of
    (*c*) in   (*d*) through

348. My elder brother lives .... Calcutta.
    (*a*) in   (*b*) into
    (*c*) within   (*d*) at

349. My wife is good .... French.
    (*a*) in   (*b*) on
    (*c*) with   (*d*) at

350. You ought to abide .... this decision.
    (*a*) with   (*b*) of
    (*c*) by   (*d*) from

351. He will have to account .... his strange behaviour.
    (*a*) for   (*b*) by
    (*c*) from   (*d*) with

352. No sane person will agree .... your proposals.
    (*a*) with   (*b*) to
    (*c*) upon   (*d*) after

353. The robbers broke .... the house and carried away all cash and jewellery with them.
    (*a*) in   (*b*) on
    (*c*) into   (*d*) after

354. He has been suffering from fever .... the last three days.
    (*a*) since   (*b*) from
    (*c*) for   (*d*) about

355. My examination starts .... Tuesday.
    (*a*) from   (*b*) about
    (*c*) since   (*d*) over

356. He jumped .... the river.
    (*a*) in   (*b*) into
    (*c*) on   (*d*) over

357. Nirmal came and sat .... his children.
    (*a*) besides   (*b*) beside
    (*c*) for   (*d*) on

358. Saurabh was destined .... the bar.
    (*a*) with   (*b*) in
    (*c*) for   (*d*) besides

ANSWERS

1	2	3	4	5	6	7	8	9	10
(b)	(a)	(c)	(b)	(b)	(d)	(a)	(c)	(b)	(d)

11	12	13	14	15	16	17	18	19	20
(a)	(b)	(c)	(a)	(c)	(a)	(c)	(c)	(b)	(d)

21	22	23	24	25	26	27	28	29	30
(a)	(a)	(b)	(c)	(b)	(a)	(d)	(b)	(a)	(c)

31	32	33	34	35	36	37	38	39	40
(d)	(a)	(a)	(a)	(d)	(b)	(a)	(c)	(c)	(c)

41	42	43	44	45	46	47	48	49	50
(c)	(b)	(c)	(c)	(c)	(d)	(a)	(c)	(b)	(c)

51	52	53	54	55	56	57	58	59	60
(b)	(c)	(a)	(c)	(d)	(b)	(a)	(c)	(d)	(a)

61	62	63	64	65	66	67	68	69	70
(c)	(d)	(b)	(a)	(d)	(c)	(a)	(b)	(d)	(b)

71	72	73	74	75	76	77	78	79	80
(d)	(d)	(a)	(c)	(d)	(a)	(b)	(a)	(c)	(c)

81	82	83	84	85	86	87	88	89	90
(c)	(b)	(a)	(c)	(b)	(a)	(c)	(d)	(c)	(b)

91	92	93	94	95	96	97	98	99	100
(c)	(d)	(c)	(b)	(c)	(b)	(d)	(a)	(c)	(b)

101	102	103	104	105	106	107	108	109	110
(a)	(a)	(c)	(d)	(b)	(d)	(d)	(a)	(d)	(a)

111	112	113	114	115	116	117	118	119	120
(c)	(b)	(c)	(a)	(b)	(c)	(b)	(c)	(d)	(b)

121	122	123	124	125	126	127	128	129	130
(a)	(d)	(a)	(c)	(b)	(a)	(a)	(a)	(c)	(c)

131	132	133	134	135	136	137	138	139	140
(a)	(c)	(d)	(a)	(d)	(a)	(a)	(d)	(a)	(a)

141	142	143	144	145	146	147	148	149	150
(b)	(a)	(a)	(c)	(a)	(c)	(b)	(a)	(b)	(a)

151	152	153	154	155	156	157	158	159	160
(a)	(b)	(a)	(c)	(d)	(a)	(b)	(c)	(b)	(a)

161	162	163	164	165	166	167	168	169	170
(d)	(b)	(c)	(a)	(c)	(d)	(c)	(c)	(d)	(b)
171	172	173	174	175	176	177	178	179	180
(d)	(b)	(c)	(a)	(b)	(a)	(c)	(c)	(a)	(c)
181	182	183	184	185	186	187	188	189	190
(d)	(a)	(c)	(b)	(d)	(c)	(b)	(a)	(d)	(c)
191	192	193	194	195	196	197	198	199	200
(b)	(a)	(c)	(b)	(d)	(c)	(b)	(a)	(a)	(c)
201	202	203	204	205	206	207	208	209	210
(d)	(c)	(b)	(b)	(c)	(b)	(d)	(c)	(b)	(a)
211	212	213	214	215	216	217	218	219	220
(c)	(a)	(c)	(d)	(b)	(a)	(a)	(b)	(a)	(c)
221	222	223	224	225	226	227	228	229	230
(b)	(c)	(a)	(b)	(a)	(d)	(c)	(b)	(c)	(b)
231	232	233	234	235	236	237	238	239	240
(c)	(a)	(b)	(d)	(a)	(c)	(d)	(b)	(a)	(b)
241	242	243	244	245	246	247	248	249	250
(c)	(a)	(b)	(d)	(c)	(a)	(b)	(a)	(d)	(c)
251	252	253	254	255	256	257	258	259	260
(d)	(a)	(d)	(b)	(b)	(c)	(d)	(a)	(c)	(a)
261	262	263	264	265	266	267	268	269	270
(c)	(b)	(a)	(c)	(a)	(b)	(d)	(a)	(a)	(d)
271	272	273	274	275	276	277	278	279	280
(c)	(a)	(a)	(a)	(c)	(a)	(c)	(a)	(c)	(b)
281	282	283	284	285	286	287	288	289	290
(c)	(a)	(c)	(d)	(a)	(a)	(d)	(c)	(b)	(a)
291	292	293	294	295	296	297	298	299	300
(d)	(c)	(b)	(a)	(c)	(d)	(c)	(b)	(b)	(d)
301	302	303	304	305	306	307	308	309	310
(b)	(a)	(b)	(d)	(d)	(a)	(d)	(c)	(d)	(c)
311	312	313	314	315	316	317	318	319	320
(d)	(b)	(b)	(a)	(c)	(b)	(d)	(b)	(d)	(d)
321	322	323	324	325	326	327	328	329	330
(b)	(a)	(a)	(d)	(c)	(a)	(c)	(c)	(a)	(b)

331	332	333	334	335	336	337	338	339	340
(*a*)	(*d*)	(*b*)	(*c*)	(*b*)	(*d*)	(*a*)	(*b*)	(*c*)	(*a*)
341	342	343	344	345	346	347	348	349	350
(*b*)	(*a*)	(*c*)	(*d*)	(*b*)	(*d*)	(*d*)	(*a*)	(*d*)	(*c*)
351	352	353	354	355	356	357	358		
(*a*)	(*b*)	(*c*)	(*c*)	(*a*)	(*b*)	(*b*)	(*d*)		

CONJUNCTION

- **A word which joins either two or more than two words/sentences is known as conjunction.**
- Neither .... nor (in negative sense)
  Either .... or (in affirmative sense)
  Both .... and
  Hardly .... when/before
  No sooner .... than
  Scarcely .... when/before
  Though .... yet
- **Some illustrations based on above guidelines**
  Illustration:

  1. Yashwant is | neither | good | nor | bad.

  2. It is | both | cheap | and | good.

  3. | No sooner | did Ashok see the police | than | he ran away.

- **'Both' and 'as well as' cannot be used together in the same sentence.**
  Illustration: Both Bangladesh and Bhutan are poor. (✓)
  Bangladesh as well as Bhutan is poor. (✓)
  Both Bangladesh   as well as Bhutan are poor. (×)
- **Never use 'that' before who, whose, whom, where, when, what, which and why.**
  Illustration:
  The director asked Mr. S.R. Kumar that why he was late. (×)
  The director asked Mr. S.R. Kumar why he was late (✓)
- Not only .... but also (verb will be according to second subject)
- Either .... or (verb will be according to second subject)

Illustration:

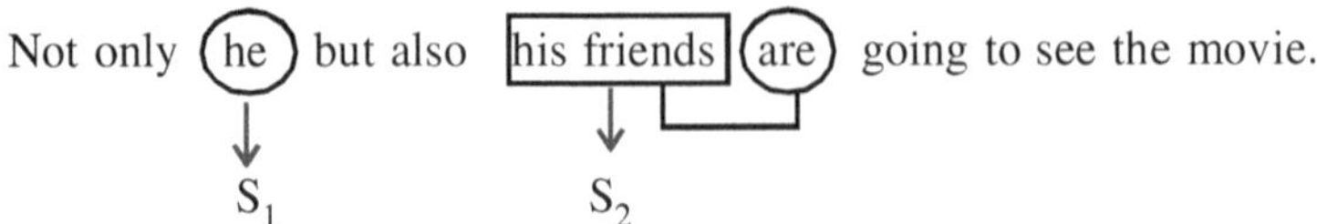

- **'But' will be used in negative sense.**
  Illustration: She worked hard but failed in the examination.

- $S_1 + \text{as well as} + S_2$

  A sentence having above structure takes verb according to first subject (S_1).

  Illustration: He as well as his friends is playing cricket.

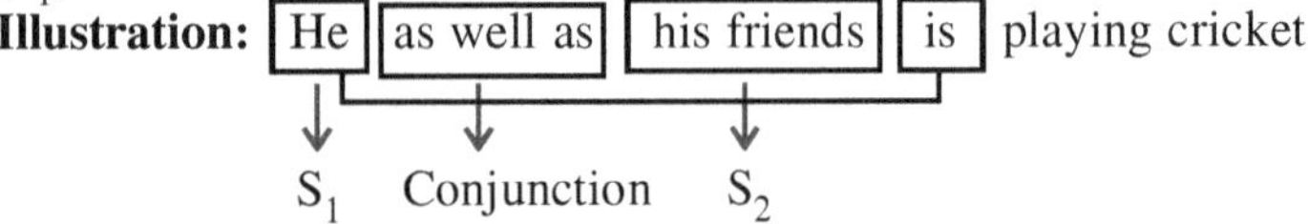

- **Use of as if (see illustration)**
  Illustration:
  Mr. Raj Prakash behaves as if he were the president of India.

  (Note : 'As if' takes always 'were')

- **If two subjects are combined with 'together with' then verb will be according to first subject.**
  Illustration:

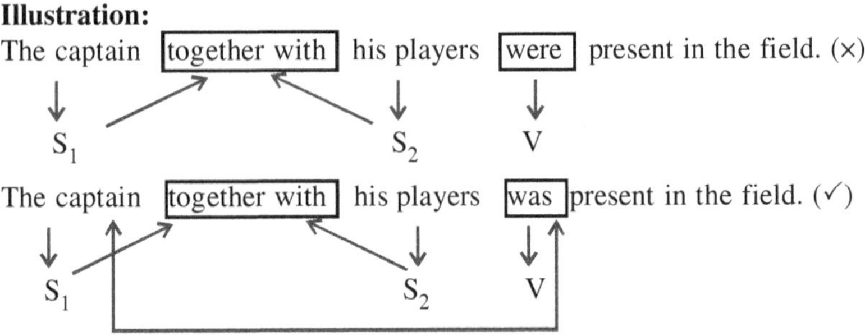

JUDGE YOURSELF

In the following questions choose the correct option to fill the blank.

1. Neither he .... his friend is good.
   - (*a*) or
   - (*b*) and
   - (*c*) but
   - (*d*) nor

2. The officer asked the peon .... why he was late.
   - (*a*) that
   - (*b*) if
   - (*c*) but
   - (*d*) no word

3. Both Ajay .... Bijay are intelligent.

(*a*) or   (*b*) nor
(*c*) and   (*d*) no word

4. No Sooner did the thief see the public .... he ran away.
(*a*) then   (*b*) and
(*c*) but   (*d*) than

5. Abhinav .... his brothers was going to Mumbai.
(*a*) but   (*b*) yet
(*c*) no word (*d*) together

6. He behaves .... he were the captain of the team.
(*a*) as if   (*b*) as
(*c*) no word (*d*) that

7. Either Rupali .... Sonali is going to attend the meeting.
(*a*) and   (*b*) but
(*c*) nor   (*d*) or

8. Neither Nirmal .... Ashwinee is going to listen the speech of A.B. Vajpayee.
(*a*) and   (*b*) but
(*c*) nor   (*d*) or

9. Ravi .... Prakash are going to Kolkata.
(*a*) or   (*b*) nor
(*c*) but   (*d*) and

10. Rice .... curry is my usual breakfast.
(*a*) and   (*b*) but
(*c*) then   (*d*) than

11. Hardly had he left .... his brother came.
(*a*) then   (*b*) than
(*c*) when   (*d*) that

12. I would rather have a copy .... a book.
(*a*) then   (*b*) than
(*c*) when   (*d*) that

13. He is no other .... my friend.
(*a*) then   (*b*) than
(*c*) when   (*d*) but

14. He saw a snake ....he awoke.
(*a*) then   (*b*) when
(*c*) than   (*d*) no word

15. Ten years have passed .... my grandmother died.
(*a*) since   (*b*) when
(*c*) then   (*d*) than

16. She is .... good .... bad.
(*a*) either, not (*b*) neither, or
(*c*) neither, nor(*d*) neither, than

17. The cellphone is both cheap .... best.
(*a*) than   (*b*) and
(*c*) then   (*d*) or

18. No sooner did the thief see the police .... he ran away.
(*a*) then   (*b*) than
(*c*) so   (*d*) because

19. Srishti will go .... Sanju goes.
(*a*) if   (*b*) than
(*c*) then   (*d*) although

ANSWERS

1	2	3	4	5	6	7	8	9	10
(*d*)	(*d*)	(*c*)	(*d*)	(*d*)	(*a*)	(*d*)	(*c*)	(*d*)	(*a*)

11	12	13	14	15	16	17	18	19
(*c*)	(*b*)	(*b*)	(*b*)	(*a*)	(*c*)	(*b*)	(*b*)	(*a*)

SECTION-II

DO'S AND DON'TS OF ARTICLE

Purple Patches

- **Two types of Articles :**
  - (i)   Indefinite Article (A, An)
  - (ii) Definite Article (The)
- **To reveal the sense of 'any one' Indefinite Article is used.**
- **To show a particular person or object Definite Article is used.**

USE OF ARTICLE

Some Do's

Indefinite Article

- **Indefinite articles are used before Singular Countable noun.**

  Illustration: He is (a) teacher.

  Indef. Art. ⸺ ⸺Sing. Count. Noun.

- **Indefinite articles are used before 'few'/'little' for showing a small number/quantity.**

  Illustration: A few students were present in the classroom.

  ⸺ (Some students)

- **For saying something related to price and speed, Indefinite articles will be used.**

  Illustration: The train is running with (a) *speed* of 40 km./hr.

  (Showing speed)

  The cost of mango is forty rupees (a) *kilo.*

  (Showing quantity)

  [**Note :** Indefinite articles are used with certain words like a dozen, a great deal of, a lot of, a million etc.]

- In exclamatory sentences, indefinite articles are used before singular countable noun.

  Illustration: What a marvellous joke!

- **Article 'A' → Consonant sound.**

  A European

  ⸺ (Uropian) produces 'U' sound which is consonant as per Hindi grammar.

46

- **Article 'An' → Vowel Sound.**
  An *FIR*
  └───────Af produces vowel sound as per Hindi grammar.

Definite Article

Definite Article is used :

1. before names of ranges of mountains, group of islands, rivers, gulfs, seas, oceans, epics, newspapers, heavenly bodies, dates of a month, ordinal numbers written in letters.
   Illustration: The Himalayas, The Ganga, The Indian Ocean, The Geeta, The Times of India, The Sun, The 4th of May, The First.
2. before the superlative degree.
   Illustration: The best girl, the highest mountain etc.
3. before the names of profession.
   Illustration: The author, the press etc.
4. before names of musical instruments, historical places or buildings.
   Illustration: The violin, The Red fort, etc.
5. before adjectives used as nouns.
   Illustration: The poor (means poor men)
6. before common nouns used as Abstract nouns.
   Illustration: The mother in her is dead.

OMISSION OF ARTICLE

Some Don'ts

Articles are not used,

1. before Material Nouns.
   Illustration: I drink milk (✓)
   I drink a milk (×)
   [Stone/wine/wood/cloth/iron never takes articles in a normal situation but when it refers a particular thing it takes article.]
2. before Abstract Nouns.
   Illustration: She is completely shaken with fear.
3. before Proper Nouns.
   Illustration: John Milton was a great poet. (✓)
   The John Milton was a great poet. (×)
4. before languages.
   Illustration: I like Hindi. (✓)
   I dislike **an** English. (×)
5. before names of relations.
   Illustration: Mother has gone out. (✓)
   The mother has gone out. (×)

6. a noun which comes before 'kind of'/'sort of' doesn't take any article.
   Illustration: She doesn't like this sort of person. (✓)
   What kind of **a** perfume do you like. (×)

JUDGE YOURSELF

In the following questions choose the correct option to fill the blank.

1. .... will have to be paid for this material.
   (*a*) Half rupee
   (*b*) Half a rupee
   (*c*) A half rupee
   (*d*) An half rupee

2. .... is taking keen interest in India.
   (*a*) The USA   (*b*) USA
   (*c*) An USA   (*d*) A USA

3. Only .... can save our country.
   (*a*) the Hitler   (*b*) a Hitler
   (*c*) Hitler   (*d*) an Hitler

4. I can run for ....
   (*a*) hundred miles
   (*b*) the hundred miles
   (*c*) a hundred miles
   (*d*) an hundred miles.

5. .... man-eater has been killed.
   (*a*) The
   (*b*) A
   (*c*) An
   (*d*) Either (*a*) or (*b*)

6. What .... fine idea!
   (*a*) the   (*b*) an
   (*c*) a   (*d*) no article

7. .... earth is moving around the sun.
   (*a*) An   (*b*) A
   (*c*) The   (*d*) No article

8. This is .... first example while I got.
   (*a*) the   (*b*) a
   (*c*) an   (*d*) no article

9. This is .... house which was built during earthquake.
   (*a*) a   (*b*) an
   (*c*) the   (*d*) no article

10. .... America is a rich country.
    (*a*) The   (*b*) An
    (*c*) A   (*d*) no article

11. .... U.S.A. is a developed country.
    (*a*) A   (*b*) An
    (*c*) The   (*d*) No article

12. .... Bible is a holy book.
    (*a*) A   (*b*) The
    (*c*) An   (*d*) No article

13. .... rich should help the poor.
    (*a*) The   (*b*) A
    (*c*) An   (*d*) No article

14. .... Gold is a costly metal.
    (*a*) The   (*b*) A
    (*c*) An   (*d*) No article

15. Kalidas is .... Shakespeare of India.
    (*a*) a   (*b*) an
    (*c*) the   (*d*) no article

16. I can not do .... difficult work.
    (*a*) a such   (*b*) the such
    (*c*) such the   (*d*) such a

17. How foolish .... plan it is!
  (*a*) a
  (*b*) an
  (*c*) the
  (*d*) no word required

18. An ink is .... useful article.
  (*a*) an
  (*b*) a
  (*c*) the
  (*d*) no word required

19. There are .... husband and wife.
  (*a*) a
  (*b*) an
  (*c*) the
  (*d*) no word required

20. He is learning .... French
  (*a*) the
  (*b*) a
  (*c*) an
  (*d*) no word required

21. I am going to by .... umbrella.
  (*a*) an
  (*b*) a
  (*c*) the
  (*d*) no word required

22. Dr. A.L. Sinha was .... University Professor.
  (*a*) the
  (*b*) a

  (*c*) an
  (*d*) no article

23. She is .... honest leader.
  (*a*) the   (*b*) an
  (*c*) a   (*d*) no article

24. .... lion is the king of a forest.
  (*a*) A   (*b*) No article
  (*c*) An   (*d*) The

25. The rose is .... Sweetest of all flowers.
  (*a*) an   (*b*) a
  (*c*) the   (*d*) no article

26. She caught him by .... arm.
  (*a*) the   (*b*) an
  (*c*) a   (*d*) no article

27. I know .... each boy.
  (*a*) an   (*b*) a
  (*c*) the   (*d*) no article

28. I love .... every bird.
  (*a*) a   (*b*) an
  (*c*) the   (*d*) no article

29. Mr. Rao is .... union leader.
  (*a*) a   (*b*) the
  (*c*) an   (*d*) no article

30. I am .... honest person.
  (*a*) the   (*b*) an
  (*c*) a   (*d*) no article

ANSWERS

1	2	3	4	5	6	7	8	9	10
(*b*)	(*a*)	(*b*)	(*c*)	(*d*)	(*c*)	(*c*)	(*a*)	(*c*)	(*d*)

11	12	13	14	15	16	17	18	19	20
(*c*)	(*b*)	(*a*)	(*d*)	(*c*)	(*d*)	(*a*)	(*b*)	(*d*)	(*d*)

21	22	23	24	25	26	27	28	29	30
(*c*)	(*a*)	(*b*)	(*d*)	(*c*)	(*a*)	(*d*)	(*d*)	(*a*)	(*b*)

SECTION-III

TENSE AT A GLANCE

- The key point is that Tense is related to the form of verb.
- Tense has three kinds :

PRESENT TENSE WITH ITS FORM

(i) Simple Present/Present Indefinite

$$S + V_1 + O + C.$$

Here,

S   = Subject
V_1 = 1st form of verb
O   = Object
C   = Compliment (one who completes the sense of a sentence.)

Relation between Person & Number

Person	Singular No.	Plural No.
1st	I	We
2nd	You	You
3rd	He, she, it name of any thing, i.e. man	They men

Illustration:

I read a novel of Premchand.
S V_1 O   C

Exception:

If the subject will be in third person, singular number then do insert *s/es* with the first form of verb.

$$S + Vs/es + O + C$$

Illustration:

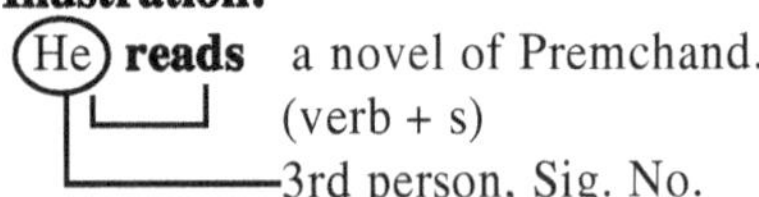

(ii) Present Continuous/Present Imperfect (Progressive)

$$S + A.V. + V_4 + O + C$$

Here,

A.V. = Auxiliary verb or Helping verb.
i.e., is; am; are; has; have; etc.

50

V_4 = V + ing (4rth form of verb)
i.e., going; playing etc.

Illustration:

I   am   reading   a novel   of Premchand.
S   A.V. V_4 O   C

(iii) Present Perfect

S + has/have + V_3 + O + C

Here,

V_3 = 3rd form of verb
i.e., Past Participle.

Relation between Subject & Auxilary Verb

Subject	A.V.
I	am
You	are
He, she, it	is
They	are
Name of any thing in singular No. i.e. book	is
Name of anything in plural no. i.e. fruits.	are

Illustration:

I   have   gone   through   a novel of Premchand.
S   A.V. V_3 Preposition   O   C

(Note : Preposition will be discussed under a separate chapter.)

Exception

If the subject will be in third person, singular number then use *has* in place of have.

Illustration:

(He) **has** gone through a novel of Premchand.
———3rd person, Singular No.

(iv) Present Perfect Continuous

S + has/have + been + V_4 + O + for/since + C

Illustration:

I have been reading a novel for two weeks of Premchand.
S V_4 O   C

Exception

If the subject will be in third person, singular number then use *has been* in place of have been.

Illustration:

(He) **has been** reading a novel for two weeks of Premchand.
3rd person, Singular No.

Use of for/since :
- *for* is used for period of time i.e., for two hours, three days etc.
- *Since* is used for point of time.
  i.e., Since Monday, Since 2005 etc.
  Illustration: They have been playing cricket (for) the last five years.
  Period of time.

  She has been writing a letter (since) 2 p.m.
  Point of time.

PAST TENSE WITH ITS FORM

(i) Simple Past/Past Indefinite

$$S + V_2 + O + C$$

Here, V_2 = 2nd form of verb.

Illustration:

He   wrote   a fiction   in Hindi.
S V_2 O   C

Form of Verb

V_1	V_2	V_3	V_4
Write	Wrote	Written	Writing
Read	Read	Read	Reading
Go	Went	Gone	Going
. . .	. . .	. . .	. . .

(ii) Past Continuous/Past Imperfect (Progressive)

$$S + A.V. + V_4 + O + C$$

Here, A.V. = Auxiliary verb or Helping verb i.e., was, were
(Note : For singular subject i.e., He it, book etc. *was* will be used and for plural subject i.e., They, we, fruits etc. *were* will be used.)

Illustration:

(I) was   reading a novel of Premchand.
Singular subject

(We) were   dancing on the floor.
Plural subject

(iii) Past Perfect

$$S + had + V_3 + O + C$$

Illustration:

I   had   gone   through   a novel   of Premchand.
S   A.V. V_3 Preposition   O   C
(Note : *Had* is also in the list of A.V. or helping verb.)

(iv) Past Prefect Continuous

$$\boxed{S + had+been + V_4 + O + for/since + C}$$

Illustration:

I had been reading a novel for two weeks of Premchand.
S V_4 O   C (period of time)

She had been writing a book since the last January.
  S V_4 O   C (point of time)

FUTURE TENSE WITH ITS FORM

(i) Simple Future/Future Indefinite

$$\boxed{S + shall/will + V_1 + O + C}$$

(Note : *shall/will* is also in the list of A.V. or helping verb.)

Illustration:

I   shall   read a novel of Premchand.

S   A.V. V_1 O   C

Use of shall/will

In general case, shall = I and will = He, you, she, it and name of any object. To make certainty or emphasis, shall = He, she, it, you and name of any object and will = I.

(ii) Future Continuous/Future Imperfect (Progressive)

$$\boxed{S + shall/will + be + V_4 + O + C}$$

Illustration:

He will be playing this match at Salt Lake Stadium.
S   A.V. V_4 O   C

(iii) Future Perfect

$$\boxed{S + will/shall + have + V_3 + O + C}$$

Illustration:

She will have sung a song on the stage.
S   A.V. V_3 O   C

(Note : Future Perfect Continuous is not in use these days.)

A comparative chart regarding Verb

Simple Present	Simple Past	Simple Future
V_1	V_2	shall/will + V_1
Present Continuous	Past Continuous	Future Continuous
is/am/are + V_4	was/were + V_4	shall/will + be + V_4
Present Perfect	Past Perfect	Future Perfect
has/have + V_3	had + V_3	shall/will + have + V_3
Present Perf. Cont.	Past Perft. Cont.	Future Perf. Cont.
has/have + been + V_4	had + been + V_4	Not in use

Some more Clues

Simple Pr.

Reveals habit or repition of work—
- He always goes to college.
- I like fruits very much.

Reveals time or condition—
- She will select if you guide her.
- Raj will stay here until Srishti comes back.

Reveals principle or eternal truth—
- The earth moves round the sun.
- Water freezes at 0°C.

Reveals future plan/programme—
- The aeroplane takes off at 4 p.m.
- She goes for Mumbai tomorrow.

Pr. Cont.

Reveals intention or likelihood of the work—
- He is going to purchase a scooter.
- The patient is going to die.

Pr. Perf.

Reveals that the said work is finished just now. So, it is not related to present time—
- I have done the task.

Pr. Perf. Cont.

Reveals that the work has started in the past but it is continue up to now—
- They have been working since 1985.

Simple Past

Reveals a habit of working of the past time—

- She used to help him.

Past Cont.

Reveals a habit of working of old days—

- Kalpana was always murmuring.

Words like could, might, would are in the past tense but their applications will be in present tense for showing request—

- Would you like to go there?

The sentence which reveals wish or desire, having past tense in its structure shows present or future time—

- I wish I were a director of this company.

JUDGE YOURSELF

In the following questions choose the correct option to fill the blank.

1. I have .... the task.
   - (a) did
   - (b) do
   - (c) done
   - (d) does

2. He has .... through the book.
   - (a) going
   - (b) went
   - (c) gone
   - (d) goes

3. I have been playing cricket .... two years.
   - (a) since
   - (b) for
   - (c) from
   - (d) of

4. He .... a beautiful sketch.
   - (a) made
   - (b) make
   - (c) makes
   - (d) either (a) or (c)

5. I have been working in this office .... 1987.
   - (a) since
   - (b) for
   - (c) from
   - (d) of

6. They will .... performed on the stage.
   - (a) had
   - (b) has
   - (c) have
   - (d) (a) & (b)

7. Ravi is .... to railway station.
   - (a) went
   - (b) going
   - (c) goes
   - (d) to

8. We will .... playing this match at Green Park Stadium.
   - (a) be
   - (b) being
   - (c) have
   - (d) has

9. He will .... a glass of water.
   - (a) drank
   - (b) drink
   - (c) drunk
   - (d) drinks

10. She has .... making a noise for two hours.
   - (a) being
   - (b) been
   - (c) will be
   - (d) be

11. We .... the target.
   - (a) hit
   - (b) hits
   - (c) hited
   - (d) heat

12. She .... a wonderful game.
   - (a) played
   - (b) will played
   - (c) will plays
   - (d) play

13. I .... the King of this locality.
   - (a) is
   - (b) are
   - (c) have
   - (d) am

14. The Sun .... in the east
  (*a*) rised   (*b*) risen
  (*c*) rose   (*d*) rises

15. I have .... a wonderful picnic spot.
  (*a*) saw   (*b*) seen
  (*c*) see   (*d*) sees

16. I have been making a noise .... two hours.
  (*a*) since
  (*b*) for
  (*c*) from
  (*d*) no word required

17. He had been .... for the last five years.
  (*a*) working   (*b*) worked
  (*c*) will work   (*d*) work

18. I wish I .... the President of India.
  (*a*) was   (*b*) were
  (*c*) had   (*d*) have

19. She will .... gone to Kolkata.
  (*a*) has
  (*b*) had
  (*c*) have
  (*d*) no word required

20. He .... a cup of tea.
  (*a*) drink   (*b*) has drink
  (*c*) have drink   (*d*) drinks

21. The Sun .... in the east.
  (*a*) rose   (*b*) rises
  (*c*) had rose   (*d*) will risen

22. People .... gone out of their houses.
  (*a*) is   (*b*) was
  (*c*) has   (*d*) have

23. I had .... coming from Mumbai.
  (*a*) been   (*b*) being
  (*c*) be   (*d*) to be

24. She .... a tremendous job for her locality.
  (*a*) make
  (*b*) making
  (*c*) will be make
  (*d*) has made

25. I have been playing cricket .... 1985.
  (*a*) for   (*b*) from
  (*c*) since   (*d*) on

26. Ranu and Neeru .... going to Mumbai.
  (*a*) has   (*b*) have
  (*c*) being   (*d*) are

27. Pratham and Priya .... play at noon.
  (*a*) Shall   (*b*) will
  (*c*) being   (*d*) been

28. Rupam .... to see a movie along with Monu.
  (*a*) goes   (*b*) gone
  (*c*) going   (*d*) has go

ANSWERS

1	2	3	4	5	6	7	8	9	10
(*c*)	(*c*)	(*b*)	(*d*)	(*a*)	(*c*)	(*b*)	(*a*)	(*b*)	(*b*)

11	12	13	14	15	16	17	18	19	20
(*a*)	(*a*)	(*d*)	(*d*)	(*b*)	(*b*)	(*a*)	(*b*)	(*c*)	(*d*)

21	22	23	24	25	26	27	28
(*b*)	(*d*)	(*a*)	(*d*)	(*c*)	(*d*)	(*b*)	(*a*)

SECTION-IV

WORLD OF VOICE

KINDS OF VOICE

(a) Active voice
(b) Passive voice
- Transformation of voice *i.e.*, from Active voice to Passive voice.
- Voice and Tense are closely associated with each other.
- Tense plays an important role while transforming the voice.
- On the basis of following points, voice can be discussed:

1. Indefinite (In Active Voice)

Illustration:

(a) Srishti writes a letter. (Simple Present)
(b) Srishti wrote a letter. (Simple Past)
(c) Srishti will write a letter. (Simple Future)

Transformations based on Voice

Subject	Object
I	me
He	him
She	her
They	them

Rule of Transformation

1st-step	:	Demarkation of sentence into S, V, O etc.
2nd-step	:	Change object into subject. (See the above chart)
3rd-step	:	Use helping verb/A.V. according to tense.

(See chart on next page)

4rth-step	:	Use 3rd form of verb.
5th-step	:	Insert 'by'.
6th-step	:	Change subject into object. (see the above chart)
7th-step	:	Use of full stop.

Demonstration of illustration based on rule

1st-step   :   (a) <u>Srishti</u> <u>writes</u> a <u>letter</u>. (Active Voice)
                     S   V   O

57

2nd-step : $\underline{\text{A letter}}$
               S

3rd-step : $\underline{\text{A letter}}$ $\underline{\text{is}}$
               S   A.V.

4th-step : $\underline{\text{A letter}}$ $\underline{\text{is}}$ $\underline{\text{written}}$
               S   A.V. V_3

5th-step : $\underline{\text{A letter}}$ $\underline{\text{is}}$ $\underline{\text{written by}}$
               S   A.V. V_3

6th-step : $\underline{\text{A letter}}$ $\underline{\text{is}}$ $\underline{\text{written}}$ by $\underline{\text{Srishti}}$
               S   A.V. V_3 O

7th-step : $\underline{\text{A letter}}$ $\underline{\text{is}}$ $\underline{\text{written}}$ by $\underline{\text{Srishti}}$ $\underline{\cdot}$ (Passive Voice).
               S   A.V. V_3 O   full stop.

Use of A.V./helping verb

Present	Past	Future
is, am, are	was, were	will be, shall be

In Passive Voice
(b) A letter was written by Srishti.

(c) A letter will be written by Srishti.

2. Continuous

Illustration:
(a) He is making a noise. (Present Continuous)

(b) He was making a noise. (Past Continuous)

Rule of Transformation :
(i) Apply all the above steps.

(ii) While doing so after 3rd step introduce one more step, *i.e.*, 3rd (A) step.

(iii) In 3rd (A) step use 'being'.

In Passive Voice
(a) A noise is **being** made by him.

(b) A noise was **being** made by him.

3. Perfect

Illustration:
(a) Sania has created a world record. (Present Perfect)

(b) Sania had created a world record. (Past Perfect)

(c) Sania will have created a world record (Future Perfect)

Rule of Transformation :
(i) Apply all the steps said earlier.
(ii) While doing so use 'been' in 3rd (A) step.

In Passive Voice :
(a) A world record has been created by Sania.
(b) A world record had been created by Sania.
(c) A world record will have been created by Sania.
(**Note :** While transforming the sentence from one voice to another voice, tense will not be changed at any cost.)

TRANSFORMATION BASED ON VARIOUS SENTENCES

Special Rules regarding Transformation of Voice

1. **Sentence having Do/Did/Does**
   Illustration:
   (a) **Do** you make this plan? (In Active Voice)
   (b) **Did** they drink tea?
   (c) **Does** she draw a figure?

   Rule of Transformation :
   1st-step   : Omit Do/Did/Does.
   2nd-step : Change in to passive form as earlier.
   3rd-step : Make the sentence interrogative. *i.e.*, use auxilary verb in the beginning of the sentence and insert(?) at the end of the sentence.

   (In Passive form)
   (a) Is this plan made by you?
   (b) Was tea drunk by them?
   (c) Is a figure drawn by her?

2. **Sentence having Helping verb in the beginning**
   Illustration:
   Is he reading a story? (In Active Voice)
   A.V.

   Rule of Transformation :
   1st-step : Change into Assertive Sentence.
   (Note : Use the process which is written earlier.)
   2nd-step : Change into passive form.
   3rd-step : Make the sentence interrogative.

   In Passive Voice
   1st-step : He is reading a story.
   2nd-step : A story is being read by him.
   3rd-step : Is a story being read by him?

3. Sentence having who in the beginning
Illustration:
<u>Who</u> gave you this cell phone? (In Active Voice)
Rule of Transformation:
1st-step : Forget who and change the rest portion into assertive sentence.
2nd-step : Change into passive form.
3rd -step : Make the sentence interrogative.
4rth-step : Insert 'By whom' in the beginning of the sentence.
In Passive Voice
1st-step : You gave this cellphone.
2nd-step : This cellphone was given to you.
3rd-step : Was the cellphone given to you?
4rth-step : By whom was this cellphone given to you?

4. Sentence having Double object
(a) If the structure of a sentence is like $\boxed{S + V + O_1 + O_2}$

Illustration: $\underset{S}{\text{She}} \quad \underset{V_2}{\text{gave}} \quad \underset{O_1}{\text{me}} \quad \underset{O_2}{\text{a novel.}}$ (In Active Voice)

Here,
O_1 = Indirect object
O_2 = Direct object
(Note : Indirect object means an object which succeeds 'to' or 'for' but Direct object hasn't such quality.)
Then, the passive form will be :
Ist- procedure : I was given a novel.
2nd-procedure : A novel was given to me.
(b) If the structure of a sentence is like $\boxed{S + V + O + O.C.}$

Illustration: $\underset{S}{\text{They}} \quad \underset{V_2}{\text{made}} \quad \underset{O}{\text{him}} \quad \underset{O.C}{\text{captain.}}$ (In Active Voice)

Here,
O.C. means a complement which comes to clarify the meaning of an object, before this object Transitive verb must be used.
Then, the passive form will be—
He was made captain.

5. If the Structure of an Active Voice is like $\boxed{S + A.V. + to + V_1 + O}$
Illustration: $\underset{S}{\text{I}} \quad \underset{A.V.}{\text{was}} \quad \underset{}{\text{to}} \quad \underset{V_1}{\text{help}} \quad \underset{O}{\text{her.}}$
(Note : Use 'to be' after helping/auxilary verb.]
In passive Voice
$\qquad$ She $\underset{A.V.}{\underline{\text{was}}}$ <u>to be</u> <u>helped</u> (by me)

6. If the structure of an Active Voice is like $S + has/have/had + to + V_1 + O$

Illustration: <u>They</u> had to <u>help</u> <u>him</u>.
            S V_1 O

(Note : Use 'to be' + V_3]

In Passive Voice

<u>He</u> had <u>to be</u> <u>helped</u>. (by them)
 S V_3

7. If the structure of an Active Voice is like $There + A.V. + N(S) + Infinitive$

Here,   N = Noun

              S = Subject

Illustration: <u>There</u> <u>is</u> no <u>money</u> <u>to</u> waste.
                   AV.   N(S) Infinitive

[Note : Use 'to be' + V_3]

In Passive Voice

There is no money <u>to be</u> <u>wasted.</u>
                           V_3

8. Active Voice in Imperative Sentence showing request/advice.

Illustration:

Help the poor.

[Note : Use should be]

In Passive Voice

The poor <u>should be</u> helped.

9. Active Voice in Imperative Sentence showing order/command

Illustration:

Ring the bell at once.

Rule of Transformation

$Let, + \ldots + be + V_3 + \ldots$

<u>Let,</u> <u>the bell</u> <u>be</u> <u>rung</u> <u>at once.</u>
     $\ldots$ V_3 $\ldots$

[Note : In such type of sentence never use 'by you'.]

10. If the structure of an Active Voice is like $S + C.V. + Infinite$ (without 'to')

Here, C.V. = Causative verb

Illustration: <u>She</u>   <u>made</u>   me   <u>laugh.</u>
           S   C.V.   Infinitive

Rules of Transformation

1st-step : Change object into subject.

2nd-step : Use of 'to' before infinitive which is concealed in Active Voice.

In Passive Voice

$$\underline{\text{I}} \text{ was made } \underline{\text{to laugh}}.$$

S   Infinitive

11. If the structure of Active Voice is like $\boxed{\text{P.C. + that + N.C. (object)}}$

Here,

P.C. = Principal clause

N.C. = Noun clause (having object)

Illustration: <u>People consider</u> <u>that</u> <u>he</u> <u>is wise.</u> (Active Voice)

                 P.C.   N.C.

                                        Subject

Rule of Transformation

1st-step : The subject of Noun clause will remain unchanged in passive form.

2nd-step : Avoid the subject of Principal clause.

3rd-step : Never use 'by + object'.

In Passive Voice

He is considered to be wise.

12. If the structure of an Active Voice is like $\boxed{\text{S + M.V. + V}_1\text{ + O + C}}$

Here,

M.V. = can, could, shall, should, may, might.

Illustration: <u>I</u>   <u>can</u>   <u>write</u>   <u>a fiction</u>   <u>in English.</u>

             S   M.V. V_1 O   C

Rule of Transformation

(Note : Use 'be' after M.V.)

In Passive Voice

A fiction in English <u>can</u> <u>be</u> written by me.

                                M.V.

$\boxed{\textbf{JUDGE YOURSELF}}$

In these questions, the sentences have been given in Active/Passive voice. From the given options, choose the one which best expresses the given sentence in Passive/Active voice.

1. Help the poor .

    (*a*) The poor should be helped.

    (*b*) The poor would be helped.

    (*c*) The poor must be helped.

    (*d*) The poor will be helped.

2. Bring a glass of water.

    (*a*) A glass of water will be brought.

    (*b*) A glass of water should be brought.

    (*c*) Let, a glass of water be brought.

    (*d*) Let, a glass of water will be brought.

3. He gave me a beautiful flower pot.
  (*a*) A beautiful flower pot was given to me by him.
  (*b*) A beautiful flower pot had given to me by him.
  (*c*) A beautiful flower pot had been giving by him.
  (*d*) I was giving him a beautiful flower pot.

4. Is he answering the question?
  (*a*) The question is answered by him.
  (*b*) The question is being answered by him.
  (*c*) Is the question being answered by him?
  (*d*) Is the question being answering by him?

5. Who gave you this letter?
  (*a*) This letter was given to you by whom?
  (*b*) This letter had given to you by whom?
  (*c*) Was this letter given to you?
  (*d*) By whom was this letter given to you?

6. The professor teaches students.
  (*a*) Students are being taught by the professor.
  (*b*) Students are taught by the professor.
  (*c*) The professor is being taught by students.
  (*d*) Students are being teaching by students.

7. M.S. Dhoni has created a world record.
  (*a*) A world record has been created by M.S. Dhoni.
  (*b*) A world record has created by M.S. Dhoni.
  (*c*) A world record is created by M.S. Dhoni.
  (*d*) A world record is being created by M.S. Dhoni.

8. Srishti sings a lovely song.
  (*a*) A lovely song had sung by Srishti.
  (*b*) A lovely song was sung by Srishti.
  (*c*) A lovely song is sung by Srishti.
  (*d*) A lovely song is sang by Srishti.

9. He was drawing a picture.
  (*a*) A picture was drawn by him.
  (*b*) A picture was being drawn by him.
  (*c*) A picture was drawing by him.
  (*d*) A picture was drew by him.

10. We made him leader.
  (*a*) He was made leader by us.
  (*b*) He was maded leader.
  (*c*) He made leader by us.
  (*d*) He was made leader.

11. There is no time to waste.
  (*a*) There is no time to be wasted.
  (*b*) No time to be wasted there.
  (*c*) No time to be wasted by there.
  (*d*) No time is to be wasted.

12. Take medicine in time.
  (*a*) In time medicine to be taken.
  (*b*) Medicine should be taken in time.

(c) Medicine in time will be taken.

(d) Medicine has to be in time taken.

13. He reads a novel.
(a) A novel was read by him.
(b) A novel has read by him.
(c) A novel is being read by him.
(d) A novel is red by him.

14. They had cleared the dues.
(a) The dues had been cleared.
(b) The dues had cleared by them.
(c) The dues had being cleared.
(d) The dues is cleared.

15. I invite you on the dinner.
(a) On the dinner, you have been invited.
(b) On the dinner, you are inviting.
(c) You are inviting by me on the dinner.
(d) You are invited by me on the dinner.

16. We chose him our leader.
(a) He was choosen our leader.
(b) He has been choosen our leader.
(c) He had choosen our leader.
(d) He have been choosen our leader.

17. Who made a maiden century?
(a) By whose was a maiden century made?

(b) By whom was a maiden century make?
(c) By whom was a maiden century made?
(d) By whom had a maiden century made?

18. I may help him in her project.
(a) He might be helped by me in her project.
(b) He may be helped in her project by me.
(c) He might be helped in her project by me.
(d) In her project, he may be help by me.

19. Take medicine in time.
(a) Medicine should be taken in time.
(b) Medicine will be taken in time.
(c) Medicine will be took in time.
(d) Medicine shall take in time.

20. I am solving the questions.
(a) The questions are being solved by me.
(b) The questions are been solved by me.
(c) The questions are be solved by me.
(d) The question are solved by me.

ANSWERS

1	2	3	4	5	6	7	8	9	10
(a)	(c)	(a)	(c)	(d)	(b)	(a)	(c)	(b)	(d)

11	12	13	14	15	16	17	18	19	20
(a)	(b)	(d)	(a)	(d)	(a)	(b)	(b)	(a)	(d)

┌─────────────┐
SECTION-V
└─────────────┘

PRESENTATION OF SPEECH

Kinds of Narration

- Narration means Statement or Speech.
- It has two kinds— (i) Direct (ii) Indirect.
- **Facts related to Narration :**

Illustration: He says to me, "I am suffering from jaundice".

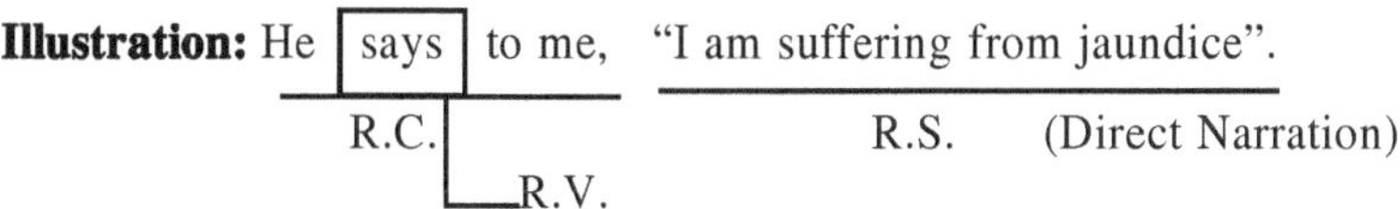

- He says to me that he is suffering from jaundice.

(Indirect-Narration)

Here,

R.C. = Reporting clause.

R.V. = Reporting verb.

R.S. = Reported Speech.

Transformation Based on General Rules

1. **Change of Person** : 'SON' is the useful formula to serve the purpose.

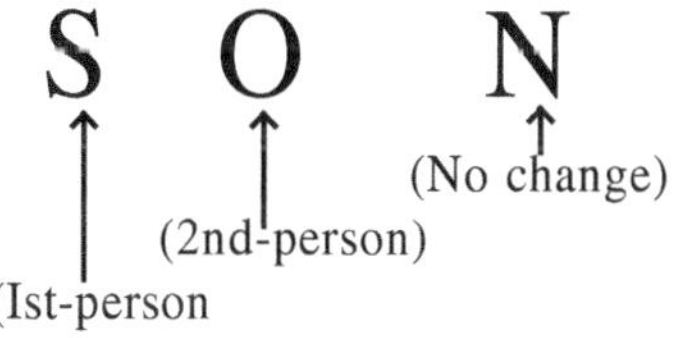

(i) If the subject/object of R.S. is in 1st person then, while transforming into indirect speech it will be according to the subject of R.C.

(ii) If the subject/object of R.S. is in 2nd person then, while transforming into indirect speech it will be according to the object of R.C.

(iii) 3rd-person requires no change.

Illustration

(i) Dhiraj told me, "I shall do my work" (Direct speech)

  - Dhiraj told me that he would do his work. (Indirect speech)

Explanation.

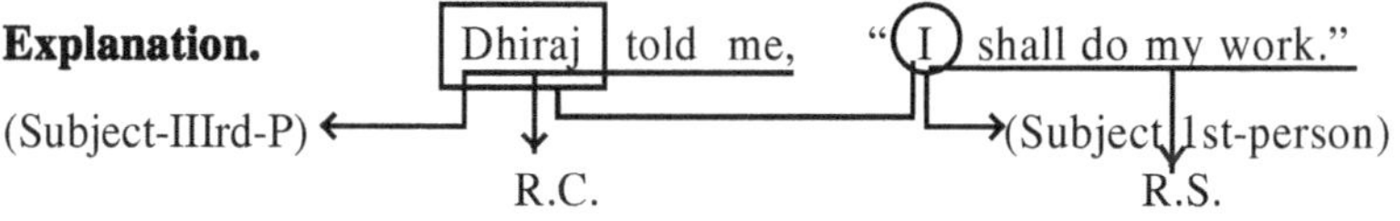

(ii) Golcha tells me, "I will help you".

- Golcha tells me that he will help me.

Explanation

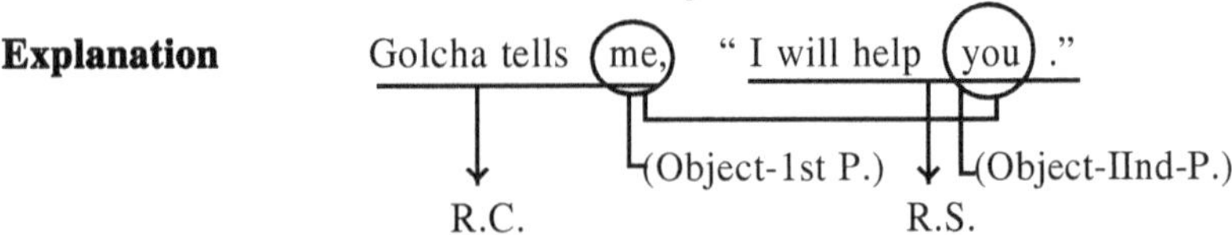

(iii) Hrithika will say to Srishti, "Survi is a very good house wife".

- Hrithika will say to Srishti that Survi is a very good house wife.

Explanation

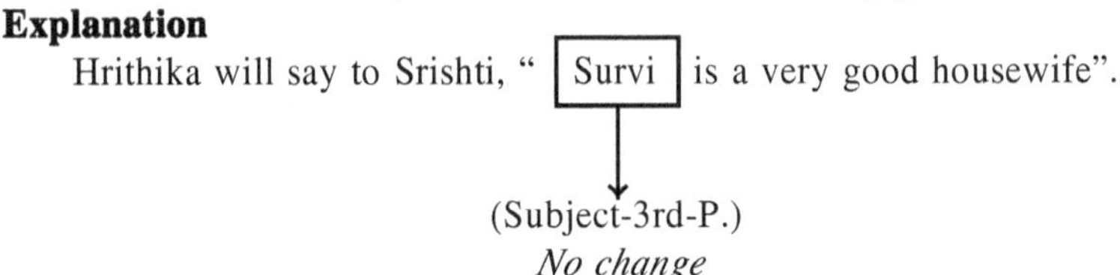

2. Change of Tense :

R.V.	R.S.	Result
Present Tense	Any Tense	No change.
Future Tense	Any Tense	No change.
Past Tense	Present/Future Tense	Change into corresponding Past Tense.
Past Tense	Past Indefinite Tense	Change into Past Perfect Tense.
Past Tense	Past Continuous Tense	Change into Past Perfect Continuous Tense
Past Tense	Past Pefect/Perfect-Continuous Tense	No change.
Past Tense	Universal Truth	No change.
Past Tense	Proverb	No change.

Other Changes (If R.V. in Past Tense)

(i) This into That
(ii) These into Those
(iii) Here into There
(iv) Now into Then
(v) Thus into So

   (vi) Hence into Thence
  (vii) To-day into That day
 (viii) Tomorrow into Next day
   (ix) Yesterday into The previous day
    (x) Last night into The previous night
   (xi) Next year into The following year.
  (xii) A year ago into A year before.

Illustration:

1. She says, "He was a good player".
   - She says that he was a good player.
2. They will say, "We are scholars".
   - They will say that they are scholars.
3. He said, "I have performed the task".
   - He said that he had performed the task.
4. They said, "We will create a history".
   - They said that they would create a history.
5. Mr. Somnath said, "I went to Mumbai".
   - Mr. Somnath said that he had gone to Mumbai.
6. Mr. Sambhunath said, "I was making a plan".
   - Mr. Sambhunath said that he had been making a plan.
7. Mrs. Kalpana said, "I had performed a stage show".
   - Mrs. Kalpana said that she had performed a stage show.
8. Miss Nutan said, "I had been teaching in this school since 2005".
   - Miss Nutan said that she had been teaching in this school since 2005.
9. The teacher said, "The sun rises in the east".
   - The teacher said that the sun rises in the east.

Transformation Based on Special Rules

I. Rule related to Interrogative Sentence

- If the answer of an interrogative sentence is possible in yes-no manner.
  Illustration. M.S. Dhoni told Rahul Dravid, "Will you help me?"

  M.S. Dhoni asked Rahul Dravid whether he would help him.

  (Note : The answer of R.S. is possible in yes-no manner)

  Rule of Transformation from Direct to Indirect speech

  Step I : Change R.V. into ask.

  Step II : In place of comma use 'if/whether'.

  Step III : Change interrogative sentence into assertive sentence.

- If the answer of an interrogative sentence is not possible in yes-no manner.
  Illustration: Rahul Dravid told Dhoni, "What do you want?"

  Rahul Dravid asked Dhoni what he wanted.

  (Note : Only in Step II, you have to avoid comma and inverted comma and rest will be same as mentioned above).

II. Rule related to Imperative Sentence

- Imperative sentence is a sentence which shows Order/Advice/Request
  Illustration: My father said to me, "Go there".

  My father ordered me to go there.

Rule of Transformation from Direct to Indirect Speech

Step I : Change R.V. as per meaning/sense of R.S. into order/request/advise.
Step II : In place of comma, use 'to'.
Step III : Rest portion will be same.

III. Rule related to Optative Sentence

- Optative sentence is a sentence which exposes the feeling of bless/curse/pray/wish.
  Illustration: Mother said to me, "May you live long!"

  Mother blessed me that I might live long.

Rule of Transformation from Direct to Indirect Speech

Step I : Change R.V. as per meaning/sense of R.S. into bless/curse/pray/wish.
Step II : In place of comma, use 'that'.
Step III : Change optative sentence into assertive sentence.

IV. Rule related to Exclamatory Sentence

- Exclamatory sentence is a sentence which takes note of exclamatory (!) mark in that sentence showing inner feeling.
  Illustration: She said, "Alas! I am ruined".

  She exclaimed with sorrow that she was ruined.

Rule of Transformation from Direct to Indirect Speech

Step I : Change R.V. as per meaning/sense of R.S. into exclaim/exclaims/exclaimed/will or shall exclaim + joy/sorrow/anger/surprise/applause/contempt.
Step II : Change comma into that.
Step III : Change note of exclamation (!) into full (.)
Step IV : Change exclamatory sentence into assertive sentence.

JUDGE YOURSELF

Each sentence (Direct) in this assignment in followed by four options, i.e., (a, b, c and d) of it (Indirect) on these four options, only one is correct. Spot the correct answer.

1. She said to me, "Keep quite and listen to my words".
   (*a*) She requested me to keep quite and listen to her words.
   (*b*) She ordered me to keep quite and listen to her words.
   (*c*) She entreated me to keep quite and listen to her words.
   (*d*) She told me to keep quite and listen to her words.

2. My brother said to me, "What are you doing here?"
   (*a*) My brother asked me that what I was doing there.
   (*b*) My brother asked me what I was doing there.
   (*c*) My brother asked me that what was I doing there.
   (*d*) My brother asked me what I was doing here.

3. Ravi said, "My father lived in this city two years ago."
   (*a*) Ravi said that his father had lived in that city two years before.
   (*b*) Ravi said that his father had lived in that city two years ago.
   (*c*) Ravi told that his father had lived in that city ago two years.
   (*d*) Ravi asked that his father had lived in that city before two years.

4. My brother said to me, "When I was young, I used to play cricket".
   (*a*) My brother told me that when I was young, I used to play cricket.
   (*b*) My brother told me that when I was young, I used to play cricket.
   (*c*) My brother told me that when he was young, I used to play cricket.
   (*d*) My brother told me that when he was young, he used to play cricket.

5. The student said, "Sir, I am not guilty".
   (*a*) The student said with respect that he was not guilty.
   (*h*) The student plcadcd that he was not guilty.
   (*c*) The student pleaded with respect that he was not guilty.
   (*d*) The student said respectfully that he was not guilty.

6. Prabha said, "I am an early-riser".
   (*a*) She regretted that she was an early-riser.
   (*b*) She said that she is an early-riser.

    (c) She said that she was an early-riser.

    (d) She regretted that she is an early-riser.

7. The police officer said to the criminal, "Speak as I tell you".

    (a) The police officer directed the criminal to speak as he told him.

    (b) The police officer told the criminal to speak as he told him.

    (c) The police officer advised the criminal to speak as he told him.

    (d) The police officer requested the criminal to speak as he told him.

8. The preacher said to me, "May God help you!"

    (a) The preacher prayed that God might help me.

    (b) The preacher prayed that God might help him.

    (c) The preacher requested that God might help me.

    (d) The preacher requested the God might help them.

9. She said to me, "Happy Diwali!"

    (a) She blessed me a happy Diwali.

    (b) She wished me a happy Diwali.

    (c) She prayed a happy Diwali.

    (d) She said to me a very happy Diwali.

10. He said, "Shall I open the gate?"

    (a) He asked that he should open the gate.

    (b) He asked if he should open the gate.

    (c) He ordered that he should open the gate.

    (d) He requested that he should open the gate.

11. I told Ravi Singh, "Do have a cup of tea".

    (a) I ordered Ravi Singh to have a cup of tea.

    (b) I advised Ravi Singh to had a cup of tea.

    (c) I requested Ravi Singh to have a cup of tea.

    (d) I said Ravi Singh to have a cup of cold tea.

12. He told me, "Shall I go to the picture?"

    (a) He asked that he should go to the picture.

    (b) He asked if he shall go to the picture.

    (c) He asked if he should go to the picture.

    (d) He requested me to go to the picture.

13. The teacher says, "Two and two makes four".

    (a) The teacher says that two and two made four.

    (b) The teacher wishes that two and two makes four.

    (c) The teacher advises that two and two makes four.

    (d) The teacher says that two and two makes four.

14. Baby said, "I will go".

    (a) Baby said that she will go.

    (b) Baby said that she could go.

(*c*) Baby say that she will go.
(*d*) Baby said that she would go.

15. A said to my sister, "Please, give me more money".
(*a*) I requested my sister to give me more money.
(*b*) I scolded my sister to give me more money.
(*c*) I advised my sister to gave me more money.
(*d*) I requested my sister to give her more money.

16. He said, "Bring a chair at once".
(*a*) He ordered to bring a chair at once.
(*b*) He requested to bring a chair at once.
(*c*) He told to bring a chair at once.
(*d*) He says to bring a chair at once.

17. The teacher said, "Don't make a noise".
(*a*) The teacher says to (me/him/her) not to make a noise.
(*b*) The teacher asked (me/him/her) not to make a noise.
(*c*) The teacher request not to make a noise.
(*d*) The teacher asked (me/him/her) not to made a noise.

18. My father said, "The earth is round".
(*a*) My father said that the earth was round.
(*b*) My father says that the earth is round.
(*c*) My father said that the earth is round
(*d*) My father ordered that the earth is round.

19. We said, "What a place it is!"
(*a*) We said that it was a very fine place.
(*b*) We said that is a very fine place.
(*c*) We said that the place is fine.
(*d*) We exclaimed with joy/surprise that it was a very fine place.

20. She said, "Shall I thread the needle?"
(*a*) She asked if she should thread the needle.
(*b*) She asked if she shall thread the needle.
(*c*) She ordered if she should thread the needle.
(*d*) She says that if she would thread the needle.

ANSWERS

1	2	3	4	5	6	7	8	9	10
(*b*)	(*b*)	(*a*)	(*d*)	(*c*)	(*c*)	(*a*)	(*a*)	(*b*)	(*b*)

11	12	13	14	15	16	17	18	19	20
(*c*)	(*c*)	(*d*)	(*d*)	(*a*)	(*a*)	(*b*)	(*c*)	(*d*)	(*a*)

SLIP OF PEN

COMMON ERRORS

JUDGE YOURSELF

Read each sentence to find out whether there is any grammatical error in it. The error, if any will be one part of the sentence. The letter of that part is the answer. If there is no error, the answer will be 'e'. (Avoid the errors of punctuation, if any).

1. Indian ocean (*a*)/ should be (*b*) / declared (*c*)/ a zone of peace (*d*)/ No error (*e*).

2. Himalayas shielded (*a*)/ India from the (*b*)/ invaders (*c*)/ in the past (*d*)/ No error (*e*) .

3. How fine (*a*)/ actor (*b*)/ Sanjeev Kumar (*c*) / was (*d*)/ No error (*e*).

4. Train will be (*a*)/ arriving at (*b*)/ the station (*c*)/ early today (*d*)/ No error (*e*).

5. Rabindra Nath Tagore is (*a*)/ famous (*b*) / as a poet (*c*)/ and essayist (*d*)/ No error (*e*).

6. Lala Lajpat Rai (*a*)/ was a (*b*)/ famous leader (*c*)/ of the Punjab (*d*)/ No error (*e*).

7. We build the roof (*a*)/ with a step slope (*b*)/ so that the rain water could (*c*)/ slide off easily (*d*)/ No error (*e*).

8. I am sorry to disappoint you (*a*)/ but I cannot let you (*b*)/ have any more money (*c*)/ till the end of this month (*d*)/ No error (*e*).

9. My brother had (*a*)/ Just come from abroad (*b*)/ He seems to have (*c*)/ enjoyed his trip very much (*d*)/ No error (*e*).

10. If I had realised (*a*)/ what a bad teacher you are (*b*)/ would not have come (*c*)/ to you for any guidance (*d*)/ No error (*e*).

11. He put his hand (*a*)/ into his pocket and was (*b*)/ astonished when he found (*c*)/ that his wallest is not there (*d*)/ No error (*e*).

12. Don't go by his appearance (*a*)/ he is capable at (*b*)/ doing any work (*c*)/ without any hesitation (*d*)/ No error (*e*).

13. The great actor was (*a*)/ angry with the treatment (*b*)/ he had received (*c*)/ without any hesitation (*d*)/ No error (*e*).

14. This book is (*a*)/ designed to increase (*b*)/ a working knowledge of (*c*)/ spoken and written English (*d*)/ No error (*e*).

15. All individuals are (*a*)/ different so their (*b*)/ tastes vary from (*c*)/ one another (*d*)/ No error (*e*).

16. According to the information received (*a*)/ each of the actors (*b*)/ made their (*c*)/ entrance on time (*d*)/ No error (*e*).

17. The student along with few (*a*)/ other students tried (*b*)/ to man handle (*c*)/ the principal in his office (*d*)/ No error (*e*).

18. After doing his matriculation (*a*)/ Prabhat went for a world tour (*b*)/ with his (*c*)/ bicycle (*d*)/ No error (*e*).

19. He gave (*a*)/ each person (*b*)/ the same medicine (*c*)/ for children (*d*)/ No error (*e*).

20. We drove (*a*)/ across (*b*)/ several towns (*c*)/ for two weeks (*d*)/ No error (*e*).

21. We must listen (*a*)/ carefully to what (*b*)/ each others say (*c*)/ on this matter (*d*)/ No error (*e*).

22. The river is (*a*)/ too wide to (*b*)/ swim over (*c*)/ during the rainy season (*d*)/ No error (*e*).

23. This ship (*a*)/ carries the people (*b*)/ over the river (*c*)/ thrice a day (*d*)/ No error (*e*).

24. The book says (*a*)/ he was forty seven (*b*)/ when he died (*c*)/ but his actually age was only forty three (*d*)/ No error (*e*).

25. A hundred years ago (*a*)/ the population of Delhi (*b*)/ was higher than (*c*)/ it actually is (*d*)/ No error (*e*).

26. Until (*a*)/ you come to class (*b*)/ regularly (*c*)/ you will fail (*d*)/ No error (*e*).

27. The planes (*a*)/ immediately took off (*b*)/ when war was declared (*c*)/ with China (*d*)/ No error (*e*).

28. If the Prime Minister (*a*)/ will issue an appeal (*b*)/ people will contribute (*c*)/ liberally (*d*)/ No error (*e*).

29. Her new dress was very pretty (*a*)/ and her colleagues gathered (*b*)/ around to admire it (*c*)/ by the time she entered the office (*d*)/ No error (*e*).

30. Informations provided here (*a*)/ is meant to add (*b*)/ to your general knowledge (*c*)/ not to make you a doctor (*d*)/ No error (*e*).

31. Not one of the children (*a*)/ has ever sang (*b*)/ on any occasion (*c*)/ in public before (*d*)/ No error (*e*).

32. If the by-stander had not been (*a*)/ familiar with first-aid techniques (*b*)/ the driver which had met (*c*)/ with the accident would have died (*d*)/ No error (*e*).

33. Even after requesting (*a*)/ him, he did not (*b*)/ tell us that how (*c*)/ he solved the problem (*d*)/ No error (*e*).

34. We never thought (*a*)/ that Mahesh is (*b*)/ oldest than the other (*c*)/ players in the team (*d*)/ No error (*e*).

35. No sooner did he (*a*)/ got up form bed (*b*)/ then he was sent (*c*)/ to the dairy (*d*)/ No error (*e*).

36. Could you (*a*)/ lend me (*b*)/ your pen (*c*)/ to write? (*d*)/ No error (*e*).

37. Come and sit down (*a*)/ for a while, Ashok, (*b*)/ your are digging (*c*)/ since lunch time (*d*)/ No error (*e*).

38. When he parted with (*a*)/ his sister (*b*)/ at the London Airport (*c*)/ there were tears in his eyes (*d*)/ No error (*e*).

39. Let us pass away (*a*)/ our time (*b*)/ in the canteen (*c*)/ (*d*)/ No error (*e*).

40. My teacher (*a*)/ has been teaching (*b*)/ poetries in this school (*c*)/ for the last five years (*d*)/ No error (*e*).

41. Seema requested (*a*)/ that I shall lend her (*b*)/ my car (*c*)/ for one week (*d*)/ No error (*e*).

42. My father (*a*)/ asked me (*b*)/ why I am late (*c*)/ from school (*d*)/ No error (*e*).

43. Swarna talked so last (*a*)/ that no other girl (*b*)/ could keep (*c*)/ pace with her (*d*)/ No error (*e*).

44. Our teacher told (*a*)/ us that the (*b*)/ earth moved (*c*)/ round the sun (*d*)/ No error (*e*).

45. He takes rest daily (*a*)/ for two hour lest (*b*)/ he will be (*c*)/ ill once again (*d*)/ No error (*e*).

46. Rakesh replied (*a*)/ that he (*b*)/ will not come (*c*)/ to my house (*d*)/ No error (*e*).

47. The servant's clothes (*a*)/ have been burnt (*b*)/ by his master's daughter (*c*)/ to punish him (*d*)/ No error (*e*).

48. Sham Lal has (*a*)/ laboured hard (*b*)/ but not been able (*c*)/ to achieve his aim (*d*)/ No error (*e*).

49. The Government promised (*a*)/ that the loyal (*b*)/ railway workers (*c*)/ shall be given promotions (*d*)/ No error (*e*).

50. This house (*a*)/ is not worth (*b*)/ buying for (*c*)/ twenty five thousand rupees (*d*)/ No error (*e*).

51. He claims (*a*)/ that he has (*b*)/ learnt the lesson (*c*)/ word by word (*d*)/ No error (*e*).

52. He says that (*a*)/ his examination (*b*)/ starts (*c*)/ from Monday (*d*)/ No error (*e*).

53. What are (*a*)/ your future (*b*)/ prospects (*c*)/ in the firm? (*d*)/ No error (*e*).

54. It is quarter (*a*)/ to ten (*b*)/ in (*c*)/ my watch (*d*)/ No error (*e*).

55. You will be glad (*a*)/ to learnt (*b*)/ that my summer vacation (*c*)/ are near (*d*)/ No error (*e*).

56. We admired the way (*a*)/ he had completed all his work (*b*)/ and appreciating the method (c) (*d*)/ adopted by him/ No error (*e*).

57. Our neighbours had repeated (*a*)/ the same illogical sequence of activities (*b*)/ if we had not brought the (*c*)/ facts to their notice (*d*)/ No error (*e*).

58. Not only the judges acquitted (*a*)/ him of all the charges (*b*)/ levelled against him, but (*c*)/ also commended all his actions (*d*)/ No error (*e*).

59. Due to certain inevitable circumstances (*a*)/ the scheduled programme had to be (*b*)/ postponed indefinite (*c*)/ but the members could not be informed (*d*)/ No error (*e*).

60. Scarcely had (*a*)/ he gone (*b*)/ when a policeman (*c*)/ knocked at the door (*d*)/ No error (*e*).

61. Do not trouble (*a*)/ yourself about writing to me (*b*)/ unless you are quite (*c*)/ in the humour for it (*d*)/ No error (*e*).

62. Telephone was (*a*)/ discovered by (*b*)/ Graham Bell (*c*)/ an American Scientist (*d*)/ No error (*e*).

63. Sohan pleased (*a*)/ at the news (*b*)/ of his success (*c*)/ in the examination (*d*)/ No error (*e*).

64. There is no doubt (*a*)/ that Ramesh (*b*)/ is best (*c*)/ student of our class (*d*)/ No error (*e*).

65. However hard you work (*a*)/ you cannot get (*b*)/ the promotion in (*c*)/ this office (*d*)/ No error (*e*).

66. Raman is (*a*)/ the most ablest (*b*)/ clerk of our office (*c*)/ in Delhi (*d*)/ No error (*e*).

67. Because he is learned (*a*)/ so he is (*b*)/ respected (*c*)/ by all (*d*)/ No error (*e*).

68. Ram (*a*)/ as well as Sham (*b*)/ are (*c*)/ intelligent (*d*)/ No error (*e*).

69. These news were (*a*)/ broadcast (*b*)/ from (*c*)/ All India Radio yesterday (*d*)/ No error (*e*).

70. I who is, (*a*)/ your friend, (*b*)/ will stand by (*c*)/ you through thick and thin (*d*)/ No error (*e*).

71. Although winter in (*a*)/ Kashmir is cold (*b*)/ but it is pleasant (*c*)/ in many ways (*d*)/ No error (*e*).

72. Less (*a*)/ books are needed (*b*)/ in the (*c*)/ library (*d*)/ No error (*e*).

73. No sooner did I (*a*)/ reach the station (*b*)/ when (*c*)/ the train steamed off (*d*)/ No error (*e*).

74. I've go five (*a*)/ brothers and (*b*)/ each (one) is (*c*)/ quite different of the others (*d*)/ No error (*e*).

75. They (*a*)/ stood looking (*b*)/ into one another's (*c*)/ eyes (*d*)/ No error (*e*).

76. In our garden (*a*)/ there are roses (*b*)/ on either side (*c*)/ of the door (*d*)/ No error (*e*).

77. Either you (*a*)/ leave this house (*b*)/ and I'll call (*c*)/ the police (*d*)/ No error (*e*).

78. I you can't (*a*)/ help me (*b*)/ I'll ask any body else (*c*)/ to help me (*d*)/ No error (*e*).

79. He speaks (*a*)/ lot of language (*b*)/ he even (*c*)/ speaks Eskimo (*d*)/ No error (*e*).

80. The car (*a*)/ didn't want to start (*b*)/ but eventually (*c*)/ I got it doing (*d*)/ No error (*e*).

81. I speak (*a*)/ English fair well (*b*)/ enough for (*c*)/ most everyday purposes (*d*)/ No error (*e*).

82. My companions (*a*)/ as well as I (*b*)/ was nicely (*c*)/ entertained (*d*)/ No error (*e*).

83. I have come to known (*a*)/ that the conference was (*b*)/ unanimous (*c*)/ in their decision (*d*)/ No error (*e*).

84. Many a (*a*)/ battle (*b*)/ were (*c*)/ fought on the soil of India (*d*)/ No error (*e*).

85. Do you think (*a*)/ it is easy to (*b*)/ pass (*c*)/ in the examination (*d*)/ No error (*e*).

86. Cholera is raging (*a*)/ in the city (*b*)/ for the last three months (*c*)/ even longer than that (*d*)/ No error (*e*).

87. Scarcely had (*a*)/ he gone a few steps (*b*)/ that he was told (*c*)/ that his mother was no more (*d*)/ No error (*e*).

88. After toiling very hard (*a*)/ over a long period (*b*)/ he found (*c*)/ he had hardly made no profit at all (*d*)/ No error (*e*).

89. Day in and day out (*a*)/ he keep telling (*b*)/ his friends that (*c*)/ he wants to go abroad (*d*)/ No error (*e*).

90. Whatever work (*a*)/ that which you undertake (*b*)/ put your best (*c*)/ efforts in it (*d*)/ No error (*e*).

91. Mrs. Kanti Mohan (*a*)/ has bought (*b*)/ one pair of shoe (*c*)/ from Bata Shoe Store (*d*)/ No error (*e*).

92. The Indian government (*a*)/ has sent (*b*)/ its force (*c*)/ to Sri Lanka (*d*)/ No error (*e*).

93. His life (*a*)/ is full of (*b*)/ grieves (*c*)/ and sorrows (*d*)/ No error (*e*).

94. He is always (*a*)/ surrounded by (*b*)/ flattering (*c*)/ hanger-ons (*d*)/ No error (*e*).

95. All his relatives (*a*)/ expect his daughter (*b*)/ have gone on (*c*)/ a month's vacation tour (*d*)/ No error (*e*).

96. All renew licences (*a*)/ may be collected from (*b*)/ the cashier's counter after (*c*)/ paying the fees (*d*)/ No error (*e*).

97. We are happy (*a*)/ to know that (*b*)/ the project completed (*c*)/ strictly as per the schedule (*d*)/ No error (*e*).

98. These things are (*a*)/ not all together (*b*)/ as they (*c*)/ seem (*d*)/ No error (*e*).

99. A five men delegation (*a*)/ waited (*b*)/ on (*c*)/ the President (*d*)/ No error (*e*).

100. We now look forward for (*a*)/ some great achievements (*b*)/ which to some extent (*c*)/ can restore the country's prestige once again (*d*)/ No error (*e*).

101. Mahatma Gandhi did not solve (*a*)/ all the problems of the future (*b*)/ but he did solve (*c*)/ problems of his own age (*d*)/ No error (*e*).

102. No country can long endure (*a*)/ if its foundations (*b*)/ were not laid deep (*c*)/ in the material prosperity (*d*)/ No error (*e*).

103. Though he suffered of fever, (*a*)/ he attended office (*b*)/ and completed all the pending (*c*)/ work by sitting late (*d*)/ No error (*e*).

104. As always have been said, (*a*)/ parents should not (*b*)/ impose their desires (*c*)/ on their wards (*d*)/ No error (*e*).

105. Being a very fast worker, (*a*)/ he is always liking (*b*)/ by all his colleagues, (*c*)/ and superiors too (*d*)/ No error (*e*).

106. It is a hard fact (*a*)/ that a miser cannot (*b*)/ part from (*c*)/ his money (*d*)/ No error (*e*).

107. Does he remember (*a*)/ where did he stop (*b*)/ the lecture (*c*)/ last week? (*d*)/ No error (*e*).

108. I will (*a*)/ fight you (*b*)/ (*c*)/ with tooth and nail (*d*)/ No error (*e*).

109. He looked after (*a*)/ his (*b*)/ watch (*c*)/ everywhere (*d*)/ No error (*e*).

110. His father (*a*)/ is a poet (*b*)/ and a (*c*)/ philosopher (*d*)/ No error (*e*).

111. When I shall go (*a*)/ to London (*b*)/ I shall meet my (*c*)/ brother-in-law (*d*)/ No error (*e*).

112. You are (*a*)/ one of those (*b*)/ who always (*c*)/ helps the others (*d*)/ No error (*e*).

113. Each of the clerks (*a*)/ in this office (*b*)/ are loyal (*c*)/ and efficient (*d*)/ No error (*e*).

114. Satish told (*a*)/ his mother (*b*)/ that he had been reading (*c*)/ for six hours (*d*)/ No error (*e*).

115. The Principal said to (*a*)/ the students (*b*)/ to go away (*c*)/ at once (*d*)/ No error (*e*).

116. He is going (*a*)/ by the (*b*)/ 7.30 o'clock (*c*)/ train to Ferozepore (*d*)/ No error (*e*).

117. The customer scarcely had (*a*)/ enough money to pay (*b*)/ to the cashier (*c*)/ at the cash counter (*d*)/ No error (*e*).

118. Neither the earthquake (*a*)/ nor the subsequent fire (*b*)/ was able to dampen (*c*)/ the spirit of the residents (*d*)/ No error (*e*).

119. He is the (*a*)/ kindest (*b*)/ and generous (*c*)/ man (*d*)/ No error (*e*).

120. He as well (*a*)/ as his brother (*b*)/ were here (*c*)/ for their dinner (*d*)/ No error (*e*).

121. I have seen my friend (*a*)/ outside the (*b*)/ cinema house (*c*)/ last night (*d*)/ No error (*e*).

122. Sooner (*a*)/ it is done (*b*)/ the better (*c*)/ it is (*d*)/ No error (*e*).

123. It has been (*a*)/ decided (*b*)/ that we shall start (*c*)/ after the breakfast (*d*)/ No error (*e*).

124. Not only all other (*a*)/ students (*b*)/ but also I (*c*)/ think it to be wrong (*d*)/ No error (*e*).

125. In the (*a*)/ medieval age (*b*)/ Rajputs preferred death (*c*)/ than dishonour (*d*)/ No error (*e*).

126. When I went to (*a*)/ his office (*b*)/ he introduced me (*c*)/ with his boss (*d*)/ No error (*e*).

127. After hearing (*a*)/ her pathetic story (*b*)/ I was (*c*)/ moved to tears (*d*)/ No error (*e*).

128. She must be (*a*)/ compensated about (*b*)/ the loss (*c*)/ suffered by her (*d*)/ No error (*e*).

129. The milk (*a*)/ was (*b*)/ very much hot (*c*)/ to drink (*d*)/ No error (*e*).

130. Nitin's nephew, who lives (*a*)/ in Bangalore, is eager to travel to (*b*)/ Delhi to have (*c*)/ a glimpse of the capital (*d*)/ No error (*e*).

131. In the last week (*a*)/ I tell him to come (*b*)/ in time but he still (*c*)/ comes late every day (*d*)/ No error (*e*).

132. He tried as he could (*a*)/ Naveen did not (*b*)/ succeed in getting (*c*)/ his car to start up (*d*)/ No error (*e*).

133. Foolishly Madhu threw (*a*)/ some water on he electric heater (*b*)/ when it catches fire (*c*)/ and she got a shock (*d*)/ No error (*e*).

134. Rajesh was expecting (*a*)/ a telegram from his uncle (*b*)/ which would inform (*c*)/ him whether he went or not (*d*)/ No error (*e*).

135. We are trying (*a*)/ to locate the (*b*)/ historical city for (*c*)/ the past two years (*d*)/ No error (*e*).

136. I love (*a*)/ to go there (*b*)/ at any time (*c*)/ of the day (*d*)/ No error (*e*).

137. I feel that (*a*)/ it is quite easy (*b*)/ doing this work (*c*)/ without the help of others (*d*)/ No error (*e*).

138. Hitler enjoyed (*a*)/ to persecute (*b*)/ the Jews (*c*)/ living in his country (*d*)/ No error (*e*).

139. It was me (*a*)/ who helped Ram (*b*)/ in establishing (*c*)/ his business (*d*)/ No error (*e*).

140. The officer received order (*a*)/ to enforce discipline (*b*)/ among (*c*)/ his subordinates (*d*)/ No error (*e*).

141. Neither of the three tables (*a*)/ is (*b*)/ worth (*c*)/ purchasing (*d*)/ No error (*e*).

142. The (*a*)/ 'Arabian Nights' (*b*)/ are an (*c*)/ interesting novel (*d*)/ No error (*e*).

143. The father (*a*)/ together with (*b*)/ all children (*c*)/ were there (*d*)/ No error (*e*).

144. Not only the Principal (*a*)/ but also (*b*)/ the students (*c*)/ was playing (*d*)/ No error (*e*).

145. Since I meet (*a*)/ Dinesh last Saturday (*b*)/ he has been contacting me (*c*)/ everyday over phone (*d*)/ No error (*e*).

146. Neither of the plans (*a*)/ suits him and therefore (*b*)/ he decided not to (*c*)/ go out yesterday (*d*)/ No error (*e*).

147. I'll try (*a*)/ to phone you (*b*)/ in the meeting (*c*)/ tomorrow (*d*)/ No error (*e*).

148. People is (*a*)/ going to (*b*)/ the Ramlila ground (*c*)/ to watch the Dussehra celebration (*d*)/ No error (*e*).

149. Bihar (*a*)/ is rich (*b*)/ in irons (*c*)/ and various other minerals (*d*)/ No error (*e*).

150. He took (*a*)/ great pains (*b*)/ to help me (*c*)/ in my difficulty (*d*)/ No error (*e*).

151. Athletics are (*a*)/ not popular (*b*)/ in our college (*c*)/ this year (*d*)/ No error (*e*).

152. The peasantry is (*a*)/ not content (*b*)/ with this (*c*)/ arrangement (*d*)/ No error (*e*).

153. My father is (*a*)/ very fond of (*b*)/ eating vegetable (*c*)/ in the morning (*d*)/ No error (*e*).

154. He told me (*a*)/ that (*b*)/ beside that pen (*c*)/ he had two more (*d*)/ No error (*e*).

155. I told Zia (*a*)/ that she should (*b*)/ avail of (*c*)/ the opportunity (*d*)/ No error (*e*).

156. Everyone (*a*)/ should (*b*)/ mind (*c*)/ one's own business (*d*)/ No error (*e*).

157. The teacher asked the student (*a*)/ if you can (*b*)/ read the book (*c*)/ without spectacles (*d*)/ No error (*e*).

158. Every chair and every desk (*a*)/ was (*b*)/ in their (*c*)/ position (*d*)/ No error (*e*).

159. I have had to work (*a*)/ at the fountain for almost (*b*)/ ten hours before it could (*c*)/ start functioning well (*d*)/ No error (*e*).

160. No sooner had the jeep (*a*)/ arrives the station (*b*)/ than a young police officer (*c*)/ jumped out of it (*d*)/ No error (*e*).

161. No girl (*a*)/ in her troupe is (*b*)/ so sprightly as (*c*)/ your daughter (*d*)/ No error (*e*).

162. It seems evidently (*a*)/ to me that (*b*)/ the visits they made to the island (*c*)/ were not very frequent (*d*)/ No error (*e*).

163. He was very disappointed (*a*)/ when he found (*b*)/ that someone else (*c*)/ had secured higher marks (*d*)/ No error (*e*).

164. A woman washer (*a*)/ washes (*b*)/ our clothes (*c*)/ daily (*d*)/ No error (*e*).

165. He brought (*a*)/ a peacock and a peacockess (*b*)/ for his garden (*c*)/ yesterday (*d*)/ No error (*e*).

166. How many (*a*)/ male and female actors (*b*)/ are working (*c*)/ in this film? (*d*)/ No error (*e*).

167. He brought (*a*)/ two pianoes (*b*)/ for his daughters (*c*)/ from the market (*d*)/ No error (*e*).

168. There are (*a*)/ many active (*b*)/ volcanoes (*c*)/ in the world (*d*)/ No error (*e*).

169. There are (*a*)/ many mouses (*b*)/ in this dilapidated (*c*)/ house (*d*)/ No error (*e*).

170. There are (*a*)/ ten steel saves (*b*)/ and two wooden almirahs (*c*)/ in this office (*d*)/ No error (*e*).

171. I have lost (*a*)/ my scissor (*b*)/ in my office (*c*)/ in the afternoon (*d*)/ No error (*e*).

172. His new (*a*)/ spectacles (*b*)/ has been broken (*c*)/ by this naughty boy (*d*)/ No error (*e*).

173. Mathematics are (*a*)/ taught (*b*)/ in his school (*c*)/ by an experienced teacher (*d*)/ No error (*e*).

174. As it was Ramesh's (*a*)/ first interview he dressed him (*b*)/ in his most (*c*)/ formal suit (*d*)/ No error (*e*).

175. A high level meeting (*a*)/ of officials is reporting (*b*)/ to have discussed (*c*)/ the issue in great detail (*d*)/ No error (*e*).

176. While going (*a*)/ through the report (*b*)/ yesterday I find (*c*)/ several factual mistakes (*d*)/ No error (*e*).

177. On his attitude (*a*)/ it seems that what he wants (*b*)/ is that the decision-making power (*c*)/ should rest with him (*d*)/ No error (*e*).

178. No sooner did (*a*)/ the chairman begin speaking (*b*)/ some participants started (*c*)/ shouting slogans (*d*)/ No error (*e*).

179. I was standing (*a*)/ at the bus stop (*b*)/ waiting for him (*c*)/ since eight o'clock (*d*)/ No error (*e*).

180. Krishna assured (*a*)/ the manager (*b*)/ with his (*c*)/ sincerity (*d*)/ No error (*e*).

181. I have never seen (*a*)/ her relaxing (*b*)/ she is always (*c*)/ busy in her work (*d*)/ No error (*e*).

182. The train (*a*)/ has come from Jammu (*b*)/ and is (*c*)/ bound to Ferozepur (*d*)/ No error (*e*).

183. You must (*a*)/ arrive at (*b*)/ some conclusion (*c*)/ before you leave (*d*)/ No error (*e*).

184. He is (*a*)/ very attached with (*b*)/ his two children (*c*)/ who live in the hostel (*d*)/ No error (*e*).

185. We must (*a*)/ adapt ourselves (*b*)/ with our (*c*)/ circumstances (*d*)/ No error (*e*).

186. God always (*a*)/ bestows his (*b*)/ blessings (*c*)/ upon his believers (*d*)/ No error (*e*).

187. He is (*a*)/ in the habit of (*b*)/ backing out from (*c*)/ his promise (*d*)/ No error (*e*).

188. I have written (*a*)/ a letter to the (*b*)/ editor of the 'Observer' (*c*)/ on behalf of my locality (*d*)/ No error (*e*).

189. I have made (*a*)/ a complaint (*b*)/ for him (*c*)/ to the police (*d*)/ No error (*e*).

190. He told me that (*a*)/ the patient died (*b*)/ before the doctor (*c*)/ came (*d*)/ No error (*e*).

191. The committee (*a*)/ is divided (*b*)/ on (*c*)/ this point (*d*)/ No error (*e*).

192. Curry and rice (*a*)/ are (*b*)/ the favourite (*c*)/ food of the Panjabis (*d*)/ No error (*e*).

193. Much of your success (*a*)/ and prosperity in life (*b*)/ depend upon (*c*)/ your own efforts (*d*)/ No error (*e*).

194. The captain with all (*a*)/ the crew (*b*)/ were (*c*)/ drowned (*d*)/ No error (*e*).

195. Both athletes (*a*)/ were cheered (*b*)/ by the (*c*)/ spectators (*d*)/ No error (*e*).

196. He was first (*a*)/ to reach (*b*)/ the station (*c*)/ that day (*d*)/ No error (*e*).

197. The students (*a*)/ did nothing (*b*)/ but laughed (*c*)/ heartily (*d*)/ No error (*e*).

198. If it (*a*)/ will rain (*b*)/ we will not (*c*)/ go out at all (*d*)/ No error (*e*).

199. Being a rainy day (*a*)/ we could (*b*)/ not go (*c*)/ to the market place (*d*)/ No error (*e*).

200. Let us (*a*)/ do nothing (*b*)/ but to wait and see (*c*)/ for the time being (*d*)/ No error (*e*).

201. I ordered (*a*)/ for soup and salad (*b*)/ when I visited (*c*)/ the Neelam restaurant (*d*)/ No error (*e*).

202. Rahim denied (*a*)/ that he had not stolen (*b*)/ the gold ring (*c*)/ of Seema (*d*)/ No error (*e*).

203. None of the two boys (*a*)/ is (*b*)/ taking interest (*c*)/ in his work (*d*)/ No error (*e*).

204. Neither of the three (*a*)/ tables (*b*)/ is (*c*)/ worth purchasing (*d*)/ No error (*e*).

205. The patient (*a*)/ died (*b*)/ before (*c*)/ the doctor came (*d*)/ No error (*e*).

206. The jury (*a*)/ is (*b*)/ divided on (*c*)/ the issue (*d*)/ No error (*e*).

207. Has (*a*)/ both (*b*)/ of you (*c*)/ been to Calcutta? (*d*)/ No error (*e*).

208. It takes (*a*)/ five days (*b*)/ to a letter (*c*)/ to go from Delhi to Oslo (*d*)/ No error (*e*).

209. Half of us (*a*)/ are free on Tuesday (*b*)/ and other half (*c*)/ on Thursday (*d*)/ No error (*e*).

210. If I was rich (*a*)/ I would (*b*)/ spend all my time travelling (*c*)/ throughout the country (*d*)/ No error (*e*).

211. Rosy admits that (*a*)/ she's no more (*b*)/ a great singer (*c*)/ than mc (*d*)/ No error (*e*).

212. I ought have (*a*)/ phoned Meena (*b*)/ this morning (*c*)/ but I forgot (*d*)/ No error (*e*).

213. He has been undergoing (*a*)/ the special training course (*b*)/ which each of the employees (*c*)/ is required to (*d*)/ No error (*e*).

214. You must had (*a*)/ a kind and gentle heart (*b*)/ if you want (*c*)/ to be a successful doctor (*d*)/ No error (*e*).

215. If you cannot (*a*)/ sympathy with the poor, (*b*)/ how will you be (*c*)/ able to do social work? (*d*)/ No error (*e*).

216. He loosened his temper (*a*)/ whenever he knows (*b*)/ things do not take place (*c*)/ as per his planning (*d*)/ No error (*e*).

217. They wanted money (*a*)/ to purchase certain things (*b*)/ for themselves and (*c*)/ for donated to their colleagues (*d*)/ No error (*e*).

218. The children (*a*)/ were playing (*b*)/ besides the road (*c*)/ in the afternoon (*d*)/ No error (*e*).

219. I could not see her face as (*a*)/ it was covered (*b*)/ with a vale (*c*)/ of silken cloth (*d*)/ No error (*e*).

220. The thief was (*a*)/ caught red handedly (*b*)/ by the police (*c*)/ in the crowded market (*d*)/ No error (*e*).

221. A clerk (*a*)/ cannot make (*b*)/ his both ends meet (*c*)/ nowadays (*d*)/ No error (*e*).

222. The news of (*a*)/ his father's death (*b*)/ came as a (*c*)/ bolt form the sky (*d*)/ No error (*e*).

223. Mohan has collected (*a*)/ assembled on the ground (*b*)/ and are waiting for (*c*)/ the Principal to come (*d*)/ No error (*e*).

224. The book is making (*a*)/ waves and the sale (*b*)/ is quite brisk in (*c*)/ all major cities (*d*)/ No error (*e*).

225. Well, I spend six or seven years (*a*)/ after high school (*b*)/ trying to find a job for me (*c*)/ but could not succeed in it (*d*)/ No error (*e*).

226. I do not recall (*a*)/ exactly what he said to me (*b*)/ but when I was quit (*c*)/ he said something to me (*d*)/ No error (*e*).

227. We wanted to purchase (*a*)/ something but all the three stores (*b*)/ in that area (*c*)/ were closed on that day (*d*)/ No error (*e*).

228. She smiled (*a*)/ at me (*b*)/ in a (*c*)/ friendly way (*d*)/ No error (*e*).

229. I used to go (*a*)/ to France (*b*)/ seven times (*c*)/ during the last seven years (*d*)/ No error (*e*).

230. He presented (*a*)/ a glass venetian ashtray (*b*)/ to his father (*c*)/ on his birthday (*d*)/ No error (*e*).

231. He placed (*a*)/ his books (*b*)/ on the glass round table (*c*)/ when he went to the library (*d*)/ No error (*e*).

232. Motivating employees with (*a*)/ traditional authority and financial (*b*)/ incentives have become (*c*)/ increasingly difficult (*d*)/ No error (*e*).

233. Several issues raising (*a*)/ in the meeting could (*b*)/ be amicably resolved (*c*)/ due to his tactful handling (*d*)/ No error (*e*).

234. The health workers are (*a*)/ being tried their best (*b*)/ to popularise (*c*)/ preventive measures (*d*)/ No error (*e*).

235. Of the two (*a*)/ sisters (*b*)/ Meena is (*c*)/ the elder (*d*)/ No error (*e*).

236. Bible (*a*)/ can be (*b*)/ regarded as (*c*)/ a great (*d*)/ No error (*e*).

237. Such (*a*)/ rules do not (*b*)/ apply to (*c*)/ you and I (*d*)/ No error (*e*).

238. If it will rain (*a*)/ I shall (*b*)/ not go (*c*)/ to college (*d*)/ No error (*e*).

239. I am quite sorry (*a*)/ to hear (*b*)/ of (*c*)/ your failure (*d*)/ No error (*e*).

240. Please wait for me (*a*)/ until (*b*)/ I do not (*c*)/ come back (*d*)/ No error (*e*).

241. I, you and he (*a*)/ should be able (*b*)/ to manage (*c*)/ our affairs (*d*)/ No error (*e*).

242. Sham neither (*a*)/ respects his father (*b*)/ nor does not (*c*)/ helps him financially (*d*)/ No error (*e*).

243. He is (*a*)/ not only (*b*)/ an honest man (*c*)/ yet also a gentleman (*d*)/ No error (*e*).

244. All the members (*a*)/ of his family opposed him (*b*)/ nevertheless he stuck to (*c*)/ his decision to go abroad (*d*)/ No error (*e*).

245. An honest man sticks (*a*)/ to his words (*b*)/ whereas a dishonest man (*c*)/ violates it (*d*)/ No error (*e*).

246. If your son (*a*)/ is not regular (*b*)/ then he will be (*c*)/ dismissed from service (*d*)/ No error (*e*).

247. It rained (*a*)/ during the (*b*)/ night for two (*c*)/ for three hours (*d*)/ No error (*e*).

248. I'll call in (*a*)/ and see you for (*b*)/ a few minutes (*c*)/ during the afternoon (*d*)/ No error (*e*).

249. I write to (*a*)/ every of my (*b*)/ children once (*c*)/ a week (*d*)/ No error (*e*).

250. If the teacher (*a*)/ is good the students (*b*)/ will respond (*c*)/ positively to them (*d*)/ No error (*e*).

251. I will put on (*a*)/ a note in this regard (*b*)/ for your consideration (*c*)/ and necessary decision (*d*)/ No error (*e*).

252. The mission provides (*a*)/ able service to all (*b*)/ the needy people in this area (*c*)/ during last few years (*d*)/ No error (*e*).

253. I am pleased to sanction (*a*)/ one special increment (*b*)/ to all the employees (*c*)/ with this month (*d*)/ No error (*e*).

254. The English defeated (*a*)/ Germans (*b*)/ in the (*c*)/ last world war (*d*)/ No error (*e*).

255. Newly acquired freedom (*a*)/ is sometimes (*b*)/ liable (*c*)/ for abuse (*d*)/ No error (*e*).

256. Neither of the (*a*)/ two boys (*b*)/ were successful (*c*)/ in the examination (*d*)/ No error (*e*).

257. Many a man (*a*)/ were (*b*)/ drowned (*c*)/ in the sea (*d*)/ No error (*e*).

258. They would not (*a*)/ have able to plan (*b*)/ the details of the job, (*c*)/ if you had no cooperated (*d*)/ No error (*e*).

259. Very few employees *(a)*/ in our company are *(b)*/ so dedicated as *(c)*/ Mahesh will *(d)*/ No error *(e)*.

260. Rajesh won the case as *(a)*/ he argued very forcefully and *(b)*/ in such the intelligent way *(c)*/ that the judge changed his opinion *(d)*/ No error *(e)*.

261. The basket of apples *(a)*/ sent by the gardener *(b)*/ contained a number of *(c)*/ green mangoes also *(d)*/ No error *(e)*.

262. In the absence of *(a)*/ clear instructions *(b)*/ one cannot be expected *(c)*/ to be functioned effectively *(d)*/ No error *(e)*.

263. They could have *(a)*/ helped him *(b)*/ had they approached by him, *(c)*/ for help well in advance *(d)*/ No error *(e)*.

264. He has in *(a)*/ his possession a *(b)*/ price collection of very old coins *(c)*/ and some ancient paintings *(d)*/ No error *(e)*.

265. Rakesh recommended for me *(a)*/ to the officer *(b)*/ for a *(c)*/ promotion *(d)*/ No error *(e)*.

266. The child *(a)*/ begged pardon *(b)*/ from his father *(c)*/ for his coming late *(d)*/ No error *(e)*.

267. Though you have *(a)*/ a strong body *(b)*/ but you are *(c)*/ a coward *(d)*/ No error *(e)*.

268. Do keep us *(a)*/ informed *(b)*/ as mother is anxious *(c)*/ for your welfare *(d)*/ No error *(e)*.

269. I am writing *(a)*/ a letter *(b)*/ with green ink *(c)*/ to my brother *(d)*/ No error *(e)*.

270. They went *(a)*/ to Faizabad *(b)*/ in bus *(c)*/ yesterday *(d)*/ No error *(e)*.

271. She congratulated *(a)*/ me for *(b)*/ my promotion *(c)*/ in the office *(d)*/ No error *(e)*.

272. Everyone agrees *(a)*/ that Kalidas *(b)*/ is Shakespeare *(c)*/ of India *(d)*/ No error *(e)*.

273. I have been *(a)*/ writing *(b)*/ this book *(c)*/ from Monday *(d)*/ No error *(e)*.

274. I am suffering *(a)*/ from fever *(b)*/ for *(c)*/ the past three days *(d)*/ No error *(e)*.

275. The English *(a)*/ is the mother tongue *(b)*/ of the *(c)*/ English *(d)*/ No error *(e)*.

276. I have not eaten *(a)*/ bananas *(b)*/ since *(c)*/ I have been a child/ No error *(e)*.

277. Foolishly Rajani opened *(a)*/ the cooker when *(b)*/ it was full steam *(c)*/ and burnt her hands *(d)*/ No error *(e)*.

278. From a tiny room in *(a)*/ the slums, they have *(b)*/ managed to move to a good *(c)*/ house in a better locality *(d)*/ No error *(e)*.

279. Even if the doctor *(a)*/ put in his best efforts, he *(b)*/ could not succeed in *(c)*/ saving the patient *(d)*/ No error *(e)*.

280. Yesterday, a visitor to (*a*)/ the part was attacked (*b*)/ by a tiger and (*c*)/ had to hospitalise (*d*)/ No error (*e*).

281. Rajdeep always introduces (*a*)/ himself by his (*b*)/ first name and never mentions (*c*)/ his family name (*d*)/ No error (*e*).

282. Ketan had a lot (*a*)/ of work to complete yesterday (*b*)/ and wishes (*c*)/ that he had my help (*d*)/ No error (*e*).

283. You, he and I (*a*)/ should (*b*)/ beat (*c*)/ him (*d*)/ No error (*e*).

284. Somanthan (*a*)/ and Bhushan's books (*b*)/ are (*c*)/ worth praising (*d*)/ No error (*e*).

285. This house is (*a*)/ built of (*b*)/ bricks (*c*)/ and not of stones (*d*)/ No error (*e*).

286. I do not (*a*)/ remember (*b*)/ the date of him (*c*)/ leaving India (*d*)/ No error (*e*).

287. I could not find (*a*)/ it anywhere (*b*)/ Where is (*c*)/ my letter's envelope? (*d*)/ No error (*e*).

288. Even at (*a*)/ this age (*b*)/ his hair is (*c*)/ not grey (*d*)/ No error (*e*).

289. He has (*a*)/ bought (*b*)/ new furnitures (*c*)/ for his flat (*d*)/ No error (*e*).

290. It's very (*a*)/ kind of you (*b*)/ to help Surinder (*c*)/ in such a manner (*d*)/ No error (*e*).

291. His father was (*a*)/ angry with (*b*)/ his leaving (*c*)/ the house in the night (*d*)/ No error (*e*).

292. We think that (*a*)/ it is no use (*b*)/ to go there (*c*)/ at this late hour (*d*)/ No error (*e*).

293. The aim and the object (*a*)/ of his association (*b*)/ is to help (*c*)/ the poor (*d*)/ No error (*e*).

294. This factory (*a*)/ is not worth (*b*)/ buying for (*c*)/ ninety five thousand rupees (*d*)/ No error (*e*).

295. Each cigarette (*a*)/ a person smoke (*b*)/ does some harm and eventually (*c*)/ it may cause a serious disease (*d*)/ No error (*e*).

296. This is one of (*a*)/ the most interesting book (*b*)/ I have (*c*)/ ever read (*d*)/ No error (*e*).

297. In my opinion (*a*)/ the balance sheet exhibits (*b*)/ a true and fair (*c*)/ view of the state of affairs of the bank (*d*)/ No error (*e*).

298. He neglects (*a*)/ attending lectures (*b*)/ regularly (*c*)/ though college was only a few yards away from his house (*d*)/ No error (*e*).

299. We have helped them not only (*a*)/ with money but also (*b*)/ with new machinery (*c*)/ and raw material (*d*)/ No error (*e*).

300. Sudha wished (*a*)/ to thoroughly revise (*b*)/ her plan (*c*)/ to construct a new house (*d*)/ No error (*e*).

301. Neither he came (*a*)/ nor did he (*b*)/ send the money (*c*)/ through his brother (*d*)/ No error (*e*).

302. See these words (*a*)/ in the dictionary (*b*)/ and write down (*c*)/ their meanings (*d*)/ No error (*e*).

303. Two of those (*a*)/ dreaded dacoits (*b*)/ were hung (*c*)/ by the neck (*d*)/ No error (*e*).

304. The school (*a*)/ is too much small (*b*)/ to accommodate (*c*)/ all the students (*d*)/ No error (*e*).

305. I am (*a*)/ quite sorry (*b*)/ to learn about (*c*)/ the death of your father (*d*)/ No error (*e*).

306. I went to see (*a*)/ the film because (*b*)/ he had told me (*c*)/ that it was too good (*d*)/ No error (*e*).

307. Everybody says that (*a*)/ Lucy resembles with (*b*)/ her mother (*c*)/ a lot (*d*)/ No error (*e*).

308. For hours (*a*)/ I discussed on (*b*)/ this point with him (*c*)/ but he could not decide anything (*d*)/ No error (*e*).

309. The last year proved (*a*)/ quite bad (*b*)/ as major industries (*c*)/ witness lot of problems (*d*)/ No error (*e*).

310. I offered him part-time work (*a*)/ but the turned it over (*b*)/ saying that he would (*c*)/ rather wait for a full-time job (*d*)/ No error (*e*).

311. The foremost criterion of selection we adopted (*a*)/ were the number of years of training (*b*)/ a dancer had received (*c*)/ under a particular guru (*d*)/ No error (*e*).

312. He fixed a metal ladder (*a*)/ for the wall below his window (*b*)/ so as to be able to (*c*)/ escape if there was a fire (*d*)/ No error (*e*).

313. Scarcely had I (*a*)/ finished washing the car (*b*)/ than the master came (*c*)/ and asked me to clean the floor of the house (*d*)/ No error (*e*).

314. Students (*a*)/ as well as the teacher (*b*)/ was (*c*)/ playing (*d*)/ No error (*e*).

315. Neither Ram (*a*)/ nor Sham (*b*)/ are (*c*)/ at fault (*d*)/ No error (*e*).

316. Neither women (*a*)/ nor (*b*) (*c*)/ children/ was admitted (*d*)/ No error (*e*).

317. If I shall (*a*)/ go to Calcutta (*b*)/ I shall bring (*c*)/ a beautiful watch for you (*d*)/ No error (*e*).

318. I told him that (*a*)/ he could (*b*)/ go home (*c*)/ by all mean (*d*)/ No error (*e*).

319. After the death (*a*)/ of their father (*b*)/ the two brothers are (*c*)/ having their hand at the daggers (*d*)/ No error (*e*).

320. He added insult (*a*)/ to his wounds (*b*)/ by making (*c*)/ sarcastic comments (*d*)/ No error (*e*).

321. He has achieved (*a*)/ success in life (*b*)/ from dint of (*c*)/ hard work (*d*)/ No error (*e*).

322. He burnt a fire (*a*)/ and started (*b*)/ roasting (*c*)/ the chicken (*d*)/ No error (*e*).

323. I have written (*a*)/ a letter (*b*)/ at him to his Delhi address (*c*)/ today (*d*)/ No error (*e*).

324. His favourite maxim (*a*)/ is — cut your shirt (*b*)/ according (*c*)/ to the cloth (*d*)/ No error (*e*).

325. His brother (*a*)/ Dharmender is (*b*)/ an excellent cook (*c*)/ is it not? (*d*)/ No error (*e*).

326. I have (*a*)/ brought a (*b*)/ he-duck and a she-duck (*c*)/ for my friend (*d*)/ No error (*e*).

327. Later on he (*a*)/ became a monk (*b*)/ and she became (*c*)/ a monkess (*d*)/ No error (*e*).

328. By arresting the local criminals (*a*)/ and encouraging good people (*b*)/ we can end (*c*)/ hostilities of that area (*d*)/ No error (*e*).

329. The apparently obvious solutions (*a*)/ to most of his problems (*b*)/ were overlook by (*c*)/ many of his friends (*d*)/ No error (*e*).

330. In spite of the difficulties (*a*)/ on the way, (*b*)/ they enjoyed their (*c*)/ trip to Gangothri (*d*)/ No error (*e*).

331. We decided not tell to (*a*)/ the patient about (*b*)/ the disease he was (*c*)/ suffering from (*d*)/ No error (*e*).

332. The principals of equal justice (*a*)/ for all is one of (*b*)/ the cornerstones of our (*c*)/ democratic way of life (*d*)/ No error (*e*).

333. The Trust has succeeded (*a*)/ admirably in raising (*b*)/ money for (*c*)/ its future programmes (*d*)/ No error (*e*).

334. Honesty, integrity and being intelligent (*a*)/ are the qualities which (*b*)/ we look for when (*c*)/ we interview applicants (*d*)/ No error (*e*).

335. In order to save petrol, (*a*)/ motorists must have to (*b*)/ be very cautious/ while driving along the highways (c) (*d*)/ No error (*e*).

336. The war of (*a*)/ Panipat was (*b*)/ won by (*c*)/ Babar in 1526 (*d*)/ No error (*e*).

337. He applied the break (*a*)/ to stop the scooter (*b*)/ and averted (*c*)/ the accident (*d*)/ No error (*e*).

338. He has recruited (*a*)/ many persons (*b*)/ to canvas for him (*c*)/ during the forth coming elections (*d*)/ No error (*e*).

339. His father is (*a*)/ suffering from (*b*)/ a serious heart attack (*c*)/ and his death is eminent (*d*)/ No error (*e*).

340. Ram and Ramesh are (*a*)/ fast friends (*b*)/ the farmer is a merchant (*c*)/ and the latter is an officer (*d*)/ No error (*e*).

341. It is a fact (*a*)/ that Ferozepore is (*b*)/ further than (*c*)/ Faridkot from Delhi (*d*)/ No error (*e*).

342. I feet that (*a*)/ I have given you (*b*)/ very trouble (*c*)/ in this matter (*d*)/ No error (*e*).

343. These two brothers (*a*)/ cannot live without (*b*)/ one another (*c*)/ for a long time (*d*)/ No error (*e*).

344. I shall (*a*)/ do your work (*b*)/ in these holidays (*c*)/ without fail (*d*)/ No error (*e*).

345. Hindustan Times (*a*)/ of Delhi (*b*)/ is the best (*c*)/ newspaper in India (*d*)/ No error (*e*).

346. Gold of South Africa (*a*)/ is exported to (*b*)/ many (*c*)/ countries (*d*)/ No error (*e*).

347. The chairman (*a*)/ as well as six other (*b*)/ members of the committee (*c*)/ were present (*d*)/ No error (*e*).

348. Whether he will be (*a*)/ able to come (*b*)/ or may not (*c*)/ depends on the train service (*d*)/ No error (*e*).

349. He requested (*a*)/ the director (*b*)/ to admit his son (*c*)/ in his institution (*d*)/ No error (*e*).

350. On his way back (*a*)/ he was absorbed with (*b*)/ his own (*c*)/ thoughts (*d*)/ No error (*e*).

ANSWERS WITH EXPLANATION

1. (*a*) Insert 'The' before 'Indian Ocean'.

2. (*a*) Insert 'The' before 'Himalayas'.

3. (*b*) 'an' should be used before 'actor'.

4. (*a*) 'the' should be used before 'train'.

5. (*e*) No error.

6. (*e*) No error.

7. (*a*) Error of verb. Use 'built' in place of 'build'.

8. (*c*) 'have any more money' is not a good expression.

9. (*a*) Instead of 'had' use of 'has' will be correct.

10. (*b*) Instead of 'are' use of 'were' will be correct.

11. (*d*) Use 'wallet' instead of 'wallest'.

12. (*b*) Replace 'capable at' by 'capable of'.

13. (*b*) Prepositional mistake 'angry at' is a correct expression.

14. (*c*) Article mistake 'a' will be replaced by 'the'.

15. (*d*) Instead of 'one another', 'one to another' will be used.

16. (*c*) 'there' will be changed into 'his'.

17. (*a*) 'few' means nothing, so it will be 'a few'.

18. (*c*) Prepositional mistake.

19. (*b*) Instead of 'each', 'every' will be used.

20. (*b*) Replace 'across' by 'through'.

21. (*c*) Replace 'each others' by 'others.'

22. (*c*) Prepositional mistake. Use 'across.'

23. (*c*) Prepositional mistake. Use 'across'.

24. (*d*) Instead of 'actually age', 'actual age' will be used.

25. (*d*) The correct expression is 'it is now'.

26. (*a*) 'Until' is the wrong expression.

27. (*b*) Error lies in tense.

28. (*b*) In a sentence double use of future tense 'will' is wrong so 'will of part 'B' should be corrected.

29. (*d*) Error lies in this part.

30. (*a*) 'Information' will be used instead of 'informations'.

31. (*b*) Third form of the verb 'sung' will be used with 'has'.

32. (*c*) 'Who' will be used in place of 'which'.

33. (*c*) Change 'that' into 'how'.

34. (*c*) 'than' will take comparative degree, i.e. 'older'.

35. (*b*) Do/Did/Does always takes first form of verb. So, replace 'got up' by 'get up'.

36. (*c*) Instead of 'to' write 'with'.

37. (*b*) Instead of 'you are digging' use 'you have been digging'.

38. (*a*) Parted with means give up and 'parted from' means separation.

39. (*a*) 'pass away' means die, therefore, only 'pass' should be written.

40. (*c*) Replace 'poetry' in place of 'poetries'.

41. (*b*) Replace 'should' in place of 'shall'.

42. (*c*) Past tense will be used, therefore, 'was' is the correct expression.

43. (*e*) No error. The sentence is correct.

44. (*c*) We cannot write the universal truth in past tense. So, 'moved' will be replaced by 'moves'.

45. (*c*) Lest will be followed by 'should' not by 'will'.

46. (*c*) Instead of 'will', 'would' will be used in past tense.

47. (*c*) The correct expression will be 'daughter of his master'.

48. (*c*) Insert 'has' between 'but' and 'not'.

49. (*d*) Since the sentence is in past tense so 'would' will replace 'shall'.

50. (*e*) The sentence is correct.

51. (*d*) The correct expression is 'word for word'.

52. (*d*) Replace 'from' by 'on'.

53. (*a*) Instead of 'are' use 'is'.

54. (*c*) Prepositional mistake use 'by'.

55. (*d*) Use 'is' instead of 'are'.

56. (c) Had take third form of the verb, i.e. 'appreciated'.

57. (a) Write 'would have' in place of 'had'.

58. (a) Rearrangement of words, i.e. 'The judges not only acquited'.

59. (c) In palce of 'indefinite' use 'indefinitely'.

60. (e) The sentence is correct.

61. (d) Replace 'humour' by 'mood'.

62. (b) 'invented' is the correct word.

63. (a) Add 'was' before 'pleased'.

64. (c) In any superlative degree, 'the' will be placed before it.

65. (e) The sentence is correct.

66. (b) Double superlative will not be used, so use only 'the ablest'.

67. (b) Use of 'So' is not required.

68. (c) Replace 'are' by 'is' as per agreement between subject and verb rule.

69. (a) 'news' takes singular verb. So 'was' will be used.

70. (a) In place of 'is', 'am' will be used.

71. (c) Although is followed by 'yet', not by 'but'.

72. (a) Always remember 'Less is used for quantity' and 'Few denotes number'.

73. (c) No sooner did is followed by 'than', not by 'when'.

74. (d) Instead of 'different of' use 'different from'.

75. (e) The sentence is correct.

76. (e) The sentence is correct.

77. (c) 'and' will be replaced by 'or'.

78. (c) 'any body' will be replaced by 'some body'.

79. (b) Plural form of language, i.e. 'languages' will be used.

80. (e) The sentence is correct.

81. (b) In place of 'fair', 'fairly' will be used.

82. (c) As well as joins to parts of the sentence, so, the verb will be according to 1st subject (apply S-S, P-P) formula. Use 'were'.

83. (d) Use 'its' in place of 'their'.

84. (c) 'Many a' will be followed by singular verb. So it will be 'was'.

85. (d) 'in' will not be used.

86. (a) Error of tense. Use 'has been' in place of 'is'.

87. (c) Scarcely is followed by 'when' not by 'that'.

88. (d) Change 'no' into 'any'.

89. (b) Apply (S-S, P-P) formula he keep's is wrong, it should be 'he keeps'.

90. (b) Omission of 'which'. Use of double conjunction is wrong here.

91. (*c*) 'Shoes' will be the correct word.

92. (*c*) 'force' will be replaced by 'forces'.

93. (*c*) Plural form of 'grief' is 'griefs', not 'grieves'.

94. (*d*) The correct plural form is 'hangers-on'.

95. (*c*) Add 'to' before 'have gone on'.

96. (*a*) Not 'renew' it will be 'renewed'.

97. (*c*) use passive voice, i.e. 'the project was completed'.

98. (*b*) 'altogether' means completely, is the correct word.

99. (*a*) Use 'man' not 'men'.

100. (*a*) 'forward for' is wrong, use 'forward to'.

101. (*b*) 'all the problems...' is wrong, use 'the problem .....' .

102. (*c*) In place of 'were' write 'are'.

103. (*a*) Prepositional mistake. Use 'from' instead of 'of'.

104. (*a*) The correct part is 'As has always been said'.

105. (*b*) 'liking' will be changed into 'liked',

106. (*c*) Part with a thing, i.e., to give up. Part from a person, i.e. to separate.

107. (*b*) 'Where had he stopped' is the correct expression.

108. (*c*) 'tooth and nail' does not require any preposition. So 'with' will not be used.

109. (*a*) The meaning of 'look after' is to take care of and 'looked for' means searched.

110. (*c*) 'a' before philosopher is wrong here.

111. (*a*) No need of 'shall' here.

112. (*d*) In place of 'helps' use 'help'.

113. (*c*) Each will be followed by singular verb 'is' not by 'are'.

114. (*e*) The sentence is correct.

115. (*a*) 'Said' is a general word. In this sentence a sense of command reveals so use of 'ordered' is the correct expression.

116. (*c*) 'O'clock' will be deleted.

117. (*a*) Re-arrangement of words, i.e. 'The customer had scarcely'.

118. (*c*) Write 'could dampen' in place of 'was able to dampen'.

119. (*c*) Use 'most' before 'generous'.

120. (*c*) Insert 'was' detet 'were'.

121. (*a*) Error of tense, use 'I saw my friend'.

122. (*a*) If two comparative degrees are use in a sentence then both should have 'the' before them, i.e. 'The sooner' will be used.

123. (*d*) See rule omission of Article. Before name of meals 'the' will not be used.

124. (*e*) The sentence is correct.

125. (*d*) Prefer always takes 'to' preposition, not 'than'.

126. (*d*) In place of 'with' use 'to'.

127. (*e*) The sentence is correct.

128. (*b*) In place of 'compensated about' use 'Compensated for'. Error of Preposition here.

129. (*c*) The correct expression is 'too hot to drink'.

130. (*e*) The sentence is correct.

131. (*b*) Error of tense. It should be 'I told him to come'.

132. (*d*) Omission of 'to' is applicable.

133. (*c*) Error of tense. It should be 'caught' instead of 'catches'.

134. (*c*) Use 'informing'.

135. (*a*) Sentence is in Present Perfect Continuous, so use 'have been' in place of 'are'.

136. (*b*) Instead of 'to go' use 'going'.

137. (*c*) In place of 'doing' use infinitive, i.e. 'to do'.

138. (*b*) 'to persecute' will be changed into 'persecuting'.

139. (*a*) 'It was I' is the right expression.

140. (*a*) Replace 'order' by 'orders'.

141. (*a*) For more than two items 'none' is used.

142. (*c*) "The Arabian Nights" is a name of novel, so it will take singular verb, i.e. 'is'.

143. (*d*) The error is based on agreement between subject and verb concept. So, use 'was' in place of 'were'.

144. (*d*) The error is based on agreement between subject and verb concept. So, use 'were' in place of 'was'

145. (*a*) The given sentence is in the past tense, so 'met' will be used.

146. (*b*) In place of 'suits', 'suited' will be used.

147. (*c*) Prepositional mistake. In place of 'in' use 'during'.

148. (*a*) People takes plural verb. So, use 'are'.

149. (*c*) 'irons' is a wrong word, use 'iron'.

150. (*e*) The sentence is correct.

151. (*a*) 'Athletics' always takes singular verb use 'is'.

152. (*a*) 'Peasantry' is plural. So, in place of 'is' write 'are'.

153. (*c*) In place of 'vegetable' use 'vegetables'.

154. (*c*) 'besides' is the correct word.

155. (*c*) In place of 'avail' write 'avail herself'.

156. (*d*) In place of 'one's' write 'his'.

157. (*b*) Change 'can' into 'could'.

158. (*c*) Change 'their' into 'its'.

159. (*a*) 'have' will be deleted.

160. (*b*) In place of 'arrives' use 'arrived at'.

161. (*c*) 'as sprightly as' will be used in place of 'so sprightly as'.

162. (*a*) 'evidenty' will be replaced by 'evident'.

163. (*e*) The sentence is correct.

164. (*a*) 'Washer woman' is the correct word. Gender mistake is here.

165. (*b*) 'peahen' is the right word. Gender mistake arises here.

166. (*b*) In place of 'male and female actors' use 'actors and actresses'.

167. (*b*) The plural form of 'piano' is 'pianos'.

168. (*e*) The sentence is correct.

169. (*b*) Here is number mistake. Write 'mice' in place of 'mouses'.

170. (*b*) 'Saves' is not the plural of 'safe'. It is 'safes'.

171. (*b*) The correct spelling is 'scissors'.

172. (*c*) Spectacles take plural verb. Therefore, 'have' should be written in place of 'has'.

173. (*a*) Mathematics is singular, use 'is' in place of 'are'.

174. (*b*) Change 'him' into 'himself'.

175. (*b*) Passive, form will be applied, i.e. 'is reported' instead of 'is reporting'.

176. (*c*) Yesterday denotes past tense, hence, in place of 'find', 'found' will be used.

177. (*a*) Change 'On' into 'From'.

178. (*c*) Use 'than' before 'some'.

179. (*a*) Change 'was' into 'had been' as per tense demand.

180. (*c*) There is prepositional mistake. Use 'of' instead of 'with'.

181. (*d*) There is prepositional mistake. Use 'with' in place of 'in'.

182. (*c*) The correct expression is 'bound for'.

183. (*e*) The sentence is correct.

184. (*b*) 'with' will be replaced by 'to'.

185. (*c*) 'with' will be replaced by 'to'.

186. (*c*) 'upon' will be replaced by 'on'.

187. (*c*) 'of' is the correct preposition.

188. (*e*) The sentence is correct.

189. (*c*) 'for' will be replaced by 'against'.

190. (*b*) It will be past perfect tense. So add 'had' before 'died'.

191. (*b*) Concept of agreement between subject and verb applies here. So, as per rule

191. 'are' will be placed instead of 'is'.

192. (*b*) 'are' will be replaced by 'is' as per agreement between subject and verb rule.

193. (*c*) Use 'depends upon' in palce of 'depend upon'.

194. (*c*) use 'was' in palce of 'were'.

195. (*a*) Apply 'the' article before 'atheletes'.

196. (*a*) Apply 'the' article before 'first'.

197. (*c*) Use 'laugh' in place of 'laughed'.

198. (*b*) In palce of 'will rain' write 'rains'.

199. (*a*) Add 'It' before 'being'.

200. (*c*) 'to' will be deleted.

201. (*b*) 'for' will be deleted.

202. (*b*) 'not' will be deleted.

203. (*a*) 'None' is used for more than two persons/items. So, 'Neither' will be used.

204. (*a*) 'Neither' is used for only two persons/items. So, 'None' will be used.

205. (*b*) Use Past perfect tense. Insert 'had' before 'died.'

206. (*b*) In place of 'is', 'are' will be used.

207. (*a*) 'Have' will be used in place of 'Has'.

208. (*c*) This is a mistake related to preposition. Use 'for' in place of 'to'.

209. (*c*) Article 'the' will be used before 'other'.

210. (*a*) The sentence is imaginative. So, use 'were' in place of 'was'.

211. (*d*) The correct expression is 'than I am'.

212. (*a*) 'ought to' wil be used.

213. (*d*) After 'to' add 'under go'.

214. (*a*) 'had' will be replaced by 'have'.

215. (*b*) Use 'Sympathise' in place of 'Sympathy'.

216. (*a*) The correct word is 'lost', not 'loosened'.

217. (*d*) Use 'donating' instead of 'donated'.

218. (*c*) 'beside' will be used which means 'by the side of'.

219. (*c*) 'vale' is not a correct word, it should be 'veil', which means 'cover'.

220. (*b*) 'handedly' will be replaced by 'handed'.

221. (*c*) The correct expression is 'both ends meets'. Avoid 'his'.

222. (*e*) 'bolt from the blue' is the correct phrase.

223. (*e*) The sentence is correct.

224. (*c*) 'quite' will be replaced by 'very'.

225. (*a*) 'spend' will be changed into 'spent'.

226. (*b*) Rearrangement of words is required. So, it should be 'what exactly he said to me'.

227. (*c*) 'that' will be replaced by 'the'.

228. (*e*) The sentence is correct.

229. (*a*) Replace 'used to go' by 'went'.

230. (*b*) The correct expression is 'venetian glass ashtray'.

231. (*c*) Rearrangement of words required. The correct expression is 'round glass table'.

232. (*c*) 'incentives' takes 'has' not 'have'.

233. (*a*) Instead of 'raising' use 'rased'.

234. (*b*) 'being tried' will be replaced by 'trying' only.

235. (*d*) Omission of article required 'the' will be deleted.

236. (*a*) An epic takes definite article. So, 'The' will be used before 'Bible'.

237. (*d*) 'I' should be replaced by 'me'.

238. (*a*) Future tense will be changed into present tense. It should be 'If it rains'.

239. (*a*) 'quite sorry' is a slang. Use 'very sorry'.

240. (*c*) 'Until' slows negative sense. So, double negative will not be used. Therefore, avoid 'do not'.

241. (*a*) Try to remember the *magic number 321* illustrated in the chapter of '*Pronoun*'. So, it will be 'He, you and I'. (In good purpose).

242. (*c*) Avoid 'does not'.

243. (*d*) not only .. but also. So, 'yet' will be replaced by 'but'.

244. (*e*) The sentence is correct.

245. (*e*) The sentence is correct.

246. (*c*) 'then' is not required here.

247. (*e*) The sentence is correct.

248. (*e*) The sentence is correct.

249. (*b*) 'every' will be replaced by 'each'.

250. (*d*) 'them' will be changed into 'him'.

251. (*a*) The correct phrase here is 'put up', not 'put on'.

252. (*a*) Error in tense. It should be 'The mission has provided'.

253. (*d*) There is a mistake related to preposition 'from' will be used in place of 'with'.

254. (*b*) 'the' will be used before 'Germans'.

255. (*d*) The mistake is related to preposition. Use 'to' in place of 'for'.

256. (*c*) 'were' will be replaced by 'was'.

257. (*b*) 'were' will be replaced by 'was'.

258. (*b*) Present perfect will be replaced by Present perfect continuous. So, use 'have been' in place of 'have'.

259. (*d*) 'will' should be avoided.

260. (*c*) Error of article here. So, 'the' will be replaced by 'an'.

261. (*e*) The sentence is correct.

262. (*d*) Wrong words are introduced. So, it will be 'to be functionally effective'.

263. (*c*) Use 'been' before 'approached'.

264. (*c*) The correct words are 'precious collections', not 'price collection'.

265. (*a*) 'Omission of 'for' is required.'

266. (*c*) The mistake is related to preposition 'from' is changed into 'of'.

267. (*c*) Though.... yet, not 'but'.

268. (*d*) Change the preposition 'for' into 'about'.

269. (*c*) The mistake is related to preposition. Use 'in' in place of 'with'.

270. (*c*) The mistake is related to preposition. Use 'by' in place of 'in.'

271. (*b*) Preposition 'for' will be changed into 'on'.

272. (*c*) When a proper noun becomes common noun or universal truth, 'the' will be used before that. So, add 'the' before 'Shakespeare'.

273. (*d*) The sentence is given in Present perfect continuous showing point of time. So, 'since' will be used in place of 'from'.

274. (*a*) In Perfect Continuous sentence 'have/has/had+been' will be used. So, in place of 'am', 'have been is required.'

275. (*a*) Before any language article is not required. So, avoid 'the' before 'English'.

276. (*d*) Replace 'have been' by 'was'.

277. (*c*) The correct expression is 'it was still steaming'.

278. (*c*) The mistake is related to preposition. Change 'to a good' into 'in to a good'.

279. (*a*) Replace 'Even if' by 'Although'.

280. (*d*) Use 'be' after 'to'.

281. (*d*) 'family name' is a slang. It should be 'surname'.

282. (*c*) Change 'wishes' into 'wished.'

283. (*a*) Try to remember the **magic number 123** illustrated in the chapter of '*Pronoun*'. So, it will be 'I, you and he' (In bad purpose.)

284. (*a*) ('s) will be used.

285. (*c*) It will be 'brick' in place of 'bricks'.

286. (*c*) Use 'his' in place of 'him'.

287. (*d*) The right expression is 'envelope of my letter'.

288. (*e*) The sentence is correct.

289. (*c*) 'furnitures' is wrong it should be 'furniture'.

290. (*e*) The sentence is correct.

291. (*b*) The mistake is related to preposition. It should be 'angry at' 'in place of angry with'.

292. (*c*) 'to go' will be replaced by 'in going'.

293. (*a*) Article 'the' will be deleted.

294. (*e*) The sentence is correct.

295. (*b*) Apply (S-S, P-P) formula. It should be 'smokes' in place of 'smoke'.

296. (*b*) Write 'books' instead of 'book'.

297. (*e*) The sentence is correct.

298. (*d*) 'Yards' will be replaced by 'yard'.

299. (*e*) The sentence is correct.

300. (*d*) Rearrangement of words required. It should be 'to revise thoroughly'.

301. (*a*) The correct expression is 'Neither did he come'.

302. (*a*) 'See' will be replaced by 'Look up'.

303. (*c*) 'The correct word will be 'hanged' not 'hung'.

304. (*b*) Rearrangement of words required. It should be 'much too small'.

305. (*b*) 'quite sorry' is a slang, use 'very sorry'.

306. (*d*) 'too' will be replaced by 'very'.

307. (*b*) 'resembles', takes no preposition. Avoid 'with'.

308. (*b*) Avoid 'on'.

309. (*d*) Make the word in past tense, i.e. 'witnessed'.

310. (*b*) 'over' is replaced by 'down'.

311. (*b*) Change 'were' into 'was'.

312. (*b*) The mistake is related to preposition. Change 'for' into 'to'.

313. (*c*) Scarcely...when, not 'than'.

314. (*c*) When two subjects are joined by 'as well as' the verb will agree with the first subject. So, it will be 'were' in place of 'was'.

315. (*c*) It is a matter of agreement between subject and verb. So, use 'is' instead of 'are'.

316. (*d*) Replace 'was' by 'were'.

317. (*a*) Avoid 'shall'. The reason is that in a single sentence future tense will be never repeated.

318. (*d*) 'by all mean' is not a correct phrase. It should be 'by all means'.

319. (*d*) Error in phrase here. Use 'at daggers drawn'.

320. (*b*) Replace 'wounds' by 'injuries'.

321. (*c*) 'by dint of' is the correct phrase.

322. (*a*) Replace 'burnt a fire' by 'kindled a fire'.

323. (*c*) 'letter to him at his Delhi address'— is the correct expression.

324. (*b*) 'Cut your coat according to the cloth'— is the correct phrase.

325. (*d*) Replace 'is it not' by 'is he not'.

326. (*c*) Error in gender here. Use 'drake' for 'he-duck' and 'duck' for 'she-duck'.

327. (*d*) Error in gender here. Use 'nun' for 'monkess'.

328. (*c*) Add 'bring to' before 'end'.

329. (*c*) Passive form will be applied. So, 'over look' will be written as 'overlooked'.

330. (*e*) The sentence is correct.

331. (*a*) Use of infinitive is required. So, transform 'to' before 'tell'.

332. (*a*) 'principals' is wrong word here, it should be 'principles' which means theories.

333. (*e*) 'The sentence is correct.'

334. (*a*) 'being' should be deleted.

335. (*b*) 'must' should be deleted.

336. (*a*) The correct word is 'battle' here. So, 'war' should be changed into 'battle'.

337. (*a*) Replace 'break' by 'brakes'.

338. (*c*) 'Canvass'— is the correct spelling.

339. (*d*) 'imminent'— is the correct spelling.

340. (*c*) Wrong word is used here. Change 'farmer' into 'former'.

341. (*c*) Wrong word is used here, 'farther' will be used in place of 'further'.

342. (*c*) 'very' will be replaced by 'much'.

343. (*c*) 'one another' will be replaced by 'each other'.

344. (*c*) Wrong preposition is used here. Replace 'in' by 'during'.

345. (*a*) Before name of any newspaper definite article 'the' will be used.

346. (*a*) Article 'The' will be inserted before 'gold' showing particular gold of a particular place.

347. (*d*) Replace 'were' by 'was' as per agreement between subject and verb rule.

348. (*c*) Avoid 'may'.

349. (*d*) Replace 'in' by 'to'.

350. (*b*) The correct expression is 'absorbed in'.

WONDER OF WORDS

SIMILAR WORDS

JUDGE YOURSELF

In the following questions, each word is followed by four options (a), (b), (c) and (d). Select the option which best expresses the meaning of the given word.

1. ABSURD
- (a) Foolish
- (b) Simple
- (c) Courageous
- (d) Silly

2. ABANDON
- (a) Lose
- (b) Profit
- (c) Vacate
- (d) Foil

3. ADULATION
- (a) Embarrassment
- (b) Fawning
- (c) Veneration
- (d) Praise

4. ABDICATE
- (a) Rude
- (b) Soft
- (c) Imperious
- (d) Give up

5. BAFFLE
- (a) Abet
- (b) Enlighten
- (c) Foil
- (d) Taciturnity

6. BUOYANT
- (a) Support
- (b) Unworthy
- (c) Desponding
- (d) Cheerful

7. BLEMISH
- (a) Eccentric
- (b) Disgrace
- (c) Fair
- (d) Youth

8. BOOTY
- (a) Buxom
- (b) Loot
- (c) Delicate
- (d) Daub

9. CUPIDITY
- (a) Shrewd
- (b) Basic
- (c) Avarice
- (d) Parody

10. CORRIGIBLE
- (a) Amendable
- (b) Oppose
- (c) Devise
- (d) Illicit

11. CONNIVE
- (a) Overlook
- (b) Grow
- (c) Censure
- (d) Defect

12. CAJOLE
- (a) Pause
- (b) Lenient
- (c) Blast
- (d) Lure

13. HAUGHTY
- (a) Imperial
- (b) Imperious
- (c) Umpire
- (d) Brave

14. OPPORTUNE
- (a) Timely
- (b) Short lived
- (c) Occasional
- (d) Temper

15. EXTERMINATE
- (a) Extensore
- (b) Rubbing
- (c) Soothing
- (d) Extirpate

16. VENERABLE
    (*a*) Watchful   (*b*) Lawful
    (*c*) Respectful (*d*) Hateful

17. VORACIOUS
    (*a*) Funny   (*b*) Venturous
    (*c*) Gluttonous (*d*) Hungry

18. INSOLVENT
    (*a*) Rich   (*b*) Poor
    (*c*) Bankrupt (*d*) Penniless

19. REPEAL
    (*a*) Pass   (*b*) Cancel
    (*c*) Sanction (*d*) Dishonour

20. LYNCH
    (*a*) Murder   (*b*) Shoot
    (*c*) Killed   (*d*) Hang

21. COMBAT
    (*a*) Fight   (*b*) Conflict
    (*c*) Shoot   (*d*) Quarrel

22. LAMENT
    (*a*) Condone
    (*b*) Console
    (*c*) Complain
    (*d*) Contribution

23. DEBACLE
    (*a*) Disgrace (*b*) Defeat
    (*c*) Collapse (*d*) Decline

24. SHIVER
    (*a*) Fear   (*b*) Tremble
    (*c*) Shake   (*d*) Ache

25. TORTURE
    (*a*) Terror   (*b*) Harassment
    (*c*) Torment (*d*) Tranquility

26. LAUDABLE
    (*a*) Lovable
    (*b*) Commendable

    (*c*) Profitable
    (*d*) Oblivious

27. FIXED
    (*a*) Sterile   (*b*) Static
    (*c*) Stubborn (*d*) Parennial

28. FANCIFUL
    (*a*) Romantic
    (*b*) Beautiful
    (*c*) Imaginative
    (*d*) Egoistic

29. QUEER
    (*a*) Unfamiliar (*b*) Cute
    (*c*) Curious   (*d*) Strange

30. OPPRESS
    (*a*) Prosecute (*b*) Trouble
    (*c*) Persecute (*d*) Perilous

31. ZEST
    (*a*) Anticipation
    (*b*) Optimistic
    (*c*) Cruel
    (*d*) Enthusiasm

32. SUFFICIENT
    (*a*) Fit   (*b*) Proper
    (*c*) Adequate (*d*) Vast

33. OBSCENE
    (*a*) Unwanted (*b*) Healthy
    (*c*) Dirty   (*d*) Indecent

34. VETERAN
    (*a*) Talented
    (*b*) Matchless
    (*c*) Proudy
    (*d*) Experienced

35. FICTITIOUS
    (*a*) Foul   (*b*) Fraud
    (*c*) Flatering (*d*) False

36. FERAL
   (*a*) Wild
   (*b*) Cultivated
   (*c*) Well-planned
   (*d*) Unwanted

37. UNCIVILIZED
   (*a*) Savage   (*b*) Obsolete
   (*c*) Insane   (*d*) Awkward

38. MATERIALISTIC
   (*a*) Wordly   (*b*) Worldly
   (*c*) Stuff   (*d*) Rich

39. PRAISE WORTHY
   (*a*) Credible   (*b*) Incredible
   (*c*) Credulous   (*d*) Creditable

40. GLOSS
   (*a*) Brightness   (*b*) Soothing
   (*c*) Rubbing   (*d*) Miracle

41. VIVACIOUS
   (*a*) Sprightly   (*b*) Sensual
   (*c*) Smart   (*d*) Honest

42. WILE
   (*a*) Docile   (*b*) Artlessness
   (*c*) Guile   (*d*) Clear

43. TRANQUIL
   (*a*) Energy   (*b*) Boost
   (*c*) Zeal   (*d*) Quiet

44. NIGGARDLY
   (*a*) Blunt   (*b*) Facing
   (*c*) Stingy   (*d*) Generous

45. LONGING
   (*a*) Prune   (*b*) Apathy
   (*c*) Curtail   (*d*) Craving

46. JEER
   (*a*) Applaud
   (*b*) Magnanimity
   (*c*) Avoid
   (*d*) Scoff

47. DEROGATE
   (*a*) Deflenerate
   (*b*) Calm
   (*c*) Ordain
   (*d*) Exaggerate

48. ZENITH
   (*a*) Minimum   (*b*) Nadir
   (*c*) Plant   (*d*) Peak

49. GARB
   (*a*) Distort   (*b*) Dress
   (*c*) Trivial   (*d*) Rage

50. PROFANE
   (*a*) Gain   (*b*) Sacred
   (*c*) Unholy   (*d*) Lavish

51. FABRICATE
   (*a*) Devise   (*b*) Represent
   (*c*) Nucleus   (*d*) Sway

52. ABHOR
   (*a*) Rude   (*b*) Reconcile
   (*c*) Crave   (*d*) Detest

53. YIELD
   (*a*) Shum   (*b*) Incisive
   (*c*) Retain   (*d*) Surrender

54. PEDANTIC
   (*a*) Lineage
   (*b*) Shipload
   (*c*) Dull
   (*d*) Pedagogical

55. AXIOM
   (*a*) Elude   (*b*) Shirk
   (*c*) Absurdity   (*d*) Maxim

56. YOKE
   (*a*) Twist   (*b*) Release
   (*c*) Link   (*d*) Extra

57. VENT
   (*a*) End   (*b*) Stode
   (*c*) Opening   (*d*) Cure

58. INDICT
   (*a*) Allege   (*b*) Condemn
   (*c*) Warn   (*d*) Accuse

59. HARBINGER
   (*a*) Harbour   (*b*) Pilot
   (*c*) Steward   (*d*) Forerunner

60. VENUE
   (*a*) Agenda   (*b*) Time
   (*c*) Distance   (*d*) Place

61. FAKE
   (*a*) Loyal
   (*b*) Original
   (*c*) Trustworthy
   (*d*) Imitation

62. PONDER
   (*a*) Pollution
   (*b*) Evaluation
   (*c*) Anticipation
   (*d*) Think

63. EMBEZZLE
   (*a*) Vivid
   (*b*) Obscure
   (*c*) Misappropriate
   (*d*) Correct

64. ADVERSITY
   (*a*) Crisis   (*b*) Failure
   (*c*) Misfortune (*d*) Bluff

65. GRATIFY
   (*a*) Pacify   (*b*) Frank
   (*c*) Appreciate (*d*) Indulge

66. UNCOUTH
   (*a*) Rough   (*b*) Dirty
   (*c*) Ungraceful (*d*) Slovenly

67. UNTIE
   (*a*) Unchain   (*b*) Unhinge
   (*c*) Unfold   (*d*) Undo

68. MELD
   (*a*) Glisten   (*b*) Purchase
   (*c*) Common   (*d*) Merge

69. RABBLE
   (*a*) Noise   (*b*) Rubbish
   (*c*) Mob   (*d*) Roar

70. CORPULENT
   (*a*) Obese   (*b*) Lean
   (*c*) Gaunt   (*d*) Emaciated

71. RANT
   (*a*) To preach noisily
   (*b*) Praise inordinately
   (*c*) Formal
   (*d*) Quick

72. LAUD
   (*a*) Praise   (*b*) Extolled
   (*c*) Lord   (*d*) Eulogy

73. SALACITY
   (*a*) Indecency (*b*) Recession
   (*c*) Bliss   (*d*) Depression

74. STERILE
   (*a*) Dry   (*b*) Arid
   (*c*) Barren   (*d*) Cultivated

75. ECSTATIC
   (*a*) Enraptured (*b*) Animated
   (*c*) Bewildered (*d*) Illful

76. ALERT
   (*a*) Observant (*b*) Intelligent
   (*c*) Watchful (*d*) Energetic

77. SYNOPSIS
   (*a*) Puzzle   (*b*) Summary
   (*c*) Index   (*d*) Mixture

78. VITIATED
   (*a*) Purged   (*b*) Purified
   (*c*) Improved (*d*) Spoiled

79. QUOTE
 (*a*) Sigh   (*b*) Sight
 (*c*) Cite   (*d*) Site

80. WISE
 (*a*) Crafty   (*b*) Judicious
 (*c*) Judicial   (*d*) Ingenuous

81. FORTITUDE
 (*a*) Courage   (*b*) Envy
 (*c*) Hope   (*d*) Falsity

82. WEARISOMENESS
 (*a*) Tedder   (*b*) Worry
 (*c*) Tedious   (*d*) Tedium

83. VULGAR
 (*a*) Bad   (*b*) Malicious
 (*c*) Crude   (*d*) Vindicative

84. EMANCIPATE
 (*a*) Stuff   (*b*) Liberate
 (*c*) Surround   (*d*) Fine

85. TAUT
 (*a*) Unrelaxed   (*b*) Foul
 (*c*) Bribe   (*d*) A bird

86. CALLOUS
 (*a*) Cruel   (*b*) Soft
 (*c*) Kind   (*d*) Haughty

87. CHATTY
 (*a*) Abusive
 (*b*) Talkative
 (*c*) Loud-spoken
 (*d*) Reticent

88. PLENTIFUL
 (*a*) Abundant   (*b*) More
 (*c*) Surplus   (*d*) Less

89. HUMANE
 (*a*) Man like   (*b*) Manly
 (*c*) Mankind   (*d*) Kind

90. DENIER
 (*a*) Game   (*b*) Surprise
 (*c*) Denies   (*d*) Neglect

91. ADORE
 (*a*) Admiration   (*b*) Loathe
 (*c*) Worship   (*d*) Despise

92. VOLUPTUOUS
 (*a*) Exalt
 (*b*) Spiritual
 (*c*) Loathe
 (*d*) Self-indulgent

93. NUPTIALS
 (*a*) Divorce   (*b*) Separation
 (*c*) Wedding   (*d*) Cheerful

94. IMPAIR
 (*a*) Saucy   (*b*) Injure
 (*c*) Polite   (*d*) Better

95. FUGITIVE
 (*a*) Weak   (*b*) Vain
 (*c*) Enduring   (*d*) Escaping

96. ELUDE
 (*a*) Sway   (*b*) Fascinate
 (*c*) Evade   (*d*) Rule

97. ABNEGATION
 (*a*) Complete   (*b*) Final
 (*c*) Indulgence   (*d*) Rejection

98. WAG
 (*a*) Capricious   (*b*) Actor
 (*c*) Prig   (*d*) Joker

99. VACILLATE
 (*a*) Prosy   (*b*) Adaptable
 (*c*) Fluctuate   (*d*) Resolve

100. VINDICATE
 (*a*) Modesty   (*b*) Brave
 (*c*) Clever   (*d*) Adoration

101. USURP
 (*a*) Seize   (*b*) Precede
 (*c*) Custom   (*d*) Repress

102. INSCRIBE
 (*a*) Distant   (*b*) Crazy
 (*c*) Greedy   (*d*) Mark

103. ASTUTE
    (*a*) Cognizant (*b*) Hostile
    (*c*) Provoke (*d*) Shrewd

104. FOMENT
    (*a*) Provoke (*b*) Abrasion
    (*c*) Extripate (*d*) Isolation

105. INSIPID
    (*a*) Delicate (*b*) Solve
    (*c*) Stupid (*d*) Gentle

106. CAJOLE
    (*a*) Doubtful (*b*) Lure
    (*c*) Warm (*d*) Suggest

107. WONT
    (*a*) Clam (*b*) Exception
    (*c*) Rigid (*d*) Habit

108. GUILE
    (*a*) Sense (*b*) Candour
    (*c*) Deceit (*d*) Wander

109. ARID
    (*a*) Accuse (*b*) Apprehend
    (*c*) Dry (*d*) Charge

110. DEXTERITY
    (*a*) Eloquent (*b*) Rucful
    (*c*) Adroitness (*d*) Shameful

111. BIZZARE
    (*a*) Eccentric (*b*) Fair
    (*c*) Normal (*d*) Young

112. FULMINATE
    (*a*) Barren (*b*) Prodigal
    (*c*) Clamour (*d*) Misfire

113. METEORIC
    (*a*) Sudden (*b*) Cowardice
    (*c*) Mean (*d*) False

114. JOCUND
    (*a*) Puzzle (*b*) Barren
    (*c*) Gay (*d*) Calm

115. YEARN
    (*a*) Release (*b*) Crave
    (*c*) Timid (*d*) Tathe

116. DON
    (*a*) Pine (*b*) Doff
    (*c*) Blithe (*d*) Assume

117. VERTIGO
    (*a*) Midst (*b*) Uniform
    (*c*) Steadiness (*d*) Dizziness

118. DECOY
    (*a*) Lead (*b*) Escape
    (*c*) Gather (*d*) Mislead

119. IMP
    (*a*) Demon (*b*) Fair
    (*c*) Fairy (*d*) Angel

120. APPELLATION
    (*a*) Pertinent
    (*b*) Anonymity
    (*c*) Respect
    (*d*) Designation

121. JARGON
    (*a*) Clear
    (*b*) Baised
    (*c*) Youth
    (*d*) Terminology

122. SPENDTHRIFT
    (*a*) Extravagent
    (*b*) Fallacious
    (*c*) Liberal
    (*d*) Waste

123. ABSONANT
    (*a*) Unnatural
    (*b*) Objectionable
    (*c*) Discordant
    (*d*) Absurd

124. UNLAWFUL
    (*a*) Scant (*b*) Elicit
    (*c*) Illicit (*d*) Draw

125. INCLINATION
    (*a*) Attitude   (*b*) Applause
    (*c*) Aptitude   (*d*) Aspiration

126. INDICT
    (*a*) Allege   (*b*) Reprimand
    (*c*) Condemn   (*d*) Accuse

127. CANNY
    (*a*) Handsome   (*b*) Stout
    (*c*) Obstinate   (*d*) Clever

128. BENEVOLENCE
    (*a*) Illness   (*b*) Vision
    (*c*) Kindness   (*d*) Ill-will

129. EXTRICATE
    (*a*) Complicate
    (*b*) Tie
    (*c*) Pull
    (*d*) Free

130. LUCRATIVE
    (*a*) Profitable
    (*b*) Attractive
    (*c*) Tempting
    (*d*) Amusement

131. TACITURNITY
    (*a*) Hesitation   (*b*) Dumbness
    (*c*) Reserve   (*d*) Creation

132. LAMENTABLE
    (*a*) Deplorable
    (*b*) Terrible
    (*c*) Upgraded
    (*d*) Unpardonable

133. RESTRAINT
    (*a*) Restriction   (*b*) Hindrance
    (*c*) Repression   (*d*) Obstacle

134. INCENSED
    (*a*) Enthused   (*b*) Excited
    (*c*) Inflamed   (*d*) Enraged

135. LUCID
    (*a*) Complex   (*b*) Noble
    (*c*) Elaborated   (*d*) Clear

136. STRINGENT
    (*a*) Stringy   (*b*) Strict
    (*c*) Shrink   (*d*) Vivid

137. DEIFY
    (*a*) Face   (*b*) Flatter
    (*c*) Challenge   (*d*) Worship

138. RUPTURE
    (*a*) Damage   (*b*) Gap
    (*c*) Break   (*d*) Distortion

139. DILIGENT
    (*a*) Hard-working
    (*b*) Introvert
    (*c*) Prospective
    (*d*) Progressive

140. LUDICROUS
    (*a*) Serious   (*b*) Recall
    (*c*) Comic   (*d*) Dissolve

141. FORAY
    (*a*) Ranger   (*b*) Contest
    (*c*) Excursion   (*d*) Intuition

142. SYCOPHANTS
    (*a*) Submissive   (*b*) Jarnor
    (*c*) Foppish   (*d*) Flatterers

143. REFECTORY
    (*a*) Parlour
    (*b*) Living Room
    (*c*) Dining Room
    (*d*) Restaurant

144. LYNCHED
    (*a*) Killed   (*b*) Mutilated
    (*c*) Captured   (*d*) Harden

145. SHALLOW
    (*a*) Artificial   (*b*) Stupid
    (*c*) Worthless   (*d*) Superficial

146. PROPENSITY
 (*a*) Aptitude
 (*b*) Quality
 (*c*) Natural tendency
 (*d*) Charm

147. BAFFLED
 (*a*) Foiled
 (*b*) Defeated
 (*c*) Thwarted
 (*d*) Circumvented

148. RETAIN
 (*a*) Preserve (*b*) Recall
 (*c*) Conserve (*d*) Keep

149. CONNOISSEUR
 (*a*) Interpreter (*b*) Delinquent
 (*c*) Ignorant (*d*) Lover of art

150. SCANDAL
 (*a*) Disgraceful action
 (*b*) Talk
 (*c*) Rumour
 (*d*) Silly notion

151. VIGILANT
 (*a*) Ambitious (*b*) Smart
 (*c*) Intelligent (*d*) Watchful

152. VORACIOUS
 (*a*) Angry (*b*) Insane
 (*c*) Hungry (*d*) Quick

153. IMPROMPTU
 (*a*) Effective (*b*) Impressive
 (*c*) Glamour (*d*) Off hand

154. ANNIHILATED
 (*a*) Split (*b*) Miracle
 (*c*) Secured (*d*) Destroyed

155. PRECARIOUS
 (*a*) Brittle (*b*) Cautious
 (*c*) Perilous (*d*) Critical

156. GARRULOUS
 (*a*) Laughs a lot
 (*b*) Talks a lot
 (*c*) Silence
 (*d*) Gossip

157. GERMANE
 (*a*) Logic
 (*b*) Relevant
 (*c*) Responsible
 (*d*) Possible

158. GUILLIBLE
 (*a*) Unrealistic
 (*b*) Fallible
 (*c*) Enthusiastic
 (*d*) Unsuspecting

159. ALLEVIATED
 (*a*) Moderated (*b*) Removed
 (*c*) Mitigated (*d*) Lightened

160. CONSEQUENCES
 (*a*) Difficulties
 (*b*) Results
 (*c*) Applications
 (*d*) Conclusions

161. FICTITIOUS
 (*a*) Unreal
 (*b*) Uncamped
 (*c*) Unreliable
 (*d*) Unbelievable

162. APPROBATION
 (*a*) Admiration
 (*b*) Understanding
 (*c*) Appreciation
 (*d*) Approval

163. TEPID
 (*a*) Cold (*b*) Hot
 (*c*) Warm (*d*) Frozen

164. SUBSEQUENT
 (*a*) Few (*b*) Earlier
 (*c*) Many (*d*) Later

165. INEBRIATE
(*a*) Unsteady (*b*) Dreamy
(*c*) Drunken (*d*) Stupefied

166. COMMENSURATE
(*a*) Beginning
(*b*) Appropriate
(*c*) Measurable
(*d*) Proportionate

167. OUTWITTED
(*a*) Cheated
(*b*) Befooled
(*c*) Defeated
(*d*) Out manoeuvred

168. TIMID
(*a*) Slow (*b*) Medium
(*c*) Fast (*d*) Shy

169. GARNISH
(*a*) Garner (*b*) Abuse
(*c*) Adorn (*d*) Paint

170. CHASTE
(*a*) Virtuous (*b*) Dignified
(*c*) Noble (*d*) Honest

171. OBJECT
(*a*) Disapprove (*b*) Disobey
(*c*) Deny (*d*) Challenge

172. INDUSTRIOUS
(*a*) Diligent (*b*) Excellent
(*c*) Energetic (*d*) Promt

173. CANDID
(*a*) Explicit (*b*) Bright
(*c*) Apparent (*d*) Frank

174. IRONIC
(*a*) Bitter
(*b*) Inflexible
(*c*) Disguisedly Sarcastic
(*d*) Normal

175. TRANSPARENT
(*a*) Witty (*b*) Verbose
(*c*) Lucid (*d*) Blocked

176. SCOLD
(*a*) Repress (*b*) Reprieve
(*c*) Reprisal (*d*) Reprimand

177. SKETCH
(*a*) Paint (*b*) Draw
(*c*) Portray (*d*) Draft

178. PROTOTYPE
(*a*) Duplicate (*b*) Triplicate
(*c*) Substitute (*d*) Original

179. SUBMISSION
(*a*) Humility
(*b*) Surrender
(*c*) Politeness
(*d*) Carnivorous

180. ERADICATE
(*a*) Resolve (*b*) Remove
(*c*) Report (*d*) Uproot

181. SHORT-LIVED
(*a*) Mortal (*b*) Tempting
(*c*) Transient (*d*) Truant

182. MELANCHOLY
(*a*) Happy (*b*) Malice
(*c*) Cruelty (*d*) Sad

183. OBESE
(*a*) Officious
(*b*) Lean and thin
(*c*) Fat and dull-looking
(*d*) Soft

184. SHREW
(*a*) Woman of violent temper
(*b*) A person who is dull
(*c*) Man of violent temper
(*d*) Rude person

185. FEROCIOUS
    (*a*) Angry   (*b*) Dangerous
    (*c*) Fierce   (*d*) Dangerous

186. VENERATION
    (*a*) Modesty   (*b*) Exhalation
    (*c*) Brave   (*d*) Adoration

187. NONCHALANT
    (*a*) Natural   (*b*) Hot
    (*c*) Excited   (*d*) Cool

188. SAGACITY
    (*a*) Swell   (*b*) Surrender
    (*c*) Wisdom   (*d*) Resolve

189. ATOM
    (*a*) Placid   (*b*) Whole
    (*c*) Mass   (*d*) Iota

190. GRATUITOUS
    (*a*) Shear   (*b*) Justified
    (*c*) Amass   (*d*) Voluntary

191. WAIVE
    (*a*) Silent   (*b*) Relinquish
    (*c*) Press   (*d*) Bore

192. WARBLING
    (*a*) Dormant   (*b*) Vigilant
    (*c*) Inert   (*d*) Active

193. MILD
    (*a*) Loud   (*b*) Pass
    (*c*) Discuss   (*d*) Balmy

194. DUBIOUS
    (*a*) Trust   (*b*) Obligatory
    (*c*) Unreliable   (*d*) Worthy

195. TRIVIAL
    (*a*) Peculiar   (*b*) Candid
    (*c*) Frivolous   (*d*) Scrious

196. BEMOAN
    (*a*) Lament   (*b*) Acclaim
    (*c*) Defect   (*d*) Perfect

197. FRUGAL
    (*a*) Thrifty   (*b*) Prolific
    (*c*) Clamour   (*d*) Efficacious

198. HIDEOUS
    (*a*) Retrad   (*b*) Charming
    (*c*) Ugly   (*d*) Embarrass

199. INVIDIOUS
    (*a*) Placate   (*b*) Alluring
    (*c*) Unfair   (*d*) Normal

200. CHAGRIN
    (*a*) Solemnity   (*b*) Brave
    (*c*) Joy   (*d*) Annoyance

201. OSCILLATORY
    (*a*) Dancing   (*b*) Swinging
    (*c*) Running   (*d*) Kissing

202. SCHOOLING
    (*a*) Instruction
    (*b*) Going to school
    (*c*) Coming from school
    (*d*) Reading

203. TORTUOUS
    (*a*) Gathering   (*b*) Binding
    (*c*) Winding   (*d*) Sending

204. SCARCELY
    (*a*) Rigid   (*b*) Closely
    (*c*) Deficiency   (*d*) Perhaps

205. DESIST
    (*a*) Discontinue
    (*b*) Dreary
    (*c*) Desertion
    (*d*) Ripeness

206. RENUNCIATION
    (*a*) Relinquishment
    (*b*) Periodical
    (*c*) Correspondence
    (*d*) Arbitration

ANSWERS

1	2	3	4	5	6	7	8	9	10
(d)	(c)	(d)	(d)	(c)	(d)	(b)	(b)	(c)	(a)

11	12	13	14	15	16	17	18	19	20
(c)	(d)	(b)	(a)	(d)	(c)	(c)	(c)	(b)	(c)

21	22	23	24	25	26	27	28	29	30
(a)	(c)	(c)	(b)	(c)	(b)	(b)	(c)	(d)	(c)

31	32	33	34	35	36	37	38	39	40
(d)	(c)	(d)	(d)	(d)	(a)	(a)	(b)	(d)	(a)

41	42	43	44	45	46	47	48	49	50
(a)	(c)	(d)	(c)	(d)	(d)	(a)	(d)	(b)	(c)

51	52	53	54	55	56	57	58	59	60
(a)	(d)	(d)	(d)	(d)	(c)	(c)	(d)	(d)	(d)

61	62	63	64	65	66	67	68	69	70
(d)	(d)	(c)	(c)	(a)	(c)	(d)	(d)	(c)	(a)

71	72	73	74	75	76	77	78	79	80
(a)	(a)	(a)	(c)	(a)	(c)	(b)	(d)	(c)	(b)

81	82	83	84	85	86	87	88	89	90
(a)	(d)	(c)	(b)	(a)	(a)	(b)	(c)	(d)	(c)

91	92	93	94	95	96	97	98	99	100
(c)	(d)	(c)	(b)	(d)	(c)	(d)	(d)	(c)	(d)

101	102	103	104	105	106	107	108	109	110
(a)	(d)	(d)	(a)	(c)	(b)	(a)	(c)	(c)	(c)

111	112	113	114	115	116	117	118	119	120
(a)	(c)	(u)	(c)	(b)	(d)	(d)	(d)	(c)	(d)

121	122	123	124	125	126	127	128	129	130
(d)	(a)	(d)	(c)	(c)	(d)	(d)	(c)	(c)	(a)

131	132	133	134	135	136	137	138	139	140
(c)	(a)	(d)	(d)	(d)	(b)	(d)	(c)	(a)	(c)

141	142	143	144	145	146	147	148	149	150
(c)	(d)	(c)	(a)	(d)	(c)	(a)	(d)	(d)	(a)

151	152	153	154	155	156	157	158	159	160
(d)	(c)	(d)	(d)	(d)	(b)	(b)	(d)	(c)	(b)

161	162	163	164	165	166	167	168	169	170
(a)	(d)	(c)	(d)	(c)	(c)	(c)	(d)	(c)	(a)
171	172	173	174	175	176	177	178	179	180
(a)	(a)	(d)	(c)	(c)	(d)	(c)	(d)	(b)	(d)
181	182	183	184	185	186	187	188	189	190
(c)	(d)	(c)	(a)	(c)	(d)	(d)	(c)	(d)	(d)
191	192	193	194	195	196	197	198	199	200
(b)	(a)	(d)	(c)	(d)	(a)	(a)	(c)	(c)	(d)
201	202	203	204	205	206				
(b)	(a)	(c)	(d)	(a)	(a)				

OPPOSITE WORDS

JUDGE YOURSELF

In the following questions, each word is followed by four options (a), (b), (c) and (d). Select the option which looks like the antonym of the given word.

1. PLUCKED
   - (a) Admired
   - (b) Adopted
   - (c) Against
   - (d) Passed

2. IMPRUDENT
   - (a) Slave
   - (b) Thrifty
   - (c) Foolish
   - (d) Prudent

3. OMINOUS
   - (a) Virtuous
   - (b) Good
   - (c) Auspicious
   - (d) Holy

4. TRAGIC
   - (a) Dramatic
   - (b) Strong
   - (c) Gentle
   - (d) Comic

5. TREACHEROUS
   - (a) Disloyal
   - (b) Goodwill
   - (c) Veteran
   - (d) Loyal

6. IMPOVERISH
   - (a) Enrich
   - (b) Weak
   - (c) Exit
   - (d) Never

7. ORAL
   - (a) Verbal
   - (b) Sane
   - (c) Minor
   - (d) Written

8. ADMIRE
   - (a) Hate
   - (b) Unlike
   - (c) Dislike
   - (d) Enough

9. NADIR
   - (a) Earth
   - (b) Fermament
   - (c) Sky
   - (d) Zenith

10. HYPOCRISY
    - (a) Honesty
    - (b) Loyalty
    - (c) Sincerity
    - (d) Wane

11. SLEEK
    - (a) Dirty
    - (b) Shabby
    - (c) Shaggy
    - (d) Deshaped

12. ELEVATE
    - (a) Dissociate
    - (b) Assist
    - (c) Associate
    - (d) Depress

13. HUMANE
- (a) Humble
- (b) Brilliant
- (c) Cruel
- (d) Soft

14. INDOLENT
- (a) Apathetic
- (b) Passive
- (c) Energetic
- (d) Lazy

15. VIOLENT
- (a) Gentle
- (b) Savage
- (c) Haughty
- (d) Decline

16. ADVERSITY
- (a) Windfall
- (b) Inprosperity
- (c) Prosperity
- (d) Slave

17. CONSIDERATE
- (a) Humane
- (b) Polite
- (c) Callous
- (d) Affection

18. EXTRAVAGANT
- (a) Quarrelsome
- (b) Thrifty
- (c) Wane
- (d) Valiant

19. EBULLIENT
- (a) Obscure
- (b) Timid
- (c) Restrained
- (d) Exuberant

20. OPAQUE
- (a) Translucent
- (h) Ominous
- (c) Transparent
- (d) Transient

21. FANATIC
- (a) Dunce
- (b) Sympathetic
- (c) Secular
- (d) Amiable

22. EMANCIPATE
- (a) Enclose
- (b) Enslave
- (c) Capture
- (d) Disclose

23. AGITATION
- (a) Angry
- (b) Calm
- (c) Irritation
- (d) Tranquility

24. GENUINE
- (a) Spurious
- (b) Obscure
- (c) Countless
- (d) Apathetic

25. FICKLE
- (a) Permanent
- (b) Inconstant
- (c) Unconstant
- (d) Constant

26. GRUDGE
- (a) Essence
- (b) Guile
- (c) Goodwill
- (d) Ill-will

27. STIFF
- (a) Soft
- (b) Courteous
- (c) Lively
- (d) Flexible

28. COLLISION
- (a) Retaliatory
- (b) Circuitous
- (c) Perfunctory
- (d) Conciliatory

29. METICULOUS
- (a) Shaggy
- (b) Mutual
- (c) Slovenly
- (d) Meretricious

30. HYPOCRITICAL
- (a) Dependable
- (b) Gentle
- (c) Amiable
- (d) Sincere

31. VANITY
- (a) Conceit
- (b) Pride
- (c) Ostentious
- (d) Humility

32. FRONT
- (a) Upper
- (b) Unusual
- (c) Back
- (d) Rear

33. SYNTHETIC
   (*a*) Cosmetic   (*b*) Affable
   (*c*) Natural   (*d*) Plastic

34. CRESTFALLEN
   (*a*) Disturbed
   (*b*) Indignant
   (*c*) Triumphant
   (*d*) Vainglorious

35. ACQUITTED
   (*a*) Burdened   (*b*) Freed
   (*c*) Entrusted   (*d*) Convicted

36. DISPARAGE
   (*a*) Be little   (*b*) Please
   (*c*) Denigrate   (*d*) Praise

37. FLIMSY
   (*a*) Filthy   (*b*) Flippant
   (*c*) Frail   (*d*) Firm

38. QUERULOUS
   (*a*) Contended   (*b*) Litigious
   (*c*) Allay   (*d*) Compain

39. IMPACTICAL
   (*a*) Difficult
   (*b*) Impossible
   (*c*) Impracticable
   (*d*) Feasible

40. INDISCREET
   (*a*) Prudent   (*b*) Honest
   (*c*) Stupid   (*d*) Reliable

41. TANGIBLE
   (*a*) Solid   (*b*) Actual
   (*c*) Concrete   (*d*) Ethereal

42. ATTRACT
   (*a*) Lured   (*b*) Longing
   (*c*) Repel   (*d*) Disguise

43. RETROGRADE
   (*a*) Brave
   (*b*) Cowardice
   (*c*) Revolutionary
   (*d*) Progressive

44. CAPACIOUS
   (*a*) Caring   (*b*) Foolish
   (*c*) Limited   (*d*) Unlimited

45. INCREDULOUS
   (*a*) Fickle   (*b*) Stylish
   (*c*) Easy   (*d*) Gullible

46. ENTANGLE
   (*a*) Palpable   (*b*) Extricate
   (*c*) Release   (*d*) Manifest

47. CLEBRITY
   (*a*) Hazy
   (*b*) Solemnity
   (*c*) Celebration
   (*d*) Obscurity

48. COMFORT
   (*a*) Discomfort   (*b*) Discontent
   (*c*) Uncomfort   (*d*) Miscomfort

49. WELCOME
   (*a*) Repel   (*b*) Accept
   (*c*) Resist   (*d*) Fight

50. TACTFUL
   (*a*) Naive
   (*b*) Loose
   (*c*) Strict
   (*d*) Uncivilized

51. DUTIFUL
   (*a*) Harmful   (*b*) Watchful
   (*c*) Forgetful   (*d*) Remiss

52. BALD
   (*a*) Erudite   (*b*) Scaly
   (*c*) Hirsute   (*d*) Quiet

53. RIGID
   (*a*) Flux   (*b*) Adoptable
   (*c*) Yielding   (*d*) Adaptable

54. PERNICIOUS
   (*a*) Beneficial (*b*) Parochial
   (*c*) Permanent (*d*) Dangerous

55. RARE
   (*a*) Petty   (*b*) Poor
   (*c*) Small   (*d*) Common

56. FRUGAL
   (*a*) Generous
   (*b*) Ostentatious
   (*c*) Copious
   (*d*) Extravagant

57. VINDICTIVE
   (*a*) Timid
   (*b*) Forgetful
   (*c*) Forgiving
   (*d*) Disobedient

58. APPLAUDED
   (*a*) Praised
   (*b*) Welcomed
   (*c*) Disapproved
   (*d*) Misunderstood

59. CORPULENT
   (*a*) Garrulous (*b*) Belligerent
   (*c*) Gaunt   (*d*) Fat

60. ZEAL
   (*a*) Despair
   (*b*) Calmness
   (*c*) Passiveness
   (*d*) Indifference

61. FAMILIAR
   (*a*) Dangerous (*b*) Strange
   (*c*) Friendly   (*d*) Unpleasant

62. HAPHAZARD
   (*a*) Unplanned
   (*b*) Extraordinary
   (*c*) Planned
   (*d*) Excellent

63. AMUSED
   (*a*) Abused   (*b*) Astonished
   (*c*) Saddened (*d*) Jolted

64. SHRINK
   (*a*) Spoil   (*b*) Expand
   (*c*) Stretch   (*d*) Contract

65. OBSCURE
   (*a*) Explicit   (*b*) Implicit
   (*c*) Obnoxious (*d*) Pedantic

66. ASSET
   (*a*) Drag   (*b*) Loss
   (*c*) Handicap   (*d*) Liability

67. IMPRACTICABLE
   (*a*) Feasible   (*b*) Easy
   (*c*) Alternate (*d*) Possible

68. GENUINE
   (*a*) Fraudulent (*b*) Direct
   (*c*) Candid   (*d*) Forthright

69. ACCIDENTAL
   (*a*) Conventional
   (*b*) Usual
   (*c*) Intentional (*d*) Permissible

70. VIOLENT
   (*a*) Tame   (*b*) Harmless
   (*c*) Humble   (*d*) Gentle

71. PATCHY
   (*a*) Clear   (*b*) Simple
   (*c*) Attractive (*d*) Uniform

72. ANNOY
   (*a*) Reward   (*b*) Rejoice
   (*c*) Praise   (*d*) Please

73. EXODUS
   (*a*) Return   (*b*) Restoration
   (*c*) Influx   (*d*) Advanced

74. HUMILITY
   (*a*) Arrogance (*b*) Insolence
   (*c*) Conceit   (*d*) Prodigal

75. SACROSANCT
- (*a*) Unethical
- (*b*) Unholy
- (*c*) Arrogant
- (*d*) Feast

76. ACRID
- (*a*) Acquit
- (*b*) Sour
- (*c*) Smooth
- (*d*) Personality

77. INTREPID
- (*a*) Mutiny
- (*b*) Doughty
- (*c*) Voracious
- (*d*) Fearful

78. RELEGATE
- (*a*) Retrogress
- (*b*) Demote
- (*c*) Promote
- (*d*) Toil

79. LAVISH
- (*a*) Gloom
- (*b*) Crude
- (*c*) Stingy
- (*d*) Extravagant

80. OPULENCE
- (*a*) Luxury
- (*b*) Wealthy
- (*c*) Comfort
- (*d*) Indigence

81. SUCCINCT
- (*a*) Brief
- (*b*) Entire
- (*c*) Concise
- (*d*) Wordy

82. MYTH
- (*a*) Innate
- (*b*) Fact
- (*c*) Parable
- (*d*) Fiction

83. EGREGIOUS
- (*a*) Acquit
- (*b*) Enchain
- (*c*) Consumate
- (*d*) Ordinary

84. PRECLUDE
- (*a*) Debar
- (*b*) Casual
- (*c*) Admit
- (*d*) Hinder

85. OBLATION
- (*a*) Option
- (*b*) Feed
- (*c*) Gift
- (*d*) Rejection

86. HUMP
- (*a*) Tumult
- (*b*) Feeble
- (*c*) Protuberance
- (*d*) Depression

87. ADAMANT
- (*a*) Adhere
- (*b*) Awkward
- (*c*) Flexible
- (*d*) Abominate

88. LACERATE
- (*a*) Afflict
- (*b*) Heat
- (*c*) Heal
- (*d*) Tear

89. HYPOCRISY
- (*a*) Naive
- (*b*) Aware
- (*c*) Busy
- (*d*) Candour

90. RABID
- (*a*) Sane
- (*b*) Pardon
- (*c*) Allied
- (*d*) Made

91. BELLICOSE
- (*a*) Pugnacious
- (*b*) Peaceful
- (*c*) Discern
- (*d*) Bound

92. COGNIZANT
- (*a*) Abridge
- (*b*) Ruminate
- (*c*) Incautious
- (*d*) Unaware

93. HEINOUS
- (*a*) Coax
- (*b*) Odious
- (*c*) Atrocious
- (*d*) Excusable

94. BIGOTED
- (*a*) Fanatic
- (*b*) Grotesque
- (*c*) Broad-minded
- (*d*) Empty

95. OBSOLETE
- (*a*) Modern
- (*b*) Tender
- (*c*) Archaic
- (*d*) Noble

96. HAZY
- (*a*) Clarify
- (*b*) Foggy
- (*c*) Vague
- (*d*) Clear

97. ENERVATE
   (*a*) Mitigate (*b*) Grappling
   (*c*) Strengthen (*d*) Relax

98. KNOTTY
   (*a*) Care   (*b*) Question
   (*c*) Tough (*d*) Easy

99. FEND
   (*a*) Friendship (*b*) Native
   (*c*) Hostility (*d*) Laxity

100. RUSTIC
   (*a*) Urban (*b*) Rural
   (*c*) Pastoral (*d*) Toil

101. THEIST
   (*a*) Frail (*b*) Obscure
   (*c*) Alienate (*d*) Atheist

102. JOYOUS
   (*a*) Pathetic (*b*) Cruel
   (*c*) Native (*d*) Gay

103. TRANSIENT
   (*a*) Discredit (*b*) Vague
   (*c*) Eternal (*d*) Meek

104. GAIETY
   (*a*) Pleasure
   (*b*) Melancholy
   (*c*) Dull
   (*d*) Warm

105. STALE
   (*a*) Fresh (*b*) Massive
   (*c*) Dirty (*d*) Amiable

106. THRIVE
   (*a*) Decline (*b*) Ruin
   (*c*) Favour (*d*) Link

107. LUSCIOUS
   (*a*) Insipid (*b*) Fickle
   (*c*) Retrograde (*d*) Relish

108. AMATEUR
   (*a*) Amiable (*b*) Staunch
   (*c*) Timid (*d*) Veteran

109. YIELD
   (*a*) Resist (*b*) Tasteful
   (*c*) Cheerful (*d*) Brimful

110. FRAIL
   (*a*) Weak (*b*) Delicate
   (*c*) Healthy (*d*) Unicorn

111. SUBLIME
   (*a*) Unholy (*b*) Ridiculous
   (*c*) Yielding (*d*) Submitting

112. WEAN
   (*a*) Resign (*b*) Artlessness
   (*c*) Guile (*d*) Art

113. PLENTY
   (*a*) Enough (*b*) Much
   (*c*) Less (*d*) Lack

114. RELISH
   (*a*) Sublimity (*b*) Relevant
   (*c*) Dislike (*d*) Love

115. SYNTHESIS
   (*a*) Unanalysis
   (*b*) Disanalysis
   (*c*) Analysis
   (*d*) Inanalysis

116. MEAGRE
   (*a*) Fabulous
   (*b*) Hard
   (*c*) Continuous
   (*d*) Small

117. PERENNIAL
   (*a*) Rare (*b*) Regular
   (*c*) Frequent (*d*) Lasting

118. REBUKED
   (*a*) Invited (*b*) Awarded
   (*c*) Praised (*d*) Received

119. BALANCE
    (*a*) Disbalance (*b*) Debalance
    (*c*) Imbalance (*d*) Misbalance

120. ALIEN
    (*a*) Resident
    (*b*) Domiciled
    (*c*) Native
    (*d*) None

121. EXPEDITE
    (*a*) Defer   (*b*) Delay
    (*c*) Postpone (*d*) Adjourn

122. STEADFAST
    (*a*) Humble   (*b*) Sincere
    (*c*) Fickle   (*d*) Brave

123. MAGNANIMITY
    (*a*) Meanness (*b*) Jealousy
    (*c*) Poverty   (*d*) Enmity

124. EXTRAVAGANCE
    (*a*) Poverty   (*b*) Alike
    (*c*) Luxury   (*d*) Economy

125. MORBID
    (*a*) Cheerful   (*b*) Insipid
    (*c*) Healthy   (*d*) Applying

126. CELESTIAL
    (*a*) Spiritual   (*b*) Psychic
    (*c*) Internal   (*d*) Material

127. MALICIOUS
    (*a*) Boastful   (*b*) Kind
    (*c*) Indifferent (*d*) Generous

128. HOLLOW
    (*a*) Strong   (*b*) Weak
    (*c*) Solid   (*d*) Perfect

129. ABHOR
    (*a*) Applaud   (*b*) Respect
    (*c*) Dislike   (*d*) Admire

130. IMPERTINENT
    (*a*) Smooth   (*b*) Healthy
    (*c*) Inadequate (*d*) Respectful

131. PRUDENT
    (*a*) Injudicious
    (*b*) Inconsiderate
    (*c*) Reckless
    (*d*) None

132. CULPABLE
    (*a*) Blameless (*b*) Careless
    (*c*) Defendable(*d*) Restoration

133. MASSIVE
    (*a*) Heavy   (*b*) Short
    (*c*) Meagre   (*d*) Complete

134. POSSESS
    (*a*) Deny   (*b*) Agree
    (*c*) Approval   (*d*) Relinquish

135. SUBTRACTION
    (*a*) Multiplication
    (*b*) Division
    (*c*) Addition
    (*d*) None

136. OBSESS
    (*a*) Divert   (*b*) Haunt
    (*c*) Notice   (*d*) Harass

137. EXTENUATE
    (*a*) Quality   (*b*) Enhance
    (*c*) Offhand   (*d*) Palliate

138. CORRIGIBLE
    (*a*) Covetous
    (*b*) Obverse
    (*c*) Docile
    (*d*) Incorrigible

139. ONEROUS
    (*a*) Visitor   (*b*) Feed
    (*c*) Irresistible (*d*) Easy

140. WANTON
    (*a*) Total   (*b*) Revolve
    (*c*) Entire   (*d*) Discreet

141. JARGON
    (*a*) Slang
    (*b*) Silly
    (*c*) Language
    (*d*) Terminology

142. ABSURD
    (*a*) Adorn   (*b*) Flourish
    (*c*) Scarcity   (*d*) Rational

143. OSTENTATIOUS
    (*a*) Centre   (*b*) Height
    (*c*) Boastful   (*d*) Modest

144. MACABRE
    (*a*) Attractive   (*b*) Trash
    (*c*) Gruesome   (*d*) Splendour

145. FALLACY
    (*a*) Error   (*b*) Truth
    (*c*) Blunder   (*d*) Abandon

146. IMBECILE
    (*a*) Heretic   (*b*) Idiotic
    (*c*) Bewitched   (*d*) Clever

147. PALLIATE
    (*a*) Aggravate   (*b*) Extenuate
    (*c*) Miraculous   (*d*) Purchase

148. LOATH
    (*a*) Reluctant   (*b*) Haste
    (*c*) Willing   (*d*) Brisk

149. FRAGILE
    (*a*) Abrasion   (*b*) Horrid
    (*c*) Strong   (*d*) Brittle

150. BLOOMING
    (*a*) Mild   (*b*) Flowering
    (*c*) Fading   (*d*) Bright

151. PROGRESSIVE
    (*a*) Unprogressive
    (*b*) Disprogressive
    (*c*) Non-progressive
    (*d*) Retrograde

152. LASTING
    (*a*) Everlasting   (*b*) Elastic
    (*c*) Transient   (*d*) Non-elastic

153. FUTILITY
    (*a*) Utility   (*b*) Fertility
    (*c*) Unfertility   (*d*) Keen

154. SENTIMENTAL
    (*a*) Callous   (*b*) Romantic
    (*c*) Prosaic   (*d*) Emotional

155. OMINOUS
    (*a*) Auspicious
    (*b*) Favourable
    (*c*) Horrible
    (*d*) Encouraging

156. VIRTUOUS
    (*a*) Corrupt   (*b*) Scandalous
    (*c*) Cunning   (*d*) Vicious

157. IMPASSE
    (*a*) Continuation
    (*b*) Combination
    (*c*) Resurgence
    (*d*) Breakthrough

158. EPILOGUE
    (*a*) Epigram   (*b*) Dialogue
    (*c*) Prelude   (*d*) Post script

159. SQUANDERING
    (*a*) Saving   (*b*) Boarding
    (*c*) Discarding   (*d*) Caring

160. FLAGITIOUS
    (*a*) Vapid   (*b*) Frivolous
    (*c*) Innocent   (*d*) Ignorant

161. LEND
    (*a*) Borrow   (*b*) Hire
    (*c*) Pawn   (*d*) Cheat

162. BENIGN
    (*a*) Friendly   (*b*) Malevolent
    (*c*) Wise   (*d*) Unwise

163. GUILE
    (*a*) Bubble   (*b*) Growl
    (*c*) Candour   (*d*) Deceit

164. CONCORD
    (*a*) Bestow
    (*b*) Discord
    (*c*) Consolidate
    (*d*) Outline

165. BUCOLIC
    (*a*) Urban   (*b*) Rustic
    (*c*) Vindictive   (*d*) Pastoral

166. JOVIAL
    (*a*) Sagacity   (*b*) Fixed
    (*c*) General   (*d*) Gloomy

167. DIDACTIC
    (*a*) Leading   (*b*) Misleading
    (*c*) Unfair   (*d*) Warbling

168. OFFICIOUS
    (*a*) Aloof   (*b*) Intrusive
    (*c*) Alight   (*d*) Blunt

169. ZEALOT
    (*a*) Moderate   (*b*) Devotee
    (*c*) Plaint   (*d*) Bigot

170. HOOT
    (*a*) Jostle   (*b*) Tint
    (*c*) Uproar   (*d*) Honour

171. CARICATURE
    (*a*) Glory   (*b*) Fidelity
    (*c*) Prim   (*d*) Painting

172. MENIAL
    (*a*) Noble   (*b*) Notion
    (*c*) Humble   (*d*) Servile

173. GLIB
    (*a*) Fluent   (*b*) Misty
    (*c*) Ready   (*d*) Hesitating

174. AXIOM
    (*a*) Angle   (*b*) Height
    (*c*) Maxim   (*d*) Absurdity

175. VIVACIOUS
    (*a*) Quickness   (*b*) Lively
    (*c*) Nice   (*d*) Dull

176. PRODIGAL
    (*a*) Preface   (*b*) Hasty
    (*c*) Frugal   (*d*) Reckless

177. IRK
    (*a*) Amuse   (*b*) Exodus
    (*c*) Iota   (*d*) Annoy

178. FABLE
    (*a*) Peevish   (*b*) Forge
    (*c*) Fact   (*d*) Devil

179. FLUX
    (*a*) Swerve   (*b*) Motion
    (*c*) Wince   (*d*) Stillness

180. SPURIOUS
    (*a*) Barren   (*b*) Dissipate
    (*c*) Genuine   (*d*) Weak

181. IMPLICATE
    (*a*) Extricate   (*b*) Hinted
    (*c*) Involve   (*d*) Lazy

182. GRUESOME
    (*a*) Grisly   (*b*) Stern
    (*c*) Disgusting   (*d*) Attractive

183. CAPRICIOUS
    (*a*) Yielding
    (*b*) Concentrate
    (*c*) Unchanging
    (*d*) Volume

184. ABJURE
    (*a*) Deny
    (*b*) Hate
    (*c*) Acknowledge
    (*d*) Disown

185. COMIC
    (*a*) Tragic
    (*b*) Fearful
    (*c*) Emotional
    (*d*) Horrible

186. MORTAL
    (*a*) Eternal   (*b*) Divine
    (*c*) Immortal   (*d*) Spiritual

187. DENSITY
    (*a*) Clarity
    (*b*) Intelligence
    (*c*) Rarity
    (*d*) Brightness

188. CERTAIN
    (*a*) Important   (*b*) Famous
    (*c*) Fixed   (*d*) Doubtful

189. DEAR
    (*a*) Worthless   (*b*) Priceless
    (*c*) Free   (*d*) Cheap

190. ENCOURAGE
    (*a*) Discourage (*b*) Disapprove
    (*c*) Warn   (*d*) Dampen

191. MITIGATE
    (*a*) Exclusion (*b*) Appease
    (*c*) Aggravate (*d*) Innate

192. LUSTRE
    (*a*) Hide   (*b*) Splendour
    (*c*) Lie   (*d*) Gloom

193. OBSCURE
    (*a*) Lucid   (*b*) Glory
    (*c*) Distinct   (*d*) Noisy

194. PROFANE
    (*a*) Holy   (*b*) Dupe
    (*c*) Divine   (*d*) Hoary

195. PRESAGE
    (*a*) Rash   (*b*) Indication
    (*c*) Benefit   (*d*) Fulfilment

196. CATACLYSM
    (*a*) Quibble   (*b*) Deluge
    (*c*) Peace   (*d*) Conjecture

197. USURP
    (*a*) Custom   (*b*) Assume
    (*c*) Inherit   (*d*) Origin

198. TACITURN
    (*a*) Loquacious
    (*b*) Unbound
    (*c*) Chattering
    (*d*) Stunted

199. RECKLESS
    (*a*) Cautious   (*b*) Careless
    (*c*) Deprave   (*d*) Headless

200. ENNOBLE
    (*a*) Degrade   (*b*) Loud
    (*c*) Dignity   (*d*) Void

201. AID
    (*a*) Agreement (*b*) Persuasion
    (*c*) Hindrance (*d*) Support

202. TRANSPARENT
    (*a*) Vivid   (*b*) Ominous
    (*c*) Opaque   (*d*) Shaggy

203. CONCEALED
    (*a*) Revealed   (*b*) Secret
    (*c*) Denied   (*d*) Quiet

204. ADORN
    (*a*) Deform   (*b*) Decorated
    (*c*) Attraction (*d*) Numbness

205. POIGNANT
    (*a*) Scarce   (*b*) Scanty
    (*c*) Frugal   (*d*) Blissful

120

206. MEEK | **207.** QUEER
- (*a*) Disabuse   (*b*) Arrogant   (*a*) Usual   (*b*) Chaos
- (*c*) Disregard   (*d*) Sharp   (*c*) Sage   (*d*) Admire

ANSWERS

1	2	3	4	5	6	7	8	9	10
(*d*)	(*d*)	(*c*)	(*d*)	(*d*)	(*a*)	(*d*)	(*c*)	(*d*)	(*c*)

11	12	13	14	15	16	17	18	19	20
(*c*)	(*d*)	(*c*)	(*c*)	(*a*)	(*c*)	(*c*)	(*b*)	(*c*)	(*c*)

21	22	23	24	25	26	27	28	29	30
(*c*)	(*b*)	(*d*)	(*a*)	(*d*)	(*c*)	(*d*)	(*d*)	(*c*)	(*d*)

31	32	33	34	35	36	37	38	39	40
(*d*)	(*d*)	(*c*)	(*c*)	(*d*)	(*d*)	(*d*)	(*a*)	(*d*)	(*a*)

41	42	43	44	45	46	47	48	49	50
(*d*)	(*c*)	(*d*)	(*c*)	(*d*)	(*b*)	(*d*)	(*a*)	(*c*)	(*a*)

51	52	53	54	55	56	57	58	59	60
(*d*)	(*c*)	(*d*)	(*a*)	(*d*)	(*d*)	(*c*)	(*c*)	(*c*)	(*d*)

61	62	63	64	65	66	67	68	69	70
(*b*)	(*c*)	(*c*)	(*c*)	(*a*)	(*d*)	(*a*)	(*a*)	(*c*)	(*d*)

71	72	73	74	75	76	77	78	79	80
(*d*)	(*d*)	(*c*)	(*a*)	(*b*)	(*c*)	(*d*)	(*c*)	(*c*)	(*d*)

81	82	83	84	85	86	87	88	89	90
(*d*)	(*b*)	(*d*)	(*c*)	(*d*)	(*d*)	(*c*)	(*c*)	(*d*)	(*a*)

91	92	93	94	95	96	97	98	99	100
(*b*)	(*d*)	(*d*)	(*c*)	(*a*)	(*d*)	(*c*)	(*d*)	(*a*)	(*a*)

101	102	103	104	105	106	107	108	109	110
(*d*)	(*a*)	(*c*)	(*b*)	(*a*)	(*a*)	(*a*)	(*d*)	(*a*)	(*c*)

111	112	113	114	115	116	117	118	119	120
(*a*)	(*b*)	(*d*)	(*c*)	(*c*)	(*d*)	(*a*)	(*c*)	(*c*)	(*c*)

121	122	123	124	125	126	127	128	129	130
(*b*)	(*c*)	(*a*)	(*d*)	(*a*)	(*d*)	(*d*)	(*c*)	(*d*)	(*d*)

131	132	133	134	135	136	137	138	139	140
(*c*)	(*c*)	(*c*)	(*d*)	(*c*)	(*a*)	(*b*)	(*d*)	(*d*)	(*d*)

141	142	143	144	145	146	147	148	149	150
(*c*)	(*d*)	(*d*)	(*a*)	(*b*)	(*b*)	(*a*)	(*c*)	(*c*)	(*c*)

151	152	153	154	155	156	157	158	159	160
(d)	(c)	(a)	(c)	(a)	(d)	(d)	(c)	(a)	(c)
161	162	163	164	165	166	167	168	169	170
(a)	(b)	(c)	(b)	(a)	(d)	(b)	(a)	(d)	(d)
171	172	173	174	175	176	177	178	179	180
(b)	(a)	(d)	(d)	(d)	(c)	(a)	(c)	(d)	(c)
181	182	183	184	185	186	187	188	189	190
(a)	(d)	(c)	(c)	(a)	(c)	(c)	(d)	(d)	(a)
191	192	193	194	195	196	197	198	199	200
(c)	(d)	(a)	(a)	(d)	(c)	(c)	(a)	(a)	(a)
201	202	203	204	205	206	207			
(c)	(c)	(a)	(a)	(d)	(b)	(a)			

SUBSTITUTE WORDS

JUDGE YOURSELF

In questions given below out of four options choose the one which can be substituted for the given words/ sentences.

1. An assembly of listeners
   (a) Audience   (b) Nostrum
   (c) Ostracise   (d) Obituary

2. That which cannot be heard
   (a) Audible   (b) Pregnant
   (c) Inaudible   (d) Bobemian

3. A person who hates mankind
   (a) Philanthropist
   (b) Misanthropist
   (c) Nihilist
   (d) Theist

4. Animals that suckle their young ones
   (a) Mammals   (b) Pisces
   (c) Amphibian   (d) Birds

5. Murder of infants
   (a) Regicide   (b) Suicide
   (c) Homicide   (d) Infancide

6. Short lived or fleeting
   (a) Permanent   (b) Ephemeral
   (c) Effeminate   (d) Optimist

7. A person whose thoughts are turned inward and who never opens his heart to others
   (a) Extrovert   (b) Introvert
   (c) Sceptic   (d) Ambivert

8. Word for word
   (a) Verbatim   (b) Compound
   (c) Synonym   (d) Oral

9. A truth which is oft repeated
   (a) Aesthetics   (b) Truism
   (c) Verbose   (d) Truant

10. Belief in the role of a strong dictator is

(a) Fanaticism (b) Fascism
(c) Nepotism (d) Dogmatism

11. A person who does things only for pleasure
(a) Professional
(b) Radical
(c) Amateur
(d) Empiric

12. A person who practices celibacy
(a) Celibate (b) Mature
(c) Married (d) Widower

13. That which can be easily carried
(a) Portable
(b) Impregnable
(c) Invisible
(d) Apostate

14. One who flirts with ladies
(a) Solvent (b) Gentleman
(c) Philanderer (d) Popular

15. An office for which no salary is paid
(a) Hospitable (b) Free
(c) Honorary (d) Gratis

16. One who firmly believes in fate or destiny
(a) Honorary
(b) Gratis
(c) Dermatologist
(d) Fatalist

17. A word which has the same meaning as another
(a) Contemporary
(b) Substitute
(c) Synonym
(d) Antonym

18. Allowance due to a wife from her husband on legal separation
(a) Wage
(b) Compensation
(c) Debt
(d) Alimony

19. Four children born at the same time
(a) Alibi
(b) Twins
(c) Allergy
(d) Quadruplets

20. An insect with many legs
(a) Biped (b) Butterfly
(c) Centipede (d) Quadruped

21. Birds moving from one place to another
(a) Migratory (b) Respiratory
(c) Obituary (d) Transitory

22. To change hostility into friendship
(a) Surrogate (b) Castigate
(c) Placate (d) Complicate

23. The study of the art of printing is
(a) Typography
(b) Phenology
(c) Astrology
(d) Graphology

24. One who studies the history of development of mankind is
(a) Anthropologist
(b) Botanist
(c) Economist
(d) Historian

25. A handwriting which cannot be easily read
(a) Lucid (b) Edible
(c) Illegible (d) Legible

26. Government in which all religions are honoured is called
(*a*) Fanatic　(*b*) Ascetic
(*c*) Secular　(*d*) Catholic

27. One who does not show favour to anyone is called
(*a*) Impartial
(*b*) Unfavourable
(*c*) Prejudiced
(*d*) Rude

28. To throw light on something difficult
(*a*) Amplify　(*b*) Expand
(*c*) Explain　(*d*) Elucidate

29. A style that is full of words is known as
(*a*) Elegant
(*b*) Complicated
(*c*) Verbose
(*d*) Bombastic

30. A book or paper written by hand is known as
(*a*) Script
(*b*) Manuscript
(*c*) Draft
(*d*) Hand-written

31. A disease which ends in death is known as
(*a*) Life-suck　(*b*) Cancer
(*c*) Fatal　(*d*) Deadly

32. Those are practised by statesmen is called
(*a*) Diplomacy
(*b*) Viewpoint
(*c*) Statesmanship
(*d*) Politics

33. What we say about a man after his death is called

(*a*) Epitome
(*b*) Elegy
(*c*) Posthumous
(*d*) Epitaph

34. One who looks at the dark side of things is known as
(*a*) A pessimist
(*b*) An inconoclast
(*c*) An optimist
(*d*) A fatalist

35. The act of speaking through one's thoughts when alone
(*a*) Bilocation
(*b*) Dialogue
(*c*) Monologue
(*d*) Soliloquey

36. To congratulate someone in a formal manner
(*a*) Solemnise (*b*) Celebrate
(*c*) Facilitate (*d*) Felicitate

37. A disease of the mind causing an uncontrollable desire to steal
(*a*) Kleptomania
(*b*) Schizophrenia
(*c*) Claustrophobia
(*d*) Megalomania

38. A person pretending to be somebody he is not
(*a*) Liar　(*b*) Magician
(*c*) Imposter　(*d*) Rogue

39. One who dabbles in fine arts for the love of it and not for monetary gains
(*a*) Dilettante
(*b*) Professional
(*c*) Connoisseur
(*d*) Amateur

40. A prima facie case is such
- (*a*) As it turns out to be at the end
- (*b*) As it seems at first sight
- (*c*) As it seems to the court after a number of hearings
- (*d*) As it is made to seem at first sight

41. Tending to move away from the centre or axis
- (*a*) Centripetal
- (*b*) Awry
- (*c*) Centrifugal
- (*d*) Axiomatic

42. A drawing on transparent paper
- (*a*) Transparency
- (*b*) Blue print
- (*c*) Red print
- (*d*) Negative

43. Somethings that relates to everyone in the world
- (*a*) Usual
- (*b*) General
- (*c*) Universal
- (*d*) Common

44. Continuing fight between parties, families, clans, etc.
- (*a*) Quarrel
- (*b*) Skirmish
- (*c*) Feud
- (*d*) Enmity

45. Extreme old age when a man behaves like a fool
- (*a*) Senility
- (*b*) Superannuation
- (*c*) Imbecility
- (*d*) Dotage

46. One who does not believe in existence of God
- (*a*) Stoic
- (*b*) Egoist
- (*c*) Atheist
- (*d*) Naive

47. That which is preceptible by touch is
- (*a*) Tenacious
- (*b*) Contagious
- (*c*) Tangible
- (*d*) Contingent

48. Words used in ancient times but no longer in general use now
- (*a*) Ancient
- (*b*) Extinct
- (*c*) Archaic
- (*d*) Antiquated

49. Incapable of being seen through
- (*a*) Potable
- (*b*) Ductile
- (*c*) Opaque
- (*d*) Obsolete

50. A fixed orbit in space in relation to earth
- (*a*) Geo-centric
- (*b*) Geological
- (*c*) Geo-stationary
- (*d*) Geo-synchronous

51. A long vehement speech
- (*a*) Abuse
- (*b*) Abhor
- (*c*) Tirade
- (*d*) Vulgar

52. The body at the state of growth between boyhood and youth, is
- (*a*) Youth
- (*b*) Adolescent
- (*c*) Mature
- (*d*) Adult

53. The doctor who specializes in the treatment of nervous system
- (*a*) Neurologist
- (*b*) Oculist
- (*c*) Opticum
- (*d*) Obstetrician

54. A person who has an extensive knowledge
- (*a*) Illiterate
- (*b*) Innocent
- (*c*) Erudite
- (*d*) Scholar

55. The science or art of conducting negotiations between nations
- (*a*) Erratic
- (*b*) Wandering
- (*c*) Diplomacy
- (*d*) Epicure

56. One who relies on experiment not on theory
- (*a*) Theoretical
- (*b*) Empiric
- (*c*) Practical
- (*d*) Scientist

57. One incredulous of human goodness
(*a*) Naxalite   (*b*) Hedonist
(*c*) Cynic   (*d*) Stoic

58. That which cannot be explained
(*a*) Ennui
(*b*) Interesting
(*c*) Emancipate
(*d*) Inexplicable

59. Animals which like to live in flocks
(*a*) Isolate   (*b*) Gregarious
(*c*) Voracious   (*d*) Precarious

60. A person blindly attached to any opinion, system or party
(*a*) Fatalist   (*b*) Bourgeois
(*c*) Bigot   (*d*) Fallible

61. One who is well versed in the knowledge of plants and vegetables
(*a*) Botanist
(*b*) Vegetarian
(*c*) Scientist
(*d*) Non-vegetarian

62. A place where one lives permanently
(*a*) Bourgeois   (*b*) Refugee
(*c*) Domicile   (*d*) Confiscate

63. A battle or a match which neither party wins
(*a*) Detergent   (*b*) Caucus
(*c*) Equal   (*d*) Draw

64. A piece of writing full of words or using more words than required
(*a*) Vociferous   (*b*) Verbose
(*c*) Sadist   (*d*) Voracity

65. The violation or profaning sacred things
(*a*) Pantheism
(*b*) Sceptic
(*c*) Sacrilege
(*d*) Opportunist

66. One who eats only vegetables and abstains from meat of animals
(*a*) Gentle
(*b*) Mercenary
(*c*) Non-vegetarian
(*d*) Vegetarian

67. One who cannot be easily pleased
(*a*) Sycophant   (*b*) Reserved
(*c*) Flatterer   (*d*) Fastidious

68. A supporter of the cause of women
(*a*) Feminist
(*b*) Effiminate
(*c*) Loquacious
(*d*) Sophist

69. A person who hates women
(*a*) Monogamy
(*b*) Misogamist
(*c*) Misogynist
(*d*) Gynaecologist

70. Without payment or free of cost
(*a*) Hedonist   (*b*) Stoic
(*c*) Precious   (*d*) Gratis

71. A person who changes sides
(*a*) Ductile   (*b*) Anarchist
(*c*) Communist (*d*) Turncoat

72. A letter or a document which does not bear the name of its writer
(*a*) Acknowledge
(*b*) Pseudonym

(c) Elite

(d) Anonymous

73. Incapable of being effaced, or cancelled or obliterated

(a) Obviously (b) Delegate

(c) Indelible (d) Delible

74. An associate in an office or institution

(a) Accomplice

(b) Crew

(c) Colleague

(d) Tyro

75. A person's first public speech

(a) Maiden speech

(b) Inaugural

(c) Libertine

(d) Final speech

76. That which is endless

(a) Irrefutable

(b) Underscore

(c) Refutable

(d) Interminable

77. One skilled in the disease of the eyes

(a) Neurologist

(b) Dentist

(c) Oculist

(d) Obstetrician

78. The study of energy is

(a) Geography (b) Biology

(c) Physics (d) Chemistry

79. Words inscribed on a tomb

(a) Alibi (b) Epitaph

(c) Writ (d) Monument

80. One who manages funerals

(a) Undertaker (b) Anarchist

(c) Agnosite (d) Belligerent

81. A style in which a writer seeks to display his knowledge is known as

(a) Superficial

(b) Pedantic

(c) Showy

(d) Extravagant

82. One who keeps guard is known as a

(a) Soldier

(b) Policeman

(c) Gate-keeper

(d) Watchman

83. One who is insensible to kind thought is known as

(a) Unsympathetic

(b) Unkind

(c) Callous

(d) Inconsiderate

84. An address poem is called

(a) Elegy (b) Sonnet

(c) Ode (d) Epic

85. One who does a job for monetary consideration is known as

(a) Materialist

(b) Trader

(c) Mercenary

(d) Businessman

86. That which cannot be changed

(a) Unchanged (b) Revocable

(c) Changeless (d) Irrevocable

87. Money paid to employees on retirement is called

(a) Advance (b) Deposit

(c) Gratuity (d) Pension

88. To make the facts known is called

(a) Message

(*b*) Information
(*c*) Intimation
(*d*) News

89. Property inherited from one's father is called
(*a*) Ancestry   (*b*) Patrimony
(*c*) Legacy   (*d*) Matrimony

90. Ordinary and common-place remarks
(*a*) Satire   (*b*) Humour
(*c*) Examples   (*d*) Platitude

91. One who is not easily pleased by anything
(*a*) Precarious (*b*) Maiden
(*c*) Mediaeval (*d*) Fastidious

92. Malafide case is one
(*a*) Which is undertaken after a long delay
(*b*) Which is not undertaken at all
(*c*) Which is undertaken in bad faith
(*d*) Which is undertaken in good faith

93. The absence of Law and order
(*a*) Revolt   (*b*) Rebellion
(*c*) Anarchy   (*d*) Mutiny

94. To slap with a flat object
(*a*) Gnaw   (*b*) Chop
(*c*) Swat   (*d*) Hew

95. A person who tries to deceive people by claiming to be able to do wonderful things
(*a*) Magician
(*b*) Trickster
(*c*) Impostor
(*d*) Mountebank

96. A government by the nobles
(*a*) Bureaucracy
(*b*) Autocracy
(*c*) Aristocracy
(*d*) Democracy

97. The custom or practice of having more than one husband at the same time
(*a*) Polyphony
(*b*) Polychromy
(*c*) Polygyny
(*d*) Polyandry

98. To issue a thunderous verbal attack
(*a*) Animate   (*b*) Invigorate
(*c*) Fulminate (*d*) Languish

99. Present opposing arguments or evidence
(*a*) Reprimand (*b*) Criticise
(*c*) Rebut   (*d*) Rebuff

100. Deriving pleasure from inflicting pain on others
(*a*) Sadism
(*b*) Malevolence
(*c*) Bigotry
(*d*) Masochism

101. The policy of extending a country's empire and influence
(*a*) Imperialism
(*b*) Communism
(*c*) Internationalism
(*d*) Capitalism

102. One who knows everythings
(*a*) Omnipotent
(*b*) Scholar
(*c*) Omniscient
(*d*) Literate

103. One who eats everything
   (*a*) Irresistible
   (*b*) Insolvent
   (*c*) Omnivorous
   (*d*) Omniscient

104. The act of violating the sanctity of the church is
   (*a*) Sacrilege
   (*b*) Desecration
   (*c*) Heresy   (*d*) Blasphemy

105. A school boy who cuts classes frequently is a
   (*a*) Sycophant (*b*) Defeatist
   (*c*) Truant   (*d*) Martinet

106. The part of a government which is concerned with making of rules
   (*a*) Bar   (*b*) Court
   (*c*) Legislature (*d*) Tribunal

107. That which cannot be corrected
   (*a*) Indelible
   (*b*) Illegible
   (*c*) Incorrigible
   (*d*) Unintelligible

108. That which cannot be believed
   (*a*) Implausible
   (*b*) Unreliable
   (*c*) Incredible
   (*d*) Incredulous

109. A small shop that sells fashionable clothes, cosmetics etc.
   (*a*) Booth   (*b*) Store
   (*c*) Stall   (*d*) Boutique

110. A large sleeping-room with many beds
   (*a*) Hostel   (*b*) Bedroom
   (*c*) Basement (*d*) Dormitory

111. One who talks too much
   (*a*) Pregnable (*b*) Quite
   (*c*) Illogical   (*d*) Garrulous

112. One that lives on another
   (*a*) Parasite
   (*b*) Eligible
   (*c*) Independent
   (*d*) Rudimentary

113. A material through which water cannot pass
   (*a*) Fragile   (*b*) Fireproof
   (*c*) Pillion   (*d*) Waterproof

114. The murderer of a King
   (*a*) Regicide   (*b*) Fanatic
   (*c*) Suicide   (*d*) Fratricide

115. Talking to one's self
   (*a*) Egotism   (*b*) Soliloquy
   (*c*) Egoism   (*d*) Ennui

116. One who is given to sensual enjoyments
   (*a*) Cynic   (*b*) Epicurean
   (*c*) Fanatic   (*d*) Eccentric

117. A lover of books
   (*a*) Brittle
   (*b*) Bibliophile
   (*c*) Biographer
   (*d*) Philosopher

118. That which is bound to happen
   (*a*) Wavering (*b*) Inevitable
   (*c*) Opaque   (*d*) Doubtful

119. A place where birds are kept
   (*a*) House   (*b*) Zoo
   (*c*) Stable   (*d*) Aviary

120. One who walks on foot
   (*a*) Rider
   (*b*) Omnipotent
   (*c*) Pedestrian
   (*d*) Traveller

121. The crime of literary theft
    (*a*) Panacea   (*b*) Partiality
    (*c*) Plagiarism (*d*) Pluralism

122. A medicine that induces sleep is known as
    (*a*) Poppy   (*b*) Opium
    (*c*) Poison   (*d*) Narcotic

123. A word no longer in use is called
    (*a*) Non-existent
    (*b*) Ancient
    (*c*) Obsolete
    (*d*) Out-dated

124. Nations engaged in war are known as
    (*a*) Enemies
    (*b*) Belligerents
    (*c*) Mongers
    (*d*) Neutrals

125. A line of persons waiting
    (*a*) Queue   (*b*) Masses
    (*c*) Passengers (*d*) Gathering

126. A dramatic performance
    (*a*) Mascot   (*b*) Mosque
    (*c*) Mask   (*d*) Mosque

127. A person who speaks many languages
    (*a*) Polyglot
    (*b*) Bilingual
    (*c*) Linguist
    (*d*) Monolingual

128. The raison d'etre of a controversy is
    (*a*) The finesse with which participants handle it
    (*b*) The unending hostility the parties concerned have towards each other
    (*c*) The enthusiasm with which it is kept alive
    (*d*) The reason or justification of its existence

129. To walk with slow or regular steps is to
    (*a*) Stride   (*b*) Pace
    (*c*) Advance   (*d*) Limp

130. A person of good understanding, knowledge and reasoning power
    (*a*) Literate
    (*b*) Expert
    (*c*) Intellectual
    (*d*) Snob

131. Teetotaller means
    (*a*) One who abstains from taking wine
    (*b*) One who abstains from theft
    (*c*) One who abstains from malice
    (*d*) One who abstains from meat

132. Very pleasing to eat
    (*a*) Sumptuous (*h*) Tantalising
    (*c*) Palatable (*d*) Appetising

133. Parts of a country behind the coast or a river's banks
    (*a*) Archipelago
    (*b*) Swamps
    (*c*) Isthmus
    (*d*) Hinterland

134. Giving undue favours to one's own kith and kin
    (*a*) Worldliness
    (*b*) Corruption
    (*c*) Nepotism
    (*d*) Favouritism

135. One who sacrifices his life for a cause

(a) Soldier
(b) Revolutionary
(c) Martyr
(d) Patriot

136. A person who eats human beings
(a) Cannibal   (b) Nostrum
(c) Cynosure   (d) Animal

137. A thing fit to be eaten
(a) Farrier   (b) Edible
(c) Eradicate   (d) Audible

138. That which cannot be limited
(a) Optimist   (b) Mimicry
(c) Inimitable (d) Genealogy

139. A territory ruled by a monarch
(a) Aristocracy (b) Monarchy
(c) Democracy (d) Plutocracy

140. That which is not subject to death
(a) Mortal   (b) Earthy
(c) Immature   (d) Immortal

141. A victory gained at too great an expense
(a) Bloody   (b) Pyrrhic
(c) Decisive   (d) Celibacy

142. The doctor who specializes in the treatment of corns
(a) Oculist
(b) Podiatrist
(c) Cardiologist
(d) Optician

143. A person who feels sorry for a wrong he has done
(a) Compunctious
(b) Overt
(c) Illiterate
(d) Literate

144. A person who advocates extreme Patriotism
(a) Atheism
(b) Chauvinism
(c) Socialism
(d) Democracy

145. To ponder over to meditate
(a) Alleviate   (b) Expedite
(c) Ruminate   (d) Ascetic

146. One who is habitually silent
(a) Chalter box
(b) Taciturn
(c) Indifferent
(d) Verbose

147. A letter which is not claimed by anyone
(a) Wasted letter
(b) Epigram
(c) Dead letter
(d) Epicure

148. A well experienced person
(a) Veteran   (b) Tyro
(c) Outlandish (d) Novice

149. Medical examination of a dead body
(a) Psychologist
(b) Post-mortem
(c) Dissection
(d) Caesarian

150. One who is all powerful
(a) Wait
(b) Embezzle
(c) Omnipotent
(d) Effigy

151. The killing of one man by another man
(a) Insecticide (b) Suicide
(c) Homicide   (d) Fillicide

152. A drug which produces sleep or stupor, torpor, etc.
(*a*) Amulet (*b*) Narcotic
(*c*) Yawning (*d*) Insomnia

153. Science of the study of old age is called
(*a*) Exbiology
(*b*) Anthropology
(*c*) Genetics
(*d*) Gerontology

154. That which cannot be understood
(*a*) Infallible
(*b*) Unintelligible
(*c*) Incorrigible
(*d*) Intelligible

155. Anything that destroys the effect of poison
(*a*) Poison-free (*b*) Preserver
(*c*) Antidote (*d*) Saver

156. One who is at home in all countries
(*a*) Universal
(*b*) International
(*c*) Cosmopolitan
(*d*) Metropolitan

157. A person who has no regard for others' feeling is known as
(*a*) Boastful
(*b*) Haughty
(*c*) Inconsiderate
(*d*) Unkind

158. A place where bees are kept is called
(*a*) A-hive (*b*) A sanctuary
(*c*) An apiary (*d*) A mole

159. An expression of mild disapproval
(*a*) Denigration

(*b*) Reproof
(*c*) Warning
(*d*) Denigration

160. A voice load enough to be heard
(*a*) Laudable
(*b*) Oral
(*c*) Audible
(*d*) Applaudable

161. A style in which a writer makes a display of his knowledge
(*a*) Ornate (*b*) Pompous
(*c*) Pedantic (*d*) Verbose

162. One who is fond of fighting
(*a*) Militant (*b*) Belligerent
(*c*) Bellicose (*d*) Aggressive

163. To take secretly in small quantities
(*a*) Theft (*b*) Defalcation
(*c*) Pilferage (*d*) Robbery

164. One who is honourably discharged from service
(*a*) Relieved
(*b*) Emancipated
(*c*) Emeritus
(*d*) Retired

165. An actor who plays humorous parts
(*a*) Fool (*b*) Joker
(*c*) Clown (*d*) Comedian

166. A building for storing threshed grain
(*a*) Store (*b*) Granary
(*c*) Hangar (*d*) Dockyard

167. To cause troops, etc., to spread out in readiness for battle
(*a*) Align (*b*) Disperse
(*c*) Deploy (*d*) Collocate

168. One who is determined to exactfull vengeance for wrongs done to him
(*a*) Vindictive (*b*) Vsurer
(*c*) Vindicator (*d*) Virulent

169. List of the business or subjects to be considered at a meeting
(*a*) Plan (*b*) Agenda
(*c*) Schedule (*d*) Time-table

170. A person who brings goods illegally into the country
(*a*) Smuggler (*b*) Importer
(*c*) Exporter (*d*) Fraud

171. To talk without respect for something sacred or holy
(*a*) Vulgarity (*b*) Rudeness
(*c*) Obscenity (*d*) Blasphemy

172. Communication between mind and mind
(*a*) Tell-tale (*b*) Telephone
(*c*) Telepathy (*d*) Amistice

173. A player, who acts, not by speaking, but wholly by gesticulations
(*a*) Pantomine (*b*) Patent
(*c*) Paronyms (*d*) Patricide

174. To set free form restraint or bondage
(*a*) Detest
(*b*) Manipulate
(*c*) Emancipate
(*d*) Conjecture

175. An elderly unmarried woman
(*a*) Spinster (*b*) Vandal
(*c*) Adult (*d*) Bachelor

176. One who makes or compiles a dictionary
(*a*) Lexicographer
(*b*) Photographer
(*c*) Publisher
(*d*) Manuscript

177. One who is deprived of the protection of law
(*a*) Iconoclast (*b*) Citizen
(*c*) Belligerent (*d*) Outlaw

178. A vain boasting fellow
(*a*) Gallant (*b*) Fool
(*c*) Braggart (*d*) Chivalrous

179. A general pardon of political offenders
(*a*) Arson (*b*) Amnesty
(*c*) Emergency (*d*) Arsenal

180. A woman of very fair complexion with light hair and light blue eyes
(*a*) Pretty (*b*) Blonde
(*c*) Beauty (*d*) Braggart

181. The principle of living and acting for the welfare of others
(*a*) Egoism
(*b*) Misogynism
(*c*) Asceticism
(*d*) Altruism

182. The study of earthquakes is
(*a*) Zoology
(*b*) Physiology
(*c*) Seismology
(*d*) Etymology

183. The study of religion is
(*a*) Philology (*b*) Astrology
(*c*) Philosophy (*d*) Theology

184. An object which has no life
(*a*) Animate (*b*) Living
(*c*) Movable (*d*) Inanimate

185. A round about way of speaking
(*a*) Circumlocution
(*b*) Gourmet
(*c*) Flamboyant
(*d*) Eccentric

186. A person who cannot pay his debts
(*a*) Arsonist (*b*) Agnostic
(*c*) Solvent (*d*) Bankrupt

187. One who is irreverent towards God
(*a*) Fatalist
(*b*) Bigot
(*c*) Blasphemers
(*d*) Fanatic

188. One who is incapable of being tired
(*a*) Indefatigable
(*b*) Extempore
(*c*) Opportunist
(*d*) Fatigable

189. A list of books
(*a*) Epilogue (*h*) Epigram
(*c*) Catalogue (*d*) Phrase

190. Animals living on plants
(*a*) Cliche
(*b*) Celibate
(*c*) Herbivorous
(*d*) Carnivorous

191. That which cannot be passed through
(*a*) Present (*b*) Passage
(*c*) Impassable (*d*) Passable

192. A thing through which rays of light cannot pass
(*a*) Transparent
(*b*) Species
(*c*) Waif
(*d*) Opaque

193. A thing which is not fresh
(*a*) Old (*b*) New
(*c*) Juicy (*d*) Stale

194. A place for invalids and convalescents
(*a*) Irony
(*b*) Hospitable
(*c*) Dipsomania
(*d*) Sanatorium

195. A child born after the death of his father
(*a*) Posthumous
(*b*) Consort
(*c*) Censer
(*d*) Premature

196. A person interested in reading books and nothing else
(*a*) Student
(*b*) Book-worm
(*c*) Book-keeper
(*d*) Scholar

197. A man of odd habits
(*a*) Introvert (*b*) Moody
(*c*) Eccentric (*d*) Cynical

198. A room for storing grains in known as
(*a*) Godown (*b*) Store
(*c*) Granary (*d*) Warehouse

199. The practice of having more than one husband at a time is
(*a*) Polygamy (*b*) Bigamy
(*c*) Biandry (*d*) Polyandry

200. A tank for fishes or water plants
(*a*) Pyrrhic (*b*) Expiate
(*c*) Aviary (*d*) Aquarium

201. *Audible* means
   (*a*) something that can be heard
   (*b*) something that can be subjected to auditing
   (*c*) something that can be avoided
   (*d*) something that can be put in an order

202. *Manuscript* means
   (*a*) something concerning the manager of a firm
   (*b*) a paper or a book written by hand
   (*c*) the menu of a hotel
   (*d*) a passage meant for translation into another language

203. *Irritable* means
   (*a*) something concerned with irrigation
   (*b*) easily made angry
   (*c*) something concerned with soil erosion
   (*d*) something that can be rotated

204. *Fatalist* means
   (*a*) a person who is unable to pay his duty
   (*b*) a person who can not convey his feelings
   (*c*) a person who believes in fate
   (*d*) a person who does not get tired

205. *Invincible* means
   (*a*) a state of complete victory
   (*b*) incapable of doing anything
   (*c*) a state of lawlessness
   (*d*) incapable of being conquered.

206. *Patricide* means
   (*a*) the murder of one's own father
   (*b*) the murder of a friend
   (*c*) the murder of one's own mother
   (*d*) the murder of one's own child

ANSWERS

1	2	3	4	5	6	7	8	9	10
(*a*)	(*c*)	(*b*)	(*a*)	(*d*)	(*b*)	(*b*)	(*a*)	(*b*)	(*b*)
11	**12**	**13**	**14**	**15**	**16**	**17**	**18**	**19**	**20**
(*c*)	(*a*)	(*a*)	(*c*)	(*c*)	(*d*)	(*c*)	(*d*)	(*d*)	(*c*)
21	**22**	**23**	**24**	**25**	**26**	**27**	**28**	**29**	**30**
(*a*)	(*c*)	(*a*)	(*d*)	(*c*)	(*c*)	(*a*)	(*d*)	(*c*)	(*b*)
31	**32**	**33**	**34**	**35**	**36**	**37**	**38**	**39**	**40**
(*c*)	(*a*)	(*d*)	(*a*)	(*d*)	(*d*)	(*a*)	(*c*)	(*d*)	(*b*)
41	**42**	**43**	**44**	**45**	**46**	**47**	**48**	**49**	**50**
(*c*)	(*a*)	(*c*)	(*c*)	(*d*)	(*c*)	(*c*)	(*c*)	(*c*)	(*c*)

51	52	53	54	55	56	57	58	59	60
(c)	(b)	(a)	(c)	(c)	(b)	(c)	(d)	(b)	(c)
61	62	63	64	65	66	67	68	69	70
(a)	(c)	(d)	(b)	(c)	(d)	(d)	(a)	(c)	(d)
71	72	73	74	75	76	77	78	79	80
(d)	(d)	(c)	(c)	(a)	(d)	(c)	(c)	(b)	(a)
81	82	83	84	85	86	87	88	89	90
(b)	(d)	(c)	(c)	(c)	(d)	(c)	(c)	(b)	(a)
91	92	93	94	95	96	97	98	99	100
(d)	(c)	(c)	(c)	(b)	(c)	(d)	(c)	(c)	(a)
101	102	103	104	105	106	107	108	109	110
(a)	(c)	(c)	(a)	(c)	(c)	(c)	(c)	(d)	(d)
111	112	113	114	115	116	117	118	119	120
(d)	(a)	(d)	(a)	(b)	(b)	(b)	(b)	(d)	(c)
121	122	123	124	125	126	127	128	129	130
(c)	(d)	(d)	(b)	(a)	(b)	(c)	(d)	(b)	(c)
131	132	133	134	135	136	137	138	139	140
(a)	(c)	(d)	(c)	(c)	(a)	(b)	(c)	(b)	(d)
141	142	143	144	145	146	147	148	149	150
(b)	(b)	(a)	(b)	(c)	(b)	(c)	(a)	(b)	(c)
151	152	153	154	155	156	157	158	159	160
(c)	(b)	(d)	(b)	(c)	(c)	(c)	(c)	(b)	(c)
161	162	163	164	165	166	167	168	169	170
(c)	(c)	(c)	(d)	(c)	(b)	(c)	(a)	(b)	(a)
171	172	173	174	175	176	177	178	179	180
(d)	(c)	(a)	(c)	(a)	(a)	(d)	(c)	(b)	(b)
181	182	183	184	185	186	187	188	189	190
(d)	(c)	(d)	(d)	(a)	(d)	(c)	(a)	(c)	(c)
191	192	193	194	195	196	197	198	199	200
(c)	(d)	(d)	(d)	(a)	(b)	(c)	(c)	(d)	(d)
201	202	203	204	205	206				
(a)	(b)	(b)	(c)	(d)	(a)				

PAIR OF WORDS

JUDGE YOURSELF

In the following questions choose the correct word to fill the blank.

1. She comes of a .... family.
   (*a*) Respectable
   (*b*) Respectful

2. It began to .... as I reached my office.
   (*a*) Reign   (*b*) Rain

3. The teacher told the students to be ....
   (*a*) Quiet   (*b*) Quite

4. The .... has gone to attend the meeting.
   (*a*) Principle (*b*) Principal

5. .... makes a man perfect.
   (*a*) Practice   (*b*) Practise

6. Uttar Pradesh is the most .... state of India.
   (*a*) Popular   (*b*) Populous

7. The bird had a .... of bread with beak.
   (*a*) Piece   (*b*) Peace

8. As she read the letter, her face turned ....
   (*a*) Pail   (*b*) Pale

9. Man is the maker of his own ....
   (*a*) Destination
   (*b*) Destiny

10. Try this medicine, it will prove ....
    (*a*) Effectual (*b*) Effective

11. Maninder has employed an .... boy for his office works.
    (*a*) Errand   (*b*) Errant

12. The soldiers wanted to .... over their victory in the battle.
    (*a*) Exalt   (*b*) Exult

13. When I asked him to accompany us, he .... illness.
    (*a*) Fained   (*b*) Feigned

14. The books are lying on the .... piece.
    (*a*) Mantal   (*b*) Mantle

15. Sohan lives a .... life.
    (*a*) Luxurious (*b*) Luxuriant

16. She is a lady of .... birth.
    (*a*) Lowly   (*b*) Low

17. We should not be ....of other's wealth.
    (*a*) Jealous   (*b*) Zealous

18. It is two days .... from Delhi to Kerala by train.
    (*a*) Journey   (*b*) Voyage

19. My father makes a .... selection of books before buying.
    (*a*) Judicial   (*b*) Judicious

20. Marconi had an .... mind.
    (*a*) Ingenious (*b*) Ingenuous

21. It is .... to spend more than what you earn.
    (*a*) Unpudent   (*b*) Unprudent

22. Orders for his arrest were issued by the .... court.
(*a*) Imperial   (*b*) Imperious

23. During the voyage she suffered from sea ....
(*a*) Sickness   (*b*) Illness

24. Akbar was a .... ruler.
(*a*) Human   (*b*) Humane

25. Gandhiji was a .... leader.
(*a*) Notorious   (*b*) Famous

26. The boys broke the window .... of the class room.
(*a*) Pain   (*b*) Pane

27. My new trousers are very ....
(*a*) Loss   (*b*) Loose

28. She has learnt her ....
(*a*) Lesson   (*b*) Lessen

29. Brutus is an .... man.
(*a*) Honorary
(*b*) Honourable

30. I have to replace the .... of my shoe.
(*a*) Heal   (*b*) Heel

31. Avadesh Singh .... from the Punjab.
(*a*) Hales   (*b*) Hails

32. Constant worry .... his health.
(*a*) Affected   (*b*) Effected

33. John refused to .... his decision.
(*a*) Altar   (*b*) Alter

34. Vivek is a .... young man.
(*a*) Handsome   (*b*) Beautiful

35. He competed in the race .... footed.
(*a*) Bear   (*b*) Bare

36. She has given .... to a son.
(*a*) Birth   (*b*) Berth

37. Stalin was .... of poor parents.
(*a*) Borne   (*b*) Born

38. Please check your ....
(*a*) Brakes   (*b*) Breaks

39. The princess ordered for a new .... dress.
(*a*) Bridle   (*b*) Bridal

40. The .... of Plassey was fought in 1757.
(*a*) War   (*b*) Battle

41. G.B. Tilak was .... from India.
(*a*) Banished   (*b*) Exeled

42. The President gave his .... to the new bill.
(*a*) Ascent   (*b*) Assent

43. A potter is a skilled ....
(*a*) Artisan   (*b*) Artist

44. The two trains started in .... directions.
(*a*) Aposite   (*b*) Opposite

45. The fight came to an .... settlement.
(*a*) Amicable   (*b*) Amiable

46. Arjun was not .... to go out of the house.
(*a*) Permit   (*b*) Allowed

47. Mirage is an ....of the eyes.
(*a*) Illusion   (*b*) Allusion

48. The doctor has advised me to .... from drinking wine.
(*a*) Refrain   (*b*) Abstain

49. At last the thief .... his guilt.
(*a*) Admitted   (*b*) Confessed

50. After a heavy downpour the rain has .... now.
(*a*) Abated   (*b*) Abeited

51. The .... of the sea became more and more furious.
(*a*) Waive   (*b*) Waves

52. The .... is pointing to the north.
(*a*) Vane   (*b*) Wane

53. I will be going to Ooty during summer ....
(*a*) Vocation   (*b*) Vacation

54. Hansraj is a member of the college cricket ....
(*a*) Team   (*b*) Teem

55. Somebody seems to have .... with the records.
(*a*) Temper   (*b*) Tampered

56. The blade of this sword is made of ....
(*a*) Steel   (*b*) Steal

57. I .... you to finish this job before, you go on leave.
(*a*) Hope   (*b*) Expect

58. She is a very .... lady.
(*a*) Gentle   (*b*) Genteel

59. Tilak said ".......... is my birthright".
(*a*) Liberty   (*b*) Freedom

60. She is .... of her shortcomings.
(*a*) Conscious
(*b*) Conscientious

61. Smallpox is a .... disease which has been eradicated in India.
(*a*) Contagious
(*b*) Infectious

62. His sister's behaviour was ....
(*a*) Contemptuous
(*b*) Contemptible

63. You can cut that .... with a blade.
(*a*) Card   (*b*) Cord

64. The educational institutions no longer give .... punishment.
(*a*) Corporal   (*b*) Corporeal

65. Her success in the I.A.S. examination is ....
(*a*) Credible   (*b*) Creditable

66. To tell a lie is a ....
(*a*) Sin   (*b*) Crime

67. The following books have been .... for M.A. final year.
(*a*) Proscribed   (*b*) Prescribed

68. Coffee is a mild ....
(*a*) Stimulant   (*b*) Stimulus

69. Param Vir Chakra is a/an .... given for the highest gallantry in war.
(*a*) Reward   (*b*) Award

70. We should not believe in .... system.
(*a*) Cast   (*b*) Caste

71. Whenever I passed the .... I thought of my dead parents.
(*a*) Cemetery   (*b*) Symmetry

72. When a man becomes .... his progress in life declines.
(*a*) Complacent
(*b*) Complaisant

73. She looks very pretty in the red ....
(*a*) Custom   (*b*) Costume

74. I am a member of the action ....
(*a*) Counsel   (*b*) Council

75. The chairman always puts on a .... dress.
(*a*) Descent   (*b*) Decent

76. The .... drops looked beautiful.
(*a*) Dew   (*b*) Due

77. I .... with my sister in this matter.
(*a*) Defer   (*b*) Differ

78. There is a lot of .... between me and my brother.
(*a*) Difference
(*b*) Deference

79. Thousands of people .... when epidemics break out.
(*a*) Dye   (*b*) Die

80. Let us go up by the .... slowly.
(*a*) Stairs   (*b*) Stares

81. The .... is immortal.
(*a*) Sole   (*b*) Soul

82. He joined the navy as a ....
(*a*) Sailor   (*b*) Sailer

83. I lost my golden .... yesterday.
(*a*) Wring   (*b*) Ring

84. Please .... legibly.
(*a*) Write   (*b*) Right

85. We should .... good books only.
(*a*) Reed   (*b*) Read

86. The sun .... blinded my eyes.
(*a*) Rays   (*b*) Raise

87. Please .... some tea into this cup also.
(*a*) Pore   (*b*) Pour

88. This surface is not ...., it is uneven.
(*a*) Plane   (*b*) Plain

89. The climate of Delhi does not .... my mother.
(*a*) Suite   (*b*) Suit

90. The beautiful lady gradually lowered her ....
(*a*) Veil   (*b*) Vale

91. Anitha is famous for her .... modesty.
(*a*) Womanish   (*b*) Womanly

92. Mr. Talwar possesses a very strong ....
(*a*) Physic   (*b*) Physique

93. The condition of the beggar was ....
(*a*) Pitiable   (*b*) Pitibil

94. The Government has issued .... prohibiting sati.
(*a*) Ordnance   (*b*) Ordinance

95. The Prime Minister paid an .... visit to Kerala.
(*a*) Official   (*b*) Officious

96. This story has a .... lesson.
(*a*) Morale   (*b*) Moral

97. The first battle of Panipat is a .... event in the history of India.
(*a*) Memorable   (*b*) Memorial

98. .... is an important crop of India.
(*a*) Maze   (*b*) Maize

99. The Sikhs are famous for their
.... spirit.
(*a*) Martial   (*b*) Marshal

100. You should not have more than
one .... of this medicine.
(*a*) Dose   (*b*) Doze

101. The ship .... into the water
(*a*) Sank   (*b*) Drowned

102. I challenged my cousin to a
....
(*a*) Dual   (*b*) Duel

103. My niece is very ....
(*a*) Fare   (*b*) Fair

104. Agarwal had no shoes on his
....
(*a*) Feet   (*b*) Feat

105. Mason has repaired the .... of
my house last week.
(*a*) Flour   (*b*) Floor

106. She stood in the .... row.
(*a*) Fourth   (*b*) Forth

107. He adopted .... means to win
the first prize.
(*a*) Fowl   (*b*) Foul

108. She .... the authority of the
Principal and was expelled from
the college.
(*a*) Deify   (*b*) Defied

109. The thief .... to disclose the
truth.
(*a*) Denied   (*b*) Refused

110. She .... her husband's
sincerity.
(*a*) Doubts   (*b*) Suspects

111. Last year there was a severe
.... in the country.
(*a*) Draft   (*b*) Drought

112. The police arrested Shankar and
his gang for .... distillation.
(*a*) Illicit   (*b*) Elicit

113. We should not talk about our
colleagues in a .... manner.
(*a*) Contemptuous
(*b*) Contemptible

114. Cholera is a/an .... disease.
(*a*) Contagious
(*b*) Infectious

115. A .... worker is respected
everywhere.
(*a*) Conscientious
(*b*) Conscious

116. The football match is scheduled
to .... at 4 p.m. today.
(*a*) Commence (*b*) Begin

117. The .... of Mumbai does not
suit my mother.
(*a*) Weather   (*b*) Climate

118. If .... is lost everything is lost.
(*a*) Character   (*b*) Conduct

119. There is a film .... board in
India to censor the films.
(*a*) Censure   (*b*) Censor

120. I have applied for two days ....
leave.
(*a*) Casual   (*b*) Causal

121. It is a/an .... to think that
honesty does not pay.
(*a*) Error   (*b*) Mistake

122. In the second World .... atom
bombs were dropped on
Nagasaki and Hiroshima.
(*a*) War   (*b*) Battle

123. Lord Rama went into .... for fourteen years.
(*a*) Banishment
(*b*) Exile

124. India Gate is a war ....
(*a*) Memorable
(*b*) Memorial

125. The .... gate of the building was closed.
(*a*) Main   (*b*) Mane

126. She was awarded a gold .... for bravery.
(*a*) Meddle   (*b*) Medal

127. .... is followed by thunder.
(*a*) Lightning   (*b*) Lightening

128. I have not received any .... from my father for the past two months.
(*a*) Latter   (*b*) Letter

129. Avoid using this .... as it is very narrow.
(*a*) Lain   (*b*) Lane

130. The lawyer quoted many .... in support of his argument.
(*a*) Precedents   (*b*) Presidents

131. The doctor has .... this medicine for my father.
(*a*) Prescribed   (*b*) Proscribed

132. Tresspassers will be ....
(*a*) Persecuted
(*b*) Prosecuted

133. My brother has no .... experience of factory life.
(*a*) Practical   (*b*) Practicable

134. Theory .... practice.
(*a*) Proceeds   (*b*) Precedes

135. I .... the house where my sister was born.
(*a*) Recollect   (*b*) Remember

136. The .... of mango trees are very deep.
(*a*) Roots   (*b*) Routes

137. Mohan is .... of his success.
(*a*) Sanguinary (*b*) Sanguine

138. A .... man like Mr. Malhotra should not have used such words.
(*a*) Sensible   (*b*) Sensitive

139. We sat in the .... of a tree.
(*a*) Shade   (*b*) Shadow

140. My eyes are ....
(*a*) Soar   (*b*) Sore

141. Our new house is very ....
(*a*) Spacious   (*b*) Specious

142. I will tell a .... to those who complete their homework.
(*a*) Storey   (*b*) Story

143. She has not sent a .... to my letter.
(*a*) Reply   (*b*) Answer

144. Shyam is .... to drinking.
(*a*) Devoted   (*b*) Addicted

145. He is the ....boy that stole your pen.
(*a*) Very   (*b*) Vary

146. This child is the .... survivor of this accident.
(*a*) Sole   (*b*) Soul

147. We should not .... others' things.
(*a*) Steel   (*b*) Steal

148. Might is ....
(*a*) Right   (*b*) Write

149. The whole shop was .... to the ground by the fire.
(*a*) Rays   (*b*) Razed

150. The Planning Commission is drawing the next five year ....
(*a*) Plan   (*b*) Plane

151. Rajputs belong to a .... race.
(*a*) Marshal   (*b*) Martial

152. Give me a blade to .... my nails.
(*a*) Pair   (*b*) Pare

153. .... were issued by the court to summon the suspects.
(*a*) Ardours   (*b*) Orders

154. This is a .... problem, you cannot solve it easily.
(*a*) Knotty   (*b*) Naughty

155. Arvind has purchased a new .... of shoes for two hundred rupees.
(*a*) Pare   (*b*) Pair

156. Madhu is full of youthful ....
(*a*) Ardour   (*b*) Order

157. My sister's child is very ....
(*a*) Knotty   (*b*) Naughty

158. Do not be tempted by .... gains.
(*a*) Momentary
(*b*) Momentous

159. About thirty .... lost their lives in an accident at Raniganj colliery.
(*a*) Minors   (*b*) Miners

160. Iron is a very useful ....
(*a*) Metal   (*b*) Mettle

161. I went to the bank and got my .... cashed.
(*a*) Check   (*b*) Cheque

162. We have revised our .... in Hindi.
(*a*) Course   (*b*) Corse

163. Please convey my .... to your brother.
(*a*) Compliments
(*b*) Complements

164. I can work for twelve hours ....
(*a*) Continually
(*b*) Continuously

165. I write my .... daily.
(*a*) Diary   (*b*) Dairy

166. Chicken pox is an infectious ....
(*a*) Decease   (*b*) Disease

167. Vasco da Gama .... the sea route to India in 1498.
(*a*) Invented   (*b*) Discovered

168. The Moon .... from behind a cloud.
(*a*) Immersed   (*b*) Emerged

169. Many Indians .... are settled in Sri Lanka.
(*a*) Emigrants
(*b*) Immigrants

170. We went on an .... to Kashmir.
(*a*) Incursion   (*b*) Excursion

171. Real .... is found only in hard work.
(*a*) Felicity   (*b*) Facility

172. The poor man had to .... his meals.
(*a*) Forego   (*b*) Forgo

173. My final year examination .... on 21st April 1988.
  (*a*) Begins
  (*b*) Commences

174. Recently there was a bus .... in Patna.
  (*a*) Collision (*b*) Collusion

175. The .... is very fine today.
  (*a*) Weather
  (*b*) Climate

176. Anand was rewarded for his good ....
  (*a*) Character (*b*) Conduct

177. Everyone made fun of him as his manner of speaking was ....
  (*a*) Childlike (*b*) Childish

178. Lalitha was .... for her objectionable remarks.
  (*a*) Censured (*b*) Censored

179. The judge made a/an .... of judgement.
  (*a*) Error   (*b*) Blunder

180. The .... from Kalka to Simla is very steep.
  (*a*) Assent   (*b*) Ascent

181. Her remarks were not .... to the occasion.
  (*a*) Apposite (*b*) Opposite

182. He is a very famous ....
  (*a*) Artisan   (*b*) Artist

183. The teacher .... her to appear for the paper again.
  (*a*) Allowed   (*b*) Permitted

184. You should .... from telling lies.
  (*a*) Refrain   (*b*) Abstain

185. I .... that you are innocent, but I am helpless.
  (*a*) Admit
  (*b*) Confers

186. My brother .... his right to the family property.
  (*a*) Waved   (*b*) Waived

187. The .... carry blood in our body.
  (*a*) Veins   (*b*) Vanes

188. What .... will you pursue in your life?
  (*a*) Vacation (*b*) Vocation

189. This lake .... with fish.
  (*a*) Teems   (*b*) Teams

190. Do not .... at pretty girls.
  (*a*) Stair   (*b*) Stare

191. Akbar was a man of deep ....
  (*a*) Insight   (*b*) Incite

192. Kanpur is an ....city.
  (*a*) Industrious (*b*) Industrial

193. This is a very .... book.
  (*a*) Idle   (*b*) Ideal

194. He has .... much wealth.
  (*a*) Hoarded   (*b*) Horde

195. The princess had a very kind ....
  (*a*) Hart   (*b*) Heart

196. There is a big .... in air school.
  (*a*) Haul   (*b*) Hall

197. We should be determined to achieve our ....
  (*a*) Goal   (*b*) Gaol

198. I always .... what I say.
  (*a*) Mean   (*b*) Mien

199. We must .... to God daily.
  (*a*) Prey   (*b*) Pray

200. The .... is the prettiest of all the flowers.
  (*a*) Rose   (*b*) Rows

201. The .... of democracy in India is not little.
  (*a*) Roll   (*b*) Role

202. This is not a .... line.
  (*a*) Straight   (*b*) Strait

203. To .... is a crime.
  (*a*) Gambol   (*b*) Gamble

204. Capt. Singh received .... wounds in the battle field.
  (*a*) Fatal   (*b*) Fateful

205. She has a very .... impression of the picture.
  (*a*) Feint   (*b*) Faint

206. I found her in ....misery.
  (*a*) Abject   (*b*) Object

207. The committee .... a resolution condemning terrorism in the country.
  (*a*) Adapt   (*b*) Adopted

208. You .... to do your duty.
  (*a*) Ought   (*b*) Aught

209. The accused was released on ....
  (*a*) Bale   (*b*) Bail

210. One must not go against the .... of morality.
  (*a*) Cannons   (*b*) Canons

211. She had very little time to .... votes.
  (*a*) Canvass   (*b*) Canvas

212. Dyanand Saraswati was the .... guide of many people.
  (*a*) Spiritual   (*b*) Spirited

213. Aarti should not approve of her .... ways.
  (*a*) Wilful   (*b*) Willing

214. Rajesh .... many instances in support of his argument.
  (*a*) have   (*b*) has

215. The .... drops on the petals of the rose looked beautiful.
  (*a*) due   (*b*) dew

216. Please .... my black shirts red.
  (*a*) die   (*b*) dye

217. This is not a .... surface.
  (*a*) plain   (*b*) plane

ANSWERS

1	2	3	4	5	6	7	8	9	10
(*a*)	(*b*)	(*a*)	(*b*)	(*a*)	(*b*)	(*a*)	(*b*)	(*b*)	(*b*)
11	**12**	**13**	**14**	**15**	**16**	**17**	**18**	**19**	**20**
(*a*)	(*b*)	(*b*)	(*b*)	(*a*)	(*b*)	(*a*)	(*a*)	(*b*)	(*a*)
21	**22**	**23**	**24**	**25**	**26**	**27**	**28**	**29**	**30**
(*b*)	(*b*)	(*a*)	(*a*)	(*b*)	(*b*)	(*b*)	(*a*)	(*b*)	(*b*)
31	**32**	**33**	**34**	**35**	**36**	**37**	**38**	**39**	**40**
(*b*)	(*a*)	(*b*)	(*a*)	(*b*)	(*a*)	(*b*)	(*a*)	(*b*)	(*b*)

41	**42**	**43**	**44**	**45**	**46**	**47**	**48**	**49**	**50**
(*a*)	(*b*)	(*a*)	(*b*)	(*a*)	(*b*)	(*a*)	(*b*)	(*b*)	(*a*)
51	**52**	**53**	**54**	**55**	**56**	**57**	**58**	**59**	**60**
(*b*)	(*a*)	(*b*)	(*a*)	(*b*)	(*a*)	(*b*)	(*a*)	(*b*)	(*a*)
61	**62**	**63**	**64**	**65**	**66**	**67**	**68**	**69**	**70**
(*a*)	(*b*)	(*b*)	(*a*)	(*b*)	(*a*)	(*b*)	(*a*)	(*b*)	(*b*)
71	**72**	**73**	**74**	**75**	**76**	**77**	**78**	**79**	**80**
(*a*)	(*a*)	(*b*)	(*b*)	(*b*)	(*a*)	(*b*)	(*a*)	(*b*)	(*a*)
81	**82**	**83**	**84**	**85**	**86**	**87**	**88**	**89**	**90**
(*b*)	(*a*)	(*b*)	(*a*)	(*b*)	(*a*)	(*b*)	(*b*)	(*b*)	(*a*)
91	**92**	**93**	**94**	**95**	**96**	**97**	**98**	**99**	**100**
(*b*)	(*b*)	(*a*)	(*b*)	(*a*)	(*b*)	(*a*)	(*b*)	(*a*)	(*a*)
101	**102**	**103**	**104**	**105**	**106**	**107**	**108**	**109**	**110**
(*a*)	(*b*)	(*b*)	(*a*)	(*b*)	(*a*)	(*b*)	(*b*)	(*b*)	(*a*)
111	**112**	**113**	**114**	**115**	**116**	**117**	**118**	**119**	**120**
(*b*)	(*a*)	(*a*)	(*b*)	(*a*)	(*b*)	(*b*)	(*a*)	(*b*)	(*a*)
121	**122**	**123**	**124**	**125**	**126**	**127**	**128**	**129**	**130**
(*b*)	(*a*)	(*b*)	(*b*)	(*a*)	(*b*)	(*a*)	(*b*)	(*b*)	(*a*)
131	**132**	**133**	**134**	**135**	**136**	**137**	**138**	**139**	**140**
(*a*)	(*b*)	(*a*)	(*b*)	(*b*)	(*a*)	(*b*)	(*a*)	(*a*)	(*b*)
141	**142**	**143**	**144**	**145**	**146**	**147**	**148**	**149**	**150**
(*a*)	(*b*)	(*a*)	(*b*)	(*a*)	(*a*)	(*b*)	(*a*)	(*b*)	(*a*)
151	**152**	**153**	**154**	**155**	**156**	**157**	**158**	**159**	**160**
(*b*)	(*b*)	(*b*)	(*a*)	(*b*)	(*a*)	(*b*)	(*a*)	(*b*)	(*a*)
161	**162**	**163**	**164**	**165**	**166**	**167**	**168**	**169**	**170**
(*b*)	(*a*)	(*a*)	(*b*)	(*a*)	(*b*)	(*b*)	(*b*)	(*a*)	(*b*)
171	**172**	**173**	**174**	**175**	**176**	**177**	**178**	**179**	**180**
(*a*)	(*b*)	(*b*)	(*a*)	(*a*)	(*b*)	(*b*)	(*a*)	(*a*)	(*b*)
181	**182**	**183**	**184**	**185**	**186**	**187**	**188**	**189**	**190**
(*a*)	(*b*)	(*b*)	(*a*)	(*a*)	(*b*)	(*a*)	(*b*)	(*a*)	(*b*)
191	**192**	**193**	**194**	**195**	**196**	**197**	**198**	**199**	**200**
(*a*)	(*b*)	(*b*)	(*a*)	(*b*)	(*b*)	(*a*)	(*a*)	(*b*)	(*a*)
201	**202**	**203**	**204**	**205**	**206**	**207**	**208**	**209**	**210**
(*b*)	(*a*)	(*b*)	(*a*)	(*b*)	(*a*)	(*b*)	(*a*)	(*b*)	(*b*)
211	**212**	**213**	**214**	**215**	**216**	**217**			
(*a*)	(*a*)	(*a*)	(*b*)	(*b*)	(*b*)	(*a*)			

IDIOMS & PHRASES

JUDGE YOURSELF

Some Proverbs/Idioms are given below together with their meanings. Choose the correct meaning of the Proverb/ Idiom.

1. Pay off old scores
   (*a*) To repay the debt
   (*b*) To have revenge
   (*c*) To invite
   (*d*) Secretly

2. To all intents and purposes
   (*a*) With utmost care
   (*b*) Bitterly
   (*c*) Gist
   (*d*) Practically

3. Rap on the knuckles
   (*a*) Severe criticism
   (*b*) Mild criticism
   (*c*) Appreciation
   (*d*) In details

4. Turn turtle
   (*a*) To cheat
   (*b*) To be lopsided
   (*c*) To frustrate
   (*d*) To dance to the tune

5. Wash one's hands of
   (*a*) To refuse
   (*b*) To assist
   (*c*) To abuse
   (*d*) To refuse to be

6. Under duress
   (*a*) Under compulsion
   (*b*) Willing
   (*c*) To elicit information
   (*d*) To demand

7. Take pot luck
   (*a*) To intrude
   (*b*) To consent to
   (*c*) Set about
   (*d*) To be satisfied with whatever one gets

8. **'To turn the tables'** means
   (*a*) to ruin someone
   (*b*) to turn the situation to one's own side
   (*c*) to reverse the situation
   (*d*) to move from one point to another

9. His moral courage **'Carried** him **through'** all difficulties. It means
   (*a*) His moral courage supported him
   (*b*) His moral courage did not support him
   (*c*) His moral courage guided him
   (*d*) His moral courage did not guide him

10. **'On the cards'** means
    (*a*) Possibly   (*b*) Probably
    (*c*) Openly   (*d*) Likely

11. To leave someone in the lurch
    (*a*) to come to compromise with someone
    (*b*) constant source of annoyance to someone
    (*c*) to put someone at ease
    (*d*) to desert someone in his difficulties

12. To play second fiddle
  (*a*) To be happy, cheerful and healthy
  (*b*) To reduce importance of one's senior
  (*c*) To support the role and view of another person
  (*d*) To do back seat driving

13. Day and night, he **'yearns for'** his beloved, means
  (*a*) He weeps for his beloved
  (*b*) He remembers his beloved
  (*c*) He admires his beloved
  (*d*) He keenly desires to meet his beloved

14. **'Call off'** means
  (*a*) to finish
  (*b*) to withdraw
  (*c*) to postpone
  (*d*) to cry

15. **'Carry out'** means
  (*a*) to take from one place to another
  (*b*) to continue
  (*c*) to obcy
  (*d*) to make efforts

16. In the same boat
  (*a*) A worn out choice
  (*b*) Indifferent
  (*c*) In identical circumstances
  (*d*) Carry off

17. In the throes of
  (*a*) A good chance
  (*b*) In the grip of
  (*c*) Acute shortage
  (*d*) Self-sufficiency

18. In one's good book
  (*a*) A costly book
  (*b*) A priceless treasure

  (*c*) In one's favour
  (*d*) An enchanting beauty

19. Keep a straight face
  (*a*) To do make up
  (*b*) To change clothes
  (*c*) Assume responsibility
  (*d*) To remain serious

20. To be above board
  (*a*) To have a good height
  (*b*) To be honest in any business deal
  (*c*) To have no debts
  (*d*) To try to be beautiful

21. Odds and ends
  (*a*) Miscellaneous articles
  (*b*) To the contrary
  (*c*) To be in a rage
  (*d*) With great difficulty

22. On the face of it
  (*a*) To agree
  (*b*) From an action
  (*c*) More than enough
  (*d*) Apparently

23. Let the bygones be bygones
  (*a*) In one's favour
  (*b*) To pretend
  (*c*) To forget the past
  (*d*) Other choice

24. Keep one's countenance
  (*a*) To test
  (*b*) To refrain from laughing
  (*c*) To desire eagerly
  (*d*) In front of

25. To split hairs
  (*a*) Major distinctions
  (*b*) Hair with two ends
  (*c*) To make minute distinction
  (*d*) Without distinction

26. 'Bread and butter' means
- (*a*) both bread and butter
- (*b*) something essential
- (*c*) livelihood
- (*d*) relevant things

27. 'To bell the cat' means
- (*a*) to catch a cat and tie a bell round its neck
- (*b*) to make an effort
- (*c*) to be quick
- (*d*) to face a risk

28. 'Hard and fast' means
- (*a*) strict
- (*b*) solid
- (*c*) fast moving
- (*d*) some hard surface

29. 'Part and parcel' means
- (*a*) the part of a parcel
- (*b*) an essential part
- (*c*) a missing parcel
- (*d*) some part of a machine sent by parcel

30. 'Null and void' means
- (*a*) something invalid
- (*b*) something that can be avoided
- (*c*) something that can be nullified
- (*d*) something evil

31. To make clean breast of
- (*a*) to gain prominence
- (*b*) to praise oneself
- (*c*) to confess without reserve
- (*d*) to destroy before it blooms

32. 'Hard competition' means
- (*a*) to help
- (*b*) to stand for
- (*c*) to understand
- (*d*) none of these

33. 'Trump card' means
- (*a*) a powerful means of achieving an object
- (*b*) resourcefulness
- (*c*) the best gamble to attain success
- (*d*) none of these

34. 'Tall talk' means
- (*a*) a discussion continued for a long time
- (*b*) a high sounding talk
- (*c*) a meaningful talk
- (*d*) a useless talk

35. 'Small talk' means
- (*a*) Gossip
- (*b*) A discussion carried on for a long time
- (*c*) A brief discussion
- (*d*) None of these

36. To keep one's temper
- (*a*) To become angry
- (*b*) To be in good mood
- (*c*) To preserve one's energy
- (*d*) To be aloof from

37. To have an axe to grind
- (*a*) A private end to serve
- (*b*) To fail to arouse interest
- (*c*) To have no result
- (*d*) To work for both sides

38. Throw out of gear
- (*a*) To replace
- (*b*) Hinder, disturb
- (*c*) To decide
- (*d*) Take up tune

39. To and fro
- (*a*) Back and forth
- (*b*) Puzzled
- (*c*) Amazed
- (*d*) Reprove

40. Tall talk
(a) A familiar person
(b) Boastful talk
(c) A sweet song
(d) Interesting story

41. To bell the cat
(a) To do an easy job
(b) To be indifferent to
(c) To undertake a difficult job
(d) To clarify

42. To be under cloud
(a) Puzzle
(b) Enjoy the favour
(c) Talk thoughtlessly
(d) To be under suspicion

43. To cast a slur upon
(a) To discuss
(b) Assume responsibility
(c) To get rid of
(d) To bring into disrepute

44. Throw up the sponge
(a) To defy the enemy
(b) To remove restrictions
(c) Abandon the struggle
(d) To be deeply moved by

45. Throw dust into one's eye
(a) Be serious
(b) To mislead, deceive
(c) To clarify
(d) Become definite

46. Salad days
(a) Leaf vegetables
(b) Youth
(c) Safe
(d) Advocate or defend

47. Mind one's P's and Q's
(a) Be careful

(b) Learn alphabets
(c) Very easy
(d) Puzzling

48. A labour of love
(a) A tragic end
(b) A funny thing
(c) Not fruitful
(d) Work done without payment

49. Spare the rod
(a) To entertain
(b) Sharpen one's weapon
(c) Refrain from punishment
(d) To severely beat

50. Follow suit
(a) Follow an example
(b) Wear a new dress
(c) Irrelevant
(d) A gay person

51. Cast the first stone
(a) To start a fight
(b) Rehearse
(c) To be first to find fault
(d) Deeply involved

52. 'This medicine is a panacea' means
(a) this medicine is not good
(b) this medicine has wonderful curing power
(c) this is medicine that can cure every disease
(d) none of these

53. 'He is a man of iron will' means
(a) he is an obstinate fellow
(b) he is a short-tempered person
(c) he is a man of strong determination
(d) none of these

54. 'Foul play' means
(a) bad intentions
(b) a play not well acted
(c) a play not liked by the audience
(d) none of these

55. To hit the right nail on the head
(a) To do the right thing
(b) To destroy one's reputation
(c) To announce one's fixed views
(d) To teach someone a lesson

56. To pick holes
(a) To find some reason to quarrel
(b) To destroy something
(c) To criticise someone
(d) To cut some part of an item

57. To smell a rat
(a) To see signs of plague epidemic
(b) To get bad smell of a dead rat
(c) To suspect foul dealings
(d) To be in a bad mood

58. To put a spoke in one's wheel
(a) To encourage
(b) Act without restraint
(c) Risk something
(d) To obstruct one's progress

59. To put one on one's mettle
(a) To put to test
(b) Get an idea
(c) Overwhelm
(d) Resemble

60. To pull one's leg
(a) To give up
(b) Take care of
(c) To befool
(d) To know

61. To play with fire
(a) Grasp the truth
(b) To handle something dangerous
(c) To ridicule
(d) To flee away

62. To poke fun at
(a) To ridicule
(b) To sing
(c) To detect
(d) To experience

63. To reckon with
(a) Take up time
(b) Make an inventory
(c) To deal with
(d) Submit to punishment

64. To run short
(a) Talk until one is tired at
(b) Apply to oneself
(c) To get rid of
(d) To have or be too little

65. To set at defiance
(a) Upset or disturb
(b) To defy
(c) Remove restrictions
(d) Invent by thinking

66. To take a fancy to
(a) To fall in a trap
(b) Refuse to see
(c) To become fond of
(d) To consider the matters

67. 'A man of letters' means
(a) a postman
(b) a learned man
(c) a hypocrite
(d) an ignorant man

68. **'A maiden speech'** is
  (*a*) a speech made in the parliament
  (*b*) a speech made before unmarried girls
  (*c*) a speech made by a political leader
  (*d*) a speech made for the first time

69. **'Order of the day'** means
  (*a*) an order passed on a particular day
  (*b*) a current law
  (*c*) something common or general
  (*d*) none of these

70. **'To and fro'** means
  (*a*) up and down
  (*b*) backward and forward
  (*c*) here and there
  (*d*) hotch and potch

71. To end in smoke
  (*a*) to make completely understand
  (*b*) to ruin oneself
  (*c*) to excite great applause
  (*d*) None of these

72. One should always look **'beyond the nose'**. It means, one should
  (*a*) care for the future
  (*b*) look ahead liberally
  (*c*) think of coming events
  (*d*) be fore-sighted

73. **'To keep the powder dry'** means
  (*a*) Not to use any weapon
  (*b*) To maintain friendship
  (*c*) To be ready for any work
  (*d*) To give up enmity

74. To give vent to
  (*a*) To allow to flow forth
  (*b*) To prove a failure
  (*c*) To amass wealth
  (*d*) To evade

75. To eat humble pie
  (*a*) To apologise or confess
  (*b*) To order
  (*c*) To flatter
  (*d*) To get rid of

76. To hang in the balance
  (*a*) To guess right
  (*b*) To manage to live
  (*c*) To be undecided
  (*d*) To withdraw

77. To leave in the lurch
  (*a*) To study
  (*b*) To leave in difficulties
  (*c*) To lay aside
  (*d*) To face the difficulty

78. To mince matters
  (*a*) To gain distinction
  (*b*) To be undecided
  (*c*) To talk thoughtlessly
  (*d*) Not to speak plainly

79. To pay the piper
  (*a*) To bear the expenses of an undertaking
  (*b*) Just right
  (*c*) Capsize
  (*d*) To reject

80. A black sheep
  (*a*) An unlucky person
  (*b*) A negro
  (*c*) An ugly person
  (*d*) None of these

81. To catch a tarter
  (*a*) To trap wanted criminal with great difficulty

(*b*) To catch a dangerous person
(*c*) To meet with disaster
(*d*) To deal with a person who is more than one's watch

82. Read between the lines
(*a*) To hit at the real meaning
(*b*) To betray
(*c*) To overshadow
(*d*) Busy person

83. Ride rough-shod
(*a*) To interfere
(*b*) To fight
(*c*) To act high handedly
(*d*) To refuse to go

84. Root and branch
(*a*) To collect
(*b*) To set ablaze
(*c*) To take hint
(*d*) Completely

85. Sum and substance
(*a*) Renew   (*b*) Retaliate
(*c*) Disregard (*d*) Gist

86. Sit on fence
(*a*) To remain neutral
(*b*) To show contempt
(*c*) To enjoy the surroundings
(*d*) To become fond of

87. Sword of Damocles
(*a*) Damage by war
(*b*) Heavy rainfall
(*c*) Threatening danger
(*d*) To submit

88. To beg the question
(*a*) To refer to
(*b*) To take for granted
(*c*) To raise objections
(*d*) To be discussed

89. To drive home
(*a*) To find one's roots
(*b*) To return to place of rest
(*c*) Back to original position
(*d*) To emphasise

90. To put the Thames on fire
(*a*) With a rare distinction
(*b*) A natural fire
(*c*) An explosive volcano
(*d*) To punish

91. Turn up one's nose at
(*a*) To encourage
(*b*) To show contempt
(*c*) To abuse
(*d*) To fight

92. Take a cue
(*a*) A thoughtfully
(*b*) Cautiously
(*c*) To gather a hint
(*d*) To sharpen weapon

93. Turn a blind eye
(*a*) To refuse to see
(*b*) Become blind
(*c*) To act
(*d*) To hesitate

94. Take it upon myself
(*a*) To abuse
(*b*) To set on fire
(*c*) To talk foolishly
(*d*) Assume responsibility

95. Take the cake
(*a*) To eat
(*b*) To defeat
(*c*) To carry off the prize
(*d*) To steal

96. Without battling an eyelash
(*a*) In every serious condition
(*b*) By God's grace

(*c*) Without the slightest effort

(*d*) Deeply involved

97. 'Crocodile tears' means

(*a*) false tears

(*b*) wrong impression

(*c*) tears shed by a crocodile

(*d*) none of these

98. 'At sea' means

(*a*) on a ship

(*b*) on a sea journey

(*c*) weak and perplexed

(*d*) something vague

99. 'At loggerheads' means

(*a*) to be enemies

(*b*) to be friends

(*c*) criticising each other

(*d*) none of these

100. 'To burn the midnight oil' means

(*a*) to work lazily

(*b*) to work very hard till late at night

(*c*) to work by fits and starts

(*d*) none of these

101. To eat one's heart out

(*a*) To cry

(*b*) To laugh

(*c*) To suffer silently

(*d*) Pretend to suffer

102. A square deal

(*a*) A masterpiece

(*b*) An antique

(*c*) Justice

(*d*) Neat and clean

103. Snap one's fingers

(*a*) To show contempt

(*b*) To rest

(*c*) To get dressed

(*d*) A long way

104. Null and void

(*a*) Not concerned with

(*b*) To avenge

(*c*) To avoid taking sides

(*d*) Not valid

105. Hang by a thread

(*a*) To be in a critical condition

(*b*) Gain courage

(*c*) Widely excited

(*d*) At once

106. Go through fire and water

(*a*) To bathe

(*b*) To lack courage

(*c*) Be prepared to face any difficulty

(*d*) Thoroughly

107. A thorn in one side

(*a*) To be victorious

(*b*) A constant source of annoyance

(*c*) Of painful death

(*d*) Make a great noise

108. To cry wolf

(*a*) to listen eagerly

(*b*) to give false alarm

(*c*) to turn pale

(*d*) to keep off starvation

109. A man of straw

(*a*) A man of no substance

(*b*) a very active person

(*c*) a worthy fellow

(*d*) an unreasonable person

110. 'A wet blanket' is a person

(*a*) who does not care for anyone

(*b*) who has certain selfish motives

    (*c*) who is slow in under standing

    (*d*) whose presence kills joy

111. 'A white lie' means
- (*a*) a lie told with a good intention
- (*b*) a lie told by a white man
- (*c*) a harmful lie
- (*d*) none of the above

112. 'To while away' means
- (*a*) to go away
- (*b*) to spend the time uselessly
- (*c*) to use the time
- (*d*) to calculate the time

113. 'An oily tongue' means
- (*a*) a flattering tongue
- (*b*) an abusive tongue
- (*c*) a tongue that slips
- (*d*) a tongue on which oil has been put

114. 'To stand in good stead' means
- (*a*) to agree
- (*b*) to come round
- (*c*) to support
- (*d*) to be useful

115. 'A square meal' means
- (*a*) a good diet
- (*b*) a full meal
- (*c*) a timely meal
- (*d*) a proper diet

116. 'To take fancy to' means
- (*a*) to have liking for
- (*b*) to make a show
- (*c*) to consider
- (*d*) to imagine

117. As soon as Mohan saw his enemy, he **'turned tail'.** It means
- (*a*) As soon as Mohan saw his enemy he ran away
- (*b*) As soon as Mohan saw his enemy, he attacked him
- (*c*) As soon as Mohan saw his enemy, he advanced bravely
- (*d*) As soon as Mohan saw his enemy, he withdrew cowardly

118. Wet blanket
- (*a*) Inflammable item
- (*b*) Orthodox
- (*c*) One who kills joy
- (*d*) To speak bluntly

119. Yeoman's service
- (*a*) A hostile service
- (*b*) Help in need
- (*c*) To fulfil
- (*d*) To guess right

120. Without rhyme or reason
- (*a*) Compared to
- (*b*) Capable of
- (*c*) Unaccountably
- (*d*) Anxious about

121. Wild goose chase
- (*a*) A futile and foolish search
- (*b*) An emergency
- (*c*) Conscious of
- (*d*) Interest in

122. Wear and tear
- (*a*) Contempt
- (*b*) Damage caused by constant use
- (*c*) Festive occasion
- (*d*) Be leisurely

123. Not let the grass grow under one's feet
- (*a*) To remain neutral
- (*b*) Not related to
- (*c*) Unconcerned
- (*d*) Waste no time in acting

124. To put one's hand to the plough
- (*a*) To take up agricultural farming
- (*b*) To take a difficult task
- (*c*) To get entangled into unnecessary things
- (*d*) Take interest in technical work

125. To get the wind of
- (*a*) The coming danger
- (*b*) To run away
- (*c*) To fight stubbornly
- (*d*) To know something

126. Gift of the gab
- (*a*) Dull person
- (*b*) An artist
- (*c*) A witty person
- (*d*) A liar

127. Head and shoulders above
- (*a*) Far inferior
- (*b*) An intelligent man
- (*c*) Far superior to others
- (*d*) A deaf person

128. To hold a brief for another
- (*a*) To speak on another's behalf
- (*b*) A top secret
- (*c*) Speak for oneself
- (*d*) To silence by talking

129. Hobson's choice
- (*a*) A choice for the rich
- (*b*) Very good choice
- (*c*) A choice that is really no choice
- (*d*) An excuse

130. Carry the day
- (*a*) Win
- (*b*) Lose
- (*c*) Evening
- (*d*) Carry in time

131. To join issue with
- (*a*) To cooperate with others for a cause
- (*b*) To join any voluntary organisation for good purpose
- (*c*) To resolve dispute and restore peace
- (*d*) To enter into argument over any issue

132. To do oneself justice
- (*a*) To dispense justice on our own
- (*b*) To treat others with due respect
- (*c*) To defend one's point of view
- (*d*) None of these

133. 'Lend your ear to what I say' means
- (*a*) you should cut your ear and give it to me
- (*b*) you should listen to me
- (*c*) you should not pay any attention to what I say
- (*d*) you should know my intentions

134. 'A lion's share' means
- (*a*) the part of a lion
- (*b*) the share of a lion
- (*c*) major part
- (*d*) prey

135. 'A scape goat' means
- (*a*) a goat that has escaped from the herd
- (*b*) a person who is made to suffer for the misdeeds of another
- (*c*) a prisoner who has run away from custody
- (*d*) a person whose company is not desirable

136. To give a piece of one's mind
   (*a*) Scold   (*b*) Praise
   (*c*) Abandon   (*d*) Discharge

137. Capital punishment
   (*a*) Object to
   (*b*) Death penalty
   (*c*) Release
   (*d*) Balance

138. A burning question
   (*a*) A present
   (*b*) An old important issue
   (*c*) A matter hotly discussed in public
   (*d*) Life imprisonment

139. A feather in one's cap
   (*a*) Something to be ashamed of
   (*b*) Something to be proud of
   (*c*) Creditable success
   (*d*) Keep silent

140. Chicken-hearted
   (*a*) Cowardly
   (*b*) Fearlessly
   (*c*) Festive occasion
   (*d*) Sincerely

141. Come off with flying colours
   (*a*) Compensate
   (*b*) Take care of
   (*c*) Achieve creditable success
   (*d*) Keep silent

142. Cut a sorry figure
   (*a*) To beat severely
   (*b*) Make a poor show
   (*c*) To venture
   (*d*) To discourage

143. Eat one's words
   (*a*) Withdraw one's words
   (*b*) to continue on

   (*c*) To persist
   (*d*) Remain valid

144. Eat a humble pie
   (*a*) Feel hungry
   (*b*) Eat greedily
   (*c*) To face humiliation
   (*d*) To face jubilation

145. Get into hot water
   (*a*) Take bath
   (*b*) Get into trouble
   (*c*) Without aim
   (*d*) A difficult problem

146. **'To miss the bus'** means
   (*a*) being not able to catch the bus
   (*b*) to miss the chance
   (*c*) to lose a thing
   (*d*) to forget something

147. **'To miss the boat'** means
   (*a*) being not able to catch the boat
   (*b*) to lose a thing
   (*c*) to miss a chance
   (*d*) none of these

148. He is a **'man of word'** means
   (*a*) he is a boastful fellow
   (*b*) he talks very less
   (*c*) a reliable person
   (*d*) none of these

149. To set one's face against
   (*a*) To oppose with determination
   (*b*) To judge by appearance
   (*c*) To get out of difficulty
   (*d*) To look at one steadily

150. Take up the gauntlet
   (*a*) To subdue
   (*b*) To accept defeat

(c) To enter the pay
(d) To accept a challenge

151. Tooth and nail
(a) Secretly
(b) Swiftly
(c) Completely
(d) With utmost effort

152. Weather the storms
(a) Tide over difficulties
(b) To manage to live
(c) To gain distinction
(d) To suffer the defeat

153. Mr. P. V. Narshimha Rao is really **'a big gun'** today in India means
(a) Mr. Narshimha Rao is very popular today in India
(b) Mr. Narshimha Rao is a seasoned statesman
(c) Mr. Narshimha Rao is an important person today in India
(d) None of these

154. **'He has given up smoking'** means
(a) he has started smoking
(b) he has stopped smoking
(c) he has increased the rate of smoking
(d) none of these

155. **'We want fairplay from the government'** means
(a) we want justice from the government
(b) we want good treatment from the government
(c) we want an impartial treatment from the government
(d) we want an assurance from the government

156. **'A bone of contention'** means
(a) a cause of quarrel
(b) a broken bone
(c) a disputed matter
(d) none of these

157. **'To carry the day'** means
(a) to work hard
(b) to win
(c) to work throughout the day
(d) none of these

158. I am of the opinion that **'capital punishment'** should be abolished
(a) I want that punishment of death should be abolished
(b) I want that punishment of whipping should be abolished
(c) I want that all punishment given for murders should be abolished
(d) none of these

159. Scot-free
(a) Unpunished
(b) Respected
(c) Give up
(d) Continue on

160. Red-letter day
(a) A day of great joy or importance
(b) A miserable day
(c) Ripe time
(d) In perfect order

161. Make hay while the sun shines
(a) To dance happily
(b) To hurry
(c) Take advantage of favourable condition
(d) To destroy

162. 'Well-to-do' means
    (*a*) a work excellently done
    (*b*) to do something in a good way
    (*c*) well done
    (*d*) rich

163. Mohan and Sohan are **'hand and glove'** with each other means
    (*a*) Mohan and Sohan shake hands with each other
    (*b*) Mohan and Sohan are fast friends
    (*c*) Mohan and Sohan wear gloves
    (*d*) Mohan and Sohan are sworn enemies

164. He is a **'bookworm'** means
    (*a*) he is in the habit of reading much
    (*b*) he is in the habit of reading less
    (*c*) he tears the pages of the book
    (*d*) he crams

165. **'The English have left India for good'** means
    (*a*) the English have left India in a good condition
    (*b*) the English have presented a good picture of India to other countries
    (*c*) the English have left India for ever
    (*d*) the English have taught good things to the Indians

166. **'Wait upon'** means
    (*a*) to serve
    (*b*) to wait for someone
    (*c*) to contact a man at his place
    (*d*) to call a man

167. To pull along with
    (*a*) To insult
    (*b*) To abuse
    (*c*) To cooperate
    (*d*) To fight

168. Primrose path
    (*a*) A tough life
    (*b*) Easy going life
    (*c*) Rich man
    (*d*) Sharp

169. A red rag to the bull
    (*a*) Helter-skelter
    (*b*) Beautiful
    (*c*) Strong
    (*d*) Something offensive and provocative

170. Raw deal
    (*a*) Unripe fruits
    (*b*) Hostility
    (*c*) Harsh treatment
    (*d*) Opportunistic

171. See eye to eye
    (*a*) Enmity
    (*b*) Friendship
    (*c*) Contempt
    (*d*) To agree in certain matters

172. Show the white feather
    (*a*) To decorate
    (*b*) To act like a coward
    (*c*) To hate
    (*d*) To admire

173. To strike when the iron is hot
    (*a*) Make implements
    (*b*) To make weapons
    (*c*) To act promptly
    (*d*) To abuse

174. To die in harness
    (*a*) Talk thoroughly

(*b*) To die while in work
(*c*) To retire
(*d*) Tit for tat

175. Dark horse
(*a*) Unexpected winner
(*b*) To be indifferent
(*c*) Natives of Africa
(*d*) Decide for good reasons

176. To egg on
(*a*) To make omelette
(*b*) To instigate
(*c*) To act as traitor
(*d*) To revolt

177. Fall through
(*a*) To begin   (*b*) To rise up
(*c*) Collapse   (*d*) To chatter

178. To fish in troubled waters
(*a*) To cash on in time of crisis
(*b*) To fish in seas
(*c*) To fight against odd
(*d*) To reconstruct

179. A fly in the ointment
(*a*) Costly medicine
(*b*) A drawback
(*c*) To discuss
(*d*) To apply with it

180. To grease the palm of
(*a*) To polish   (*b*) To repair
(*c*) To bribe   (*d*) To reward

181. **'To make bare'** means
(*a*) to sleep without clothes
(*b*) to be frank
(*c*) to remove clothes
(*d*) to expose

182. **'To put off'** means
(*a*) to remove
(*b*) to extinguish

(*c*) to postpone
(*d*) none of the above

183. **'Turn-down'** means
(*a*) to reject
(*b*) to dismiss
(*c*) to disappear
(*d*) to waste

184. **'An underdog'** is
(*a*) a notorious fellow
(*b*) a starving person
(*c*) the poor and needy
(*d*) the neglected class

185. Mohan and Sohan are **'thick as thieves.'** It means
(*a*) they are intimate friends
(*b*) they are sworn enemies
(*c*) they work together
(*d*) they help each other

186. Be at one's beck and call
(*a*) Under one's absolute control
(*b*) To get into trouble
(*c*) To improve
(*d*) To lay aside

187. Burn one's fingers
(*a*) Become reconciled
(*b*) To hurry
(*c*) To get into trouble
(*d*) Make it difficult for

188. Burn the candles at both ends
(*a*) A wealthy person
(*b*) A lazy person
(*c*) Treat as important
(*d*) Use up too much energy

189. To cut the Gordian knot
(*a*) To do an easy thing
(*b*) To solve a difficulty

(*c*) Ready made
(*d*) To have no effect

190. Face the music
(*a*) Love music
(*b*) To avoid
(*c*) Face the consequence of one's action
(*d*) To delay

191. Keep abreast of
(*a*) To be informed of something
(*b*) A crisis
(*c*) To welcome
(*d*) To turn hostile

192. Kick the bucket
(*a*) To drop the bucket
(*b*) To destroy a thing
(*c*) To breathe one's last
(*d*) To reveal a secret

193. Loaves and fishes
(*a*) A gift
(*b*) A show piece
(*c*) To get rid of
(*d*) Material gains

194. A launching stock
(*a*) A chemical
(*b*) An object of ridicule
(*c*) To encourage
(*d*) To discourage

195. Make a clean sweep of
(*a*) To face a problem
(*b*) To amass wealth
(*c*) To rob
(*d*) To admit one's guilt fully

196. **'A hard nut to crack'** means
(*a*) A problem difficult to solve
(*b*) a nut which cannot be broken with hands
(*c*) a nut which is not easily available
(*d*) none of these

197. **'To hold good'** means
(*a*) to be useful (*b*) to be valid
(*c*) to be good (*d*) to be clear

198. **'Hallmark'** means
(*a*) a big mark
(*b*) a spot
(*c*) genuine excellence
(*d*) grand

199. Smell a rat
(*a*) To act unfairly
(*b*) To talk boastfully
(*c*) To have reason to suspect
(*d*) To discourage

200. Pick holes in another's coat
(*a*) To insult
(*b*) to applaud
(*c*) To waste time
(*d*) To find fault with another

201. In vogue
(*a*) In action
(*b*) In fashion
(*c*) In play
(*d*) In full cooperation

202. In memoriam
(*a*) In memory of
(*b*) To forget
(*c*) Without happiness
(*d*) With happiness

203. Via media
(*a*) Right course
(*b*) Left course
(*c*) Extreme course
(*d*) Middle course

204. Vini, Vidi, Vice
  (*a*) Without victory
  (*b*) I came, I fell, I died
  (*c*) She came, she went, the end
  (*d*) I came, I saw, I conquered

205. Vis-a-vis
  (*a*) In good faith
  (*b*) Face to face
  (*c*) Contrary to the fact
  (*d*) Similar

206. In toto
  (*a*) Unknown
  (*b*) On the whole
  (*c*) Isolated
  (*d*) Part by part

207. Exempli gratia
  (*a*) Without examples
  (*b*) Theoretically
  (*c*) Through mass contact
  (*d*) By way of example

ANSWERS

1	2	3	4	5	6	7	8	9	10
(*b*)	(*d*)	(*a*)	(*b*)	(*d*)	(*a*)	(*d*)	(*c*)	(*a*)	(*d*)

11	12	13	14	15	16	17	18	19	20
(*d*)	(*c*)	(*d*)	(*b*)	(*c*)	(*c*)	(*b*)	(*c*)	(*d*)	(*b*)

21	22	23	24	25	26	27	28	29	30
(*a*)	(*d*)	(*c*)	(*b*)	(*c*)	(*c*)	(*d*)	(*a*)	(*b*)	(*a*)

31	32	33	34	35	36	37	38	39	40
(*c*)	(*d*)	(*c*)	(*b*)	(*a*)	(*b*)	(*a*)	(*b*)	(*a*)	(*b*)

41	42	43	44	45	46	47	48	49	50
(*c*)	(*d*)	(*d*)	(*c*)	(*b*)	(*b*)	(*a*)	(*d*)	(*c*)	(*a*)

51	52	53	54	55	56	57	58	59	60
(*c*)	(*c*)	(*c*)	(*a*)	(*a*)	(*c*)	(*c*)	(*d*)	(*a*)	(*c*)

61	62	63	64	65	66	67	68	69	70
(*h*)	(*a*)	(*c*)	(*d*)	(*b*)	(*c*)	(*b*)	(*d*)	(*c*)	(*h*)

71	72	73	74	75	76	77	78	79	80
(*d*)	(*b*)	(*c*)	(*a*)	(*a*)	(*c*)	(*b*)	(*d*)	(*a*)	(*d*)

81	82	83	84	85	86	87	88	89	90
(*b*)	(*a*)	(*c*)	(*d*)	(*d*)	(*a*)	(*c*)	(*b*)	(*d*)	(*a*)

91	92	93	94	95	96	97	98	99	100
(*b*)	(*c*)	(*a*)	(*d*)	(*c*)	(*c*)	(*a*)	(*c*)	(*a*)	(*b*)

101	102	103	104	105	106	107	108	109	110
(*c*)	(*c*)	(*a*)	(*d*)	(*a*)	(*c*)	(*b*)	(*b*)	(*a*)	(*d*)

111	112	113	114	115	116	117	118	119	120
(a)	(b)	(a)	(d)	(b)	(a)	(a)	(c)	(b)	(c)
121	122	123	124	125	126	127	128	129	130
(a)	(b)	(d)	(b)	(b)	(c)	(c)	(a)	(c)	(a)
131	132	133	134	135	136	137	138	139	140
(b)	(d)	(b)	(c)	(b)	(a)	(b)	(c)	(b)	(a)
141	142	143	144	145	146	147	148	149	150
(c)	(b)	(a)	(c)	(b)	(b)	(c)	(c)	(a)	(d)
151	152	153	154	155	156	157	158	159	160
(d)	(a)	(c)	(b)	(a)	(a)	(b)	(a)	(a)	(a)
161	162	163	164	165	166	167	168	169	170
(c)	(d)	(b)	(a)	(c)	(a)	(c)	(b)	(d)	(c)
171	172	173	174	175	176	177	178	179	180
(d)	(b)	(c)	(b)	(a)	(b)	(c)	(a)	(b)	(c)
181	182	183	184	185	186	187	188	189	190
(d)	(c)	(a)	(c)	(a)	(a)	(c)	(d)	(b)	(c)
191	192	193	194	195	196	197	198	199	200
(a)	(c)	(d)	(b)	(d)	(a)	(b)	(c)	(c)	(d)
201	202	203	204	205	206	207			
(b)	(a)	(d)	(d)	(b)	(b)	(d)			

SPELLING TEST

JUDGE YOURSELF

Find the correctly spelt word.

1. (a) Discriminate
   (b) Discremineta
   (c) Discrimenate
   (d) Discriminate

2. (a) Juddicious (b) Judiceous
   (c) Judicious (d) Judiceus

3. (a) Accompalish
   (b) Ackmplesh
   (c) Acomplush
   (d) Accomplish

4. (a) Damage (b) Dammage
   (c) Damaige (d) Dammege

5. (a) Lackdaisical
   (b) Lackadaisical
   (c) Lckadaisicle
   (d) Lackadisical

6. (a) Efficiant (b) Effecent
   (c) Efficient (d) Eficient

7. (a) Survellance
   (b) Surveilance

(*c*) Surveillance
(*d*) Survaillance

8. (*a*) Schedule   (*b*) Schdule
    (*c*) Schedale   (*d*) Schedeule

9. (*a*) Occurad   (*b*) Occurred
    (*c*) Ocurred   (*d*) Occured

10. (*a*) Licentious (*b*) Licontious
    (*c*) Licenttious (*d*) Licientious

11. (*a*) Chancelery
    (*b*) Chancellery
    (*c*) Chancellary
    (*d*) Chancelary

12. (*a*) Itenerary   (*b*) Itinarery
    (*c*) Itinarary   (*d*) Itinerary

13. (*a*) Grieff   (*b*) Grief
    (*c*) Grieef   (*d*) Grrief

14. (*a*) Indipenseble
    (*b*) Indispansible
    (*c*) Indispensable
    (*d*) Indipensable

15. (*a*) Guarantee (*b*) Garuntee
    (*c*) Guaruntee (*d*) Gaurantee

16. (*a*) Meddicine (*b*) Medicine
    (*c*) Medicene (*d*) Medicinne

17. (*a*) Benefeted (*b*) Benefitted
    (*c*) Benifited (*d*) Benefited

18. (*a*) Kleptomonia
    (*b*) Kleptemonia
    (*c*) Kleptomania
    (*d*) Klaptomania

19. (*a*) Sepalchrle (*b*) Sepalchral
    (*c*) Sepulchrle (*d*) Sepulchral

20. (*a*) Acommodation
    (*b*) Acomodation
    (*c*) Accomodation
    (*d*) Accommodation

21. (*a*) Teracherous
    (*b*) Treacherous
    (*c*) Treacheraus
    (*d*) Treachereans

22. (*a*) Querrelsome
    (*b*) Quarrelsame
    (*c*) Quarrelsome
    (*d*) Querralsome

23. (*a*) Farmament
    (*b*) Farmement
    (*c*) Fermament
    (*d*) Fremament

24. (*a*) Sympathetic
    (*b*) Smypathetic
    (*c*) Sympothetic
    (*d*) Sympethetic

25. (*a*) Pecification
    (*b*) Pacification
    (*c*) Pecifacation
    (*d*) Pecefication

26. (*a*) Meritricious
    (*b*) Merefrecious
    (*c*) Meretricious
    (*d*) Merritricious

27. (*a*) Hypocritical
    (*b*) Hypocretical
    (*c*) Hypocriticel
    (*d*) Hypocirticel

28. (*a*) Vaingloriaus
    (*b*) Vaniglorious
    (*c*) Vaniglerious
    (*d*) Vaingloreus

29. (*a*) Imp-recticability
    (*b*) Impracticebility
    (*c*) Impracticibility
    (*d*) Impracticability

30. (*a*) Prograssive
(*b*) Progressive
(*c*) Progresive
(*d*) Prograsive

31. (*a*) Incradulous
(*b*) Incredulous
(*c*) Incridulous
(*d*) Incredalous

32. (*a*) Uncivilized
(*b*) Uncevilized
(*c*) Uncivillized
(*d*) Uncevelized

33. (*a*) Osttentatious
(*b*) Ostentetious
(*c*) Ostentatious
(*d*) Ostenttatious

34. (*a*) Extravagant
(*b*) Extreragent
(*c*) Extreregant
(*d*) Extravegent

35. (*a*) Missunderstood
(*b*) Miesunderstood
(*c*) Misunderstood
(*d*) Misunderstod

36. (*a*) Belligerent
(*b*) Beligirent
(*c*) Belligarant
(*d*) Belligerrent

37. (*a*) Pasiveness
(*b*) Passiveness
(*c*) Passeveniss
(*d*) Passivines

38. (*a*) Astonished
(*b*) Astronished
(*c*) Astoneshed
(*d*) Asstonished

39. (*a*) Obnosious
(*b*) Obnoxeous
(*c*) Obnoxious
(*d*) Obnoseous

40. (*a*) Uncivilised
(*b*) Uncivelized
(*c*) Uncevelized
(*d*) Uncivilized

41. (*a*) Sincerely   (*b*) Sencerely
(*c*) Sincerelly   (*d*) Sincerrely

42. (*a*) Efflorascence
(*b*) Eflorescene
(*c*) Effllorescence
(*d*) Efflorescence

43. (*a*) Vulnarable   (*b*) Valnerable
(*c*) Velnerable   (*d*) Vulnerable

44. (*a*) Rigourous   (*b*) Rigerous
(*c*) Rigorous   (*d*) Regerous

45. (*a*) Omenous
(*b*) Ominous
(*c*) Ommineous
(*d*) Omineous

46. (*a*) Puerille   (*b*) Puerrile
(*c*) Puerile   (*d*) Purrile

47. (*a*) Satellite   (*b*) Sattellite
(*c*) Satelite   (*d*) Sattelite

48. (*a*) Pesanger   (*b*) Passenger
(*c*) Pessenger   (*d*) Pasanger

49. (*a*) Humurous   (*b*) Humorous
(*c*) Humoreus   (*d*) Humorrous

50. (*a*) Equinimity
(*b*) Equanimmity
(*c*) Equannimity
(*d*) Equanimity

51. (*a*) Exeggerate
(*b*) Exaggerate
(*c*) Exadgerate
(*d*) Exagerate

52. (a) Fariegn   (b) Forein
    (c) Foriegn   (d) Foreign

53. (a) Rennaissance
    (b) Rennaisance
    (c) Renaisance
    (d) Renaissance

54. (a) Excesive   (b) Excessive
    (c) Exccessive   (d) Exccesive

55. (a) Forcaust   (b) Forcast
    (c) Forecast   (d) Forecaste

56. (a) Valuptuous
    (b) Volluptous
    (c) Voluptuous
    (d) Volupttuous

57. (a) Entrepraneur
    (b) Entreprenuer
    (c) Entrapreneur
    (d) Entrepreneur

58. (a) Paralleted   (b) Paralelled
    (c) Parralleled   (d) Parallelled

59. (a) Ocasion   (b) Occassion
    (c) Occasion   (d) Ocassion

60. (a) Boquet   (b) Bouquet
    (c) Bouquete   (d) Bouquette

61. (a) Loquacieous
    (b) Lequacious
    (c) Loquacious
    (d) Lequocious

62. (a) Cataclysm   (b) Cataclism
    (c) Catacilysm   (d) Cataclesm

63. (a) Chettering   (b) Chaterring
    (c) Chattering   (d) Chatering

64. (a) Fulfilment   (b) Fulffilment
    (c) Fulfilmient   (d) Fullfilment

65. (a) Conjectore   (b) Conjecture
    (c) Cenjecture   (d) Cenjectire

66. (a) Endication
    (b) Endicaltion
    (c) Indication
    (d) Indicetion

67. (a) Splendour   (b) Spllendour
    (c) Splandour   (d) Splendeur

68. (a) Excllusion   (b) Exclussion
    (c) Exclusion   (d) Exclosion

69. (a) Discourage
    (b) Disscourage
    (c) Discourege
    (d) Discaurage

70. (a) Curageous
    (b) Courageous
    (c) Courrageous
    (d) Couregeous

71. (a) Abandon   (b) Abanddon
    (c) Abendon   (d) Abbandon

72. (a) Embarassment
    (b) Emberrassement
    (c) Embarrassment
    (d) Embbaresment

73. (a) Veneration
    (b) Venration
    (c) Venneration
    (d) Venerration

74. (a) Tacciturnity
    (b) Taciturnity
    (c) Taciturrnity
    (d) Tacitturnity

75. (a) Despponding
    (b) Despending
    (c) Desponding
    (d) Dessponding

76. (a) Bueyant   (b) Buoyant
    (c) Bueeyant   (d) Buoyent

77. (*a*) Eccintric (*b*) Eccentrie
    (*c*) Eccentric (*d*) Eccintrie

78. (*a*) Corrigible (*b*) Corigible
    (*c*) Corregible (*d*) Corrigiblle

79. (*a*) Amandable
    (*b*) Amendable
    (*c*) Amenddable
    (*d*) Amendablle

80. (*a*) Occasional
    (*b*) Occassional
    (*c*) Occesional
    (*d*) Occessional

81. (*a*) Exttirpate (*b*) Extirpete
    (*c*) Extirpate (*d*) Exterpate

82. (*a*) Vorecious (*b*) Varacious
    (*c*) Voarcious (*d*) Voracious

83. (*a*) Insolvent (*b*) Insolvant
    (*c*) Insollvent (*d*) Insolvvent

84. (*a*) Querrel (*b*) Querral
    (*c*) Quarrel (*d*) Quarel

85. (*a*) Contrebution
    (*b*) Contribution
    (*c*) Contributtion
    (*d*) Conterbution

86. (*a*) Desgrace (*b*) Disgrece
    (*c*) Disgrice (*d*) Disgrace

87. (*a*) Harassment
    (*b*) Herassment
    (*c*) Harasment
    (*d*) Harassmient

88. (*a*) Tranquilitty
    (*b*) Tranquility
    (*c*) Trenquility
    (*d*) Tranquillity

89. (*a*) Imaginative
    (*b*) Imeginative
    (*c*) Imagenative
    (*d*) Imaginetive

90. (*a*) Suficient (*b*) Suficiant
    (*c*) Sufficient (*d*) Sufficiant

91. (*a*) Adequate (*b*) Edequate
    (*c*) Adaquete (*d*) Edaquete

92. (*a*) Exparienced
    (*b*) Experianced
    (*c*) Experienced
    (*d*) Experrienced

93. (*a*) Flatering (*b*) Fletering
    (*c*) Flattering (*d*) Fletaring

94. (*a*) Cuttiveted
    (*b*) Culltrivated
    (*c*) Cultivated
    (*d*) Caltivated

95. (*a*) Materialistic
    (*b*) Materielistic
    (*c*) Meterialistic
    (*d*) Matterialistic

96. (*a*) Praiceworthy
    (*b*) Peiseworthy
    (*c*) Praiseworthy
    (*d*) Praisaworthy

97. (*a*) Tranquil (*b*) Trenquil
    (*c*) Tranquel (*d*) Trinquil

98. (*a*) Neggardly (*b*) Nigardly
    (*c*) Niggerdly (*d*) Niggardly

99. (*a*) Magnanimity
    (*b*) Megnanimity
    (*c*) Magnenimity
    (*d*) Magnanimety

100. (*a*) Darogate (*b*) Derogate
     (*c*) Derogeta (*d*) Deragate

101. (*a*) Philanthropist
     (*b*) Philenthropist

(c) Phelanthropist
(d) Philanthropest

102. (a) Ephameral
(b) Ephimeral
(c) Ephemeral
(d) Ephemerel

103. (a) Fanaticism (b) Fenaticism
(c) Faneticism (d) Fanatecism

104. (a) Profesional
(b) Professionel
(c) Professional
(d) Profissional

105. (a) Ameteur (b) Amateur
(c) Amataur (d) Amateor

106. (a) Philenderer
(b) Philandarer
(c) Philanderer
(d) Philonderer

107. (a) Honorary (b) Henorary
(c) Honerary (d) Honorery

108. (a) Darmatologist
(b) Dermatologist
(c) Dcrmetologist
(d) Dermatologest

109. (a) Compansation
(b) Compensetion
(c) Compensotion
(d) Compensation

110. (a) Quadruplets
(b) Quedruplets
(c) Quadroplets
(d) Quadruplats

111. (a) Economist (b) Economest
(c) Economist (d) Econimist

112. (a) Catholic (b) Cetholic
(c) Cathelic (d) Cathilic

113. (a) Unfevourable
(b) Unfevaurable
(c) Unfavourable
(d) Unfivourable

114. (a) Bombastic (b) Bombestic
(c) Bombostic (d) Bombastie

115. (a) Posthumaus
(b) Posthomous
(c) Posthumous
(d) Pasthumous

116. (a) Epitaph (b) Epetaph
(c) Epiteph (d) Epitoph

117. (a) Falicitate (b) Felicitate
(c) Falecitate (d) Falecetate

118. (a) Schezophrenia
(b) Schizaphrenia
(c) Schizophrenia
(d) Schizophrania

119. (a) Claustrophobia
(b) Cloustrophobia
(c) Claustraphobia
(d) Claustrophabia

120. (a) Connoiseur
(b) Connaisseur
(c) Connaissour
(d) Connoisseur

121. (a) Transperency
(b) Transparency
(c) Transpirency
(d) Tranporency

122. (a) Superanuation
(b) Superennuation
(c) Superannuation
(d) Superannuetion

123. (a) Antiquated
(b) Antiqueted

(c) Antequated
(d) Antiquatted

124. (a) Adalescent (b) Addescant
(c) Adolescent (d) Adolascent

125. (a) Newrologist
(b) Neurologist
(c) Neurologest
(d) Newrologest

126. (a) Obstatricion
(b) Obstitricion
(c) Obstetricion
(d) Obstetracion

127. (a) Illiterate (b) Iliterate
(c) Illitarate (d) Illiterete

128. (a) Thioretical (b) Theoretical
(c) Theoratical (d) Theoritical

129. (a) Mersenary (b) Marcenary
(c) Marcenery (d) Mercenary

130. (a) Belligerent (b) Beligerent
(c) Belligarent (d) Belligerant

131. (a) Extrevagant
(b) Extravegant
(c) Extravagant
(d) Extravagent

132. (a) Aristocracy
(b) Arestocracy
(c) Arestocracy
(d) Aristocrecy

133. (a) Lagislature
(b) Legislature
(c) Lageslature
(d) Legesleture

134. (a) Dormetory (b) Dormitery
(c) Dormitory (d) Dermitory

135. (a) Garulous (b) Garrulaus
(c) Gorrulous (d) Garrulous

136. (a) Regecide (b) Regicide
(c) Rigecide (d) Ragicide

137. (a) Epicurean (b) Epecurean
(c) Epicurian (d) Epicorean

138. (a) Commetti (b) Commitee
(c) Committee (d) Comitte

139. (a) Inemitable (b) Inimitable
(c) Inimetable (d) Inimitabli

140. (a) Pletocray (b) Plitocracy
(c) Plotocracy (d) Plutocracy

141. (a) Immortal (b) Emortal
(c) Immortel (d) Immortol

142. (a) Perrhic (b) Pyrrhic
(c) Pyrrhec (d) Porrhec

143. (a) Chauvinism
(b) Chouvinism
(c) Chevinism
(d) Cauvinism

144. (a) Rumenate (b) Ruminote
(c) Rimunote (d) Ruminate

145. (a) Teciturn (b) Tociturn
(c) Tecitorn (d) Taciturn

146. (a) Verteran (b) Viteran
(c) Veterain (d) Veteran

147. (a) Antitode (b) Antedote
(c) Antidote (d) Autitote

148. (a) Audeble (b) Audible
(c) Audcble (d) Audebli

149. (a) Bellicose (b) Billicose
(c) Bellecose (d) Belicose

150. (a) Pilferage (b) Peliferage
(c) Pilfarege (d) Poliferage

151. (a) Arestocracy
(b) Aristocracy
(c) Aristocracy
(d) Aristocy

152. (a) Sychologist
(b) Psycologist
(c) Psychologist
(d) Psychogist

153. (a) Neucteus   (b) Neucleus
(c) Nucleus   (d) Neocleus

154. (a) Negotcate   (b) Negociate
(c) Negotiate   (d) Nagotiate

155. (a) Skelled   (b) Skilled
(c) Skiled   (d) Skillid

156. (a) Logecal   (b) Logical
(c) Lagical   (d) Logicle

157. (a) Effeciency   (b) Efficiency
(c) Eficiency   (d) Efficency

158. (a) Cumpartment
(b) Compartment
(c) Compartant
(d) Comportent

159. (a) Continuous
(b) Cuntinuous
(c) Continus
(d) Contineuous

160. (a) Valuable   (b) Valueable
(c) Valuabel   (d) Valoble

161. (a) Courteous   (b) Curteous
(c) Corteous   (d) Courtus

162. (a) Prophecy   (b) Phropecy
(c) Propecy   (d) Propheci

163. (a) Lonesome   (b) Lonsome
(c) Lonesum   (d) Lonsum

164. (a) Formedable
(b) Formidable
(c) Formidabul
(d) Formdable

165. (a) Inibriated   (b) Enibrited
(c) Inebriated   (d) Inubrited

166. (a) Guellible   (b) Guiellible
(c) Guillibel   (d) Guillible

167. (a) Subsequent
(b) Subsiquent
(c) Subsequint
(d) Subquent

168. (a) Alein   (b) Alien
(c) Abein   (d) Abien

169. (a) Misogynesm
(b) Mesogynism
(c) Misogynism
(d) Misosogesim

170. (a) Sanguini   (b) Sangune
(c) Sangiune   (d) Sanguine

171. (a) Exemplary   (b) Eximplary
(c) Exemplari   (d) Examplary

172. (a) Sycophants
(b) Sicophants
(c) Sycopants
(d) Sycophints

173. (a) Petchy   (b) Patchy
(c) Patchi   (d) Patche

174. (a) Impassi   (b) Impasse
(c) Impase   (d) Inpassi

175. (a) Aceelerate   (b) Accilerate
(c) Accelerate   (d) Accelerati

176. (a) Vendictive   (b) Vindective
(c) Vindictive   (d) Vindictivi

177. (a) Prudint   (b) Prudient
(c) Prudente   (d) Prudent

178. (a) Superfluons
(b) Superfleos
(c) Superflous
(d) Superfluous

179. (a) Expidite   (b) Expedeti
(c) Expedite   (d) Expedit

180. (a) Livity   (b) Levity
      (c) Levety   (d) Levite

181. (a) Reluctant   (b) Riluctant
      (c) Reluctent   (d) Relictunt

182. (a) Desparge   (b) Disparage
      (c) Disperage   (d) Disparege

183. (a) Maegre   (b) Meager
      (c) Meagre   (d) Megre

184. (a) Accedental
      (b) Aceedent
      (c) Accidantle
      (d) Accidental

185. (a) Cheapiness (b) Chaepness
      (c) Chepness   (d) Cheapness

186. (a) Febulous   (b) Fabulus
      (c) Fabulous   (d) Fibulous

187. (a) Colusion   (b) Collision
      (c) Colision   (d) Collison

188. (a) Eradicated
      (b) Erradicated
      (c) Eradecated
      (d) Eradiceted

189. (a) Ageonise   (b) Agonise
      (c) Agonice   (d) Agonisee

190. (a) Comit   (b) Commiet
      (c) Commit   (d) Commite

191. (a) Corigible
      (b) Corregible
      (c) Coorigible
      (d) Corrigible

192. (a) Tasiturn   (b) Taciturn
      (c) Taceturn   (d) Tacitorn

193. (a) Omnevorous
      (b) Omnivorous
      (c) Omniverous
      (d) Omnivarous

194. (a) Feud   (b) Fued
      (c) Fiud   (d) Feued

195. (a) Regicide   (b) Rigicide
      (c) Regecide   (d) Regicedi

196. (a) Pselm   (b) Slam
      (c) Psalm   (d) Salm

197. (a) Ribut   (b) Rebit
      (c) Rebut   (d) Rebute

198. (a) Dormetory (b) Durmitory
      (c) Dormitori (d) Dormitory

199. (a) Archeic   (b) Arcaic
      (c) Archeic   (d) Archaic

200. (a) Polyendry (b) Poliendry
      (c) Pollyendry (d) Polyandry

201. (a) Haphazard
      (b) Hapahazard
      (c) Haphzard
      (d) Haphazrd

202. (a) Peevishness
      (b) Pievishness
      (c) Peivishness
      (d) Peeveshness

203. (a) Gelactic   (b) Galectic
      (c) Galactic   (d) Galactec

204. (a) Imbibision
      (b) Imbision
      (c) Embibition
      (d) Imbibition

205. (a) Zoparasite
      (b) Zooparaset
      (c) Zooparasite
      (d) Zoprasite

206. (a) Neuralgia
      (b) Nuraliga
      (c) Neurolgia
      (d) Neuraltia

ANSWERS

1	2	3	4	5	6	7	8	9	10
(a)	(c)	(d)	(a)	(b)	(c)	(c)	(a)	(b)	(a)

11	12	13	14	15	16	17	18	19	20
(c)	(d)	(b)	(c)	(a)	(b)	(b)	(c)	(d)	(d)

21	22	23	24	25	26	27	28	29	30
(b)	(c)	(c)	(a)	(b)	(c)	(a)	(b)	(d)	(b)

31	32	33	34	35	36	37	38	39	40
(b)	(a)	(c)	(a)	(c)	(a)	(b)	(a)	(c)	(d)

41	42	43	44	45	46	47	48	49	50
(a)	(d)	(d)	(c)	(b)	(c)	(a)	(b)	(b)	(d)

51	52	53	54	55	56	57	58	59	60
(b)	(d)	(d)	(b)	(c)	(c)	(d)	(a)	(c)	(b)

61	62	63	64	65	66	67	68	69	70
(c)	(a)	(c)	(a)	(b)	(c)	(a)	(c)	(a)	(b)

71	72	73	74	75	76	77	78	79	80
(a)	(c)	(a)	(b)	(c)	(b)	(c)	(a)	(b)	(a)

81	82	83	84	85	86	87	88	89	90
(c)	(d)	(a)	(c)	(b)	(d)	(a)	(b)	(a)	(c)

91	92	93	94	95	96	97	98	99	100
(a)	(c)	(a)	(c)	(a)	(c)	(a)	(d)	(a)	(b)

101	102	103	104	105	106	107	108	109	110
(a)	(c)	(a)	(c)	(b)	(c)	(a)	(b)	(d)	(a)

111	112	113	114	115	116	117	118	119	120
(c)	(u)	(c)	(a)	(c)	(a)	(b)	(c)	(a)	(d)

121	122	123	124	125	126	127	128	129	130
(b)	(c)	(a)	(c)	(b)	(c)	(a)	(b)	(d)	(a)

131	132	133	134	135	136	137	138	139	140
(c)	(a)	(b)	(c)	(d)	(b)	(a)	(c)	(b)	(d)

141	142	143	144	145	146	147	148	149	150
(a)	(b)	(a)	(d)	(d)	(d)	(c)	(b)	(a)	(a)

151	152	153	154	155	156	157	158	159	160
(c)	(c)	(c)	(c)	(b)	(b)	(b)	(b)	(a)	(a)

161	162	163	164	165	166	167	168	169	170
(a)	(a)	(a)	(b)	(c)	(d)	(a)	(b)	(c)	(d)

171	172	173	174	175	176	177	178	179	180
(a)	(a)	(b)	(b)	(c)	(c)	(d)	(d)	(c)	(b)

181	182	183	184	185	186	187	188	189	190
(a)	(b)	(c)	(d)	(d)	(c)	(b)	(a)	(b)	(c)

191	192	193	194	195	196	197	198	199	200
(d)	(b)	(b)	(a)	(a)	(c)	(c)	(d)	(d)	(d)

201	202	203	204	205	206
(a)	(a)	(d)	(d)	(c)	(a)

SECTION-VIII

COMPREHENSION

Directions : *Five questions following each passage is given here with four alternatives. Read the passage carefully and choose the best answer to each question.*

PASSAGE - 1

United States software maker Oracle is considering launching a version of the Linux operating system and has looked at buying one of the two firms dominating the technology, the Financial Times newspaper reported on Monday.

The report, citing an interview with Oracle's chief executive officer Larry Ellision, said the move would redraw the software landscape and open a new front in Oracle's long rivalry with Microsoft.

It said Ellision told the newspaper that Oracle wanted to sell a full range of software that, like Microsoft, included both operating system and applications.

"I'd like to have a complete stack," Ellison was quoted as saying. "We're missing an operating system. You could argue that it makes a lot of sense for us to look at distributing and supporting Linux."

The report said that like IBM, Oracle has counted on Linux— an open source system whose code is open to anyone to view and adapt— to act as a counterweight to Microsoft's Windows, which has expanded rapidly from desktop PCs into corporate IT systems.

1. Oracle considered launching a version of the Linux operating system because :
   (*a*) it is more user friendly
   (*b*) it is cheap
   (*c*) it has an open source system
   (*d*) it is easily available

2. Apart from Oracle the other company that used Linux was
   (*a*) Microsoft
   (*b*) Ellision
   (*c*) Corporate Groups
   (*d*) IBM

3. This integration of Oracle with Linux would refuel
   (*a*) Domination of Linux
   (*b*) Oracle market
   (*c*) Microsoft's rivalry with IBM
   (*d*) Oracle's fight with Micro-soft

4. Which of the following post did Larry Ellison held?
   (*a*) CEO of Oracle
   (*b*) CEO of IBM
   (*c*) Chief executive of Oracle
   (*d*) CEO of Microsoft

173

5. Microsoft is the rapidly expanding its business from
   - (*a*) network servers to Internet
   - (*b*) operating system to small business
   - (*c*) desktop PCs into corporate IT systems
   - (*d*) other competing companies

PASSAGE - 2

India and Pakistan failed to achieve a thaw on Siachen issue despite hectic back-room diplomatic efforts that continued well past midnight last night, though the two unclear neighbours did take a step forward in resolving the Sir Creek maritime boundary dispute.

The two issues — Siachen and Sir Creek — had been discussed at length both at the Foreign Minister-level and delegation-level talks yesterday and there was expectancy in the air that External Affairs Minister Natwar Singh might return home after securing a framework agreement on working out modalities or eventual withdrawal of troops from the world's highest battlefield. The situation changed after Mr. Natwar Singh called on Pakistan President Pervez Musharraf at his official residence at Rawalpindi. Ministry of External Affairs spokesman told reporters after this meeting that Gen. Musharraf and Mr. Natwar Singh welcomed the ongoing diplomatic initiative as a framework to promote settlement.

1. (1) India and Pakistan were not able to solve any issues.
   - (2) India and Pakistan were able to solve Siachen and Sir Creek issue.
   - (3) India and Pakistan were able to solve Siachen issue only.
   - (4) India and Pakistan were able to solve Sir Creek issue only.
   - (*a*) Only 1 is true
   - (*b*) Only 2 is true
   - (*c*) All are true
   - (*d*) Only 4 is true

2. (1) A day before Foreign Minister-level and delegation-level talks were not held.
   - (2) A day after Foreign Minister-level and delegation-level talks were held.
   - (3) A day before Foreign Minister-level was held.
   - (4) A day before delegation-level talks were held.
   - (*a*) Only 3 is true
   - (*b*) Both 3 and 4 are true
   - (*c*) All are false
   - (*d*) Only 1 is true

3. (1) The talks were held in Nepal.
   - (2) The talks were held in India.
   - (3) The talks were held in Pakistan.
   - (4) The talks were held in Bangladesh.
   - (*a*) Only 3 is true
   - (*b*) Both 2 and 3 are true
   - (*c*) All are true
   - (*d*) All are false

4. What is the synonym of the word "diplomatic"?
(*a*) rational   (*b*) political
(*c*) tactful   (*d*) quiet

5. What is the antonym of the word "promote"?
(*a*) remote   (*b*) pass
(*c*) degrade   (*d*) demote

PASSAGE - 3

US intelligence chief John Negroponte has said Iran's resumption of uranium enrichment is 'troublesome' but the country is still years away from having enough fissile material to make a nuclear weapon.

Negroponte on Thursday expressed concern both about Iran's claim to have resumed uranium enrichment with a cascade of 164 centrifuges in Natanz and extreme statements made by Iranian President Mahmoud Ahmadinejad.

"The developments in Iran — clearly show that they're troublesome," he said in response to questions after a speech to the National Press Club.

"By the same token, our assessment at the moment is that even though we believe that Iran is determined to acquire or obtain a nuclear weapon, that we believe that it is still many years off before they are likely to have enough fissile material to assemble into, or to put into a nuclear weapon; perhaps into the next decade," he said.

"So I think it is important that this issue be kept in perspective," he said.

Negroponte is marking his first year in office as the director of national intelligence, a post created in the wake of the intelligence fiasco over Iraq's weapons of mass destruction.

Critics have complained that the new intelligence directorate, which is supposed to coordinate the work of some 15 US intelligence agencies, is developing into another bloated bureaucracy with nearly 1,000 people reportedly working for it.

1. Iran was still years away from having nukes because
(*a*) it has infighting going on
(*b*) it does not have such wealth
(*c*) it has an open source system
(*d*) It doesn't have required material to make a nuclear weapon

2. The post created because of the intelligence fiasco over Iraq's weapons of mass destruction is
(*a*) Director of intelligence
(*b*) Director of international intelligence
(*c*) Director of FBI
(*d*) Director of national intelligence

3. The U.S. Intelligence chief was
(*a*) John M.
(*b*) N. John
(*c*) John N.
(*d*) President Negroponte

4. The new intelligence directorate is suppose to co-ordinate the work of
(*a*) 15 U.N. secretaries
(*b*) 15 U.N. Intelligence agencies
(*c*) 15 U.N. Intelligence secretaries
(*d*) 15 U.N. Intelligence agencies

5. Critics have complained that the new intelligence directorate is developing into

    (*a*) bloated bureaucracy

    (*b*) another liability

    (*c*) bloated diplomacy

    (*d*) another bloated mockery

PASSAGE - 4

The HC on Wednesday revoked the ban on dance bars and upheld dance to be a form of expression, recognised by the Supreme Court as a fundamental right. The court said the government's failure to secure even a single conviction in the obscenity cases against dance bars proved there was no annoyance caused to those visiting these bars.

"How that (dance bars) could cause annoyance to those who do not watch it, or could affect public order is not understood. It is like saying that watching a Hindu movie, which has a dance sequence with dancers skimpily dressed, would affect public order," Justice FI Rebello and Justice Roshan Dalvi stated.

Taking a dig at the government's moral stand, the HC said, "If the notion of the state about dancing are to be accepted, we would have reached a stage where skimpy dressing and belly gyrations, which today is the Bollywood norm for dancing, will have to be banned as inherently pernicious".

Upholding the fundamental right of every citizen to earn a living with dignity by carrying out a lawful profession, the judges asked, "Are our fundamental rights so fickle that a citizen has to dance to the state's tune?"

The judges warned that if the state's argument was accepted then any establishment in the entertainment industry employing a large number of women, or any profession of amusement where women are open to gazes form men, would be considered to be exploiting women.

"Inebriated men in dance bars or other bars are a nuisance. Maintaining law and order is the responsibility of the state," the order stated.

Criticising the government's knee-jerk move to ban dancing in bars, the judges noted that no survey had been carried out to test the allegations and neither was a rehabilitation scheme worked out for the dancers, most of whom were the only earning members in their families. A still from Chandni Bar, which told the tale of a bar dancer.

1. The court said that

    (*a*) case was like a different Bollywood movie

    (*b*) Dancing to tunes to bollywood

    (*c*) Belly gyration is Hollywood norm

    (*d*) Belly gyration is a Bollywood norm

2. Government's failure to secure even a single conviction in the

    (*a*) obscenity cases against dance bars

    (*b*) human rights cases against dance bars

(c) obscenity cases against bar girls

(d) obscenity cases against men visiting dance bars

3. The court said that maintaining law and order is the responsibility of
(a) of the center
(b) the police
(c) of the army
(d) of the state

4. The court upheld the funda-mental right of every citizen to
(a) speak
(b) livelihood
(c) dance anywhere they want
(d) do whatever they want

5. Taking a dig at the government's
(a) moral stand
(b) physical stand
(c) immoral stand
(d) political stand

PASSAGE - 5

Dashing India stumper Mahendra Singh Dhoni's dazzling display with the bat has catapulted him to the second spot — next only to Ricky Ponting — while after drubbing England 5-1 in the recent home series, the Men in Blue have reached their highest-ever third place in the latest LG ICC ODI rankings.

Dhoni began the series in fifth position in the listings but 177 runs at an average of 59, including 96 in Jamshedpur, pushed him up the list and he is now seven rating points behind Australia's Ricky Ponting who tops the rankings.

India's triumph, which means they have won 17 of their last 22 ODIs, saw them leapfrog New Zealand and Pakistan in the Championship table and they are now three rating points behind second-placed South Africa.

Third place is India's highest position since the Championship table was launched. In April 2005, they were in eighth spot. Dhoni is one of our India players in the top 20 for batsmen. Yuvraj Singh is ninth, Dravid is 11th and Sachin Tendulkar, who missed the entire series due to injury, is 18th.

Virender Sehwag, who scored 78 runs in five innings during the ODI series, has dropped seven places in the rankings and is now 28th in the batting list.

Harbhajan Singh, the leading wicket-taker in the ODI series, is up six places to seventh in the Player Rankings for ODI bowlers while, further down that list, Shanthakumaran Sreesanth, who took 6-55 in Indore, has moved up 32 places to joint 66th with his best-ever haul of rating points.

1. MS Dhoni became
(a) The number one team in the world
(b) The number one player in India
(c) The number two player in World
(d) The number 5th player in the World

2. The current ranking order of the top three teams are
(a) Australia-India-Pakistan
(b) Australia-Pakistan-India

   (*c*) Australia-South Africa-India

   (*d*) Pakistan-Australia-India

3. It is India's highest position since

   (*a*) India started playing cricket

   (*b*) Championship table was launched

   (*c*) India won the World Cup

   (*d*) The last World Cup

4. Harbhajan Singh is the leading wicket taker for India in the

   (*a*) India A England A series

   (*b*) India Pakistan Series

   (*c*) India South Africa Series

   (*d*) India England Series

5. Apart from Dhoni, the other players in the top 20 features

   (*a*) Sehwag, Tendulkar, Dravid, and Dhoni

   (*b*) Sehwag, Tendulkar, Dravid

   (*c*) Dhoni, Yuvraj, Tendulkar and Dravid

   (*d*) Yuvraj, Tendulkar and Dravid

PASSAGE - 6

World oil prices hit record peaks on Tuesday above $72 in London and close to $71 in New York as the market fretted over possible military conflict between the US and Iran.

The price of New York's light sweet crude hit a historic high of $70.88 per barrel, beating the previous record $70.85 set on August 30, 2005, when Hurricane Katrina had ravaged oil facilities on the US Gulf Coast.

Also on Tuesday, the price of Brent North Sea crude oil hit a record $72.20 per barrel as the market feared that an attack on Iran could lead to a disruption of its oil exports.

Washington accuses Iran, the world's fourth biggest crude producer, of working secretly to build nuclear weapons under cover of a nuclear energy programme it is developing with Russian assistance.

Iran denies this charge and says the programme is strictly for producing nuclear energy.

The organisation of Petroleum Exporting Countries said on Tuesday that global oil demand grew by almost one million barrels per day in 2005.

At about 1120 GMT New York's main contract, light sweet crude for delivery in May, had climbed 30 cents from Monday's close to $70.70 in electronic deals before the market's official opening.

Brent crude for June delivery jumped 35 cents to $71.81 in electronic deals.

Adjusted for inflation, current oil prices remain below levels reached after the 1979 Iranian revolution when they surged to upwards of $80 per barrel in today's money.

"People are still concerned about Iran and potential military action," Global Insight analyst Simon Wardell said Tuesday.

" It looks like there's going to be a run towards $75," he added.

But he warned that prices could rocket to above $150 per barrel should Iran retaliate to any US attack by disrupting the world's busiest oil shipping lanes.

1. Which rank Iran holds among the world's biggest crude producers?
   (*a*) First   (*b*) Fourth
   (*c*) Fifth   (*d*) No rank

2. Who accussed Iran of secretly building nuclear weapons?
   (*a*) Iraq   (*b*) U.K.
   (*c*) Russia   (*d*) U.S.A.

3. What did the Organisation of Petroleum Exporting countries said?
   (*a*) Global oil prices grew by 1 million barrels per day
   (*b*) Global oil supply grew by 1 million barrels per day
   (*c*) Global oil demand grew by 1 million barrels per day
   (*d*) Global oil demand grew by 1 million barrels per weak.

4. What is the highest level of oil pricess till date.
   (*a*) $ 150 per barrel
   (*b*) $ 70.85 per barrel
   (*c*) $ 72 per barrel
   (*d*) $ 80 per barrel

5. Which charge did Iran deny?
   (*a*) They denied that they were building nuclear weapons
   (*b*) They denied that they were increasing crude prices
   (*c*) They denied that they were in war with U.S.
   (*d*) They denied that Russia and Iran were friends.

PASSAGE - 7

The US administration said on Monday that Iran's announcement that it was working on advanced P-2 centrifuges to enrich uranium was a further signal that the Islamic republic's nuclear programme was not purely civilian.

Further fuelling tensions in the Middle East region was a suicide bomb attack in Israel's commercial capital of Tel Aviv late on Monday that left nine people dead and dozens wounded, dealers said.

1. World oil prices strike historic highs because of the possibility
   (*a*) of war between UN and Iran
   (*b*) of military conflict between the US and Iraq increased
   (*c*) of war between Iraq and Iran
   (*d*) of military conflict between the US and Iran increased

2. The highest price of New York's light sweet crude previously was
   (*a*) $70.85 per barrel
   (*b*) $70.88 per barrel
   (*c*) £70.88 per barrel
   (*d*) £70.89 per barrel

3. What fueled tensions in the Middle East region?
   (*a*) Anti-Islamic policy of US
   (*b*) A suicide bomb attack in Israel's commercial capital
   (*c*) A suicide bomb attack in Iran
   (*d*) A suicide attack in Israel's President

4. The global oil demanded grew by almost
   (*a*) one million barrels per month in 2005
   (*b*) one million litres per day in 2005

(*c*) one million barrels per day in 2004

(*d*) one million barrels per day in 2005

5. The world's fourth biggest crude producer is

(*a*) Washington

(*b*) Iraq

(*c*) Iran

(*d*) Saudi Arabia

PASSAGE - 8

The new airports being developed at Delhi and Mumbai will have to gear up for a new challenge that is staring Indian aviation in its face.

Some international airlines are planning to bring the gigantic A-380 to India by the end of this year or early 2007.

The warning to gear up came from Union civil aviation secretary Ajay Prasad recently, when he said that airports needed parking bays and boarding bridges built specially for the A-380.

"No Indian carrier will be getting this plane for some time but international carriers are getting it. So we need to act fast." Prasad had said. Lufthansa and Singapore Airlines have already told Delhi airport of their plan to bring A-380 here next year. Moreover, the new aircraft will fly over India on the Europe-Southeast Asia or Australia sectors and in case of an emergency, Indian airports need to be ready to receive them. Since Delhi and Mumbai are being rebuilt, said sources, best would be make a start with them now itself.

The Delhi airport's main runway is 45-metre-wide and 3,810-metre-long and belongs to E category.

"The runway's length is fine but it needs to be 60-metre-wide. There is over 15 metres of green area on both sides of the runway and landing or taking off from here with some minor changes should not be a problem," said sources.

The biggest problem is going to be of taxiways as they need to be widened by 15 metres on both sides. And above all, new passenger terminal building would be required as the A-380 is a double-decker throughout, with doors on both levels. So two-level aerobridges would be required. Depending on its configuration, said sources, the A-380 would have anywhere between 555 and 900 passengers.

1. A new challenge is staring

(*a*) Indian aviation in Delhi only

(*b*) Indian aviation in Delhi and Mumbai

(*c*) Indian aviation in the world

(*d*) Indian air force in Delhi and Mumbai

2. Some international airlines are planning to bring the

(*a*) gigantic train A-380 to India

(*b*) gigantic plane A-380 to world

(*c*) B-380 to India

(*d*) A-380 to India

3. The biggest problem is of

(*a*) taxiways as they need to be narrowed by 15 m.

(*b*) subways as they need to be widened by 15 m.

(*c*) taxiways as they need to be widened by 15 m.

(*d*) flyovers as they need to be widened by 15 m.

4. The Delhi airport's main runway

(*a*) belongs to A Category

(*b*) belongs to B Category

(*c*) belongs to Y Category

(*d*) belongs to E Category

5. Which airlines have already begun planning to bring A-380 to India?

(*a*) Lufthansa and Singapore Airlines

(*b*) Air India and Indian Airlines

(*c*) Lufthansa and Thai Airlines

(*d*) British and Singapore Airlines

PASSAGE - 9

If there is a widespread consensus on economic reforms, as everyone says, why are there such frustrating delays in implementing them? If we are agreed on what is to be done, why don't we just do it? One reason is that we haven't had a true reformer at the top, such as a Deng or a Thatcher. The agenda of our political class is also at odds with what the world believes is necessary for the prosperity and well being of our citizens. Moreover, we haven't had reformers heading our ministries dealing with infrastructure. The most important reason, however, is that our discourse is disfunctional. We continue to waste our energies in debating "the what" when we ought to focus on "the how". How to reform is a more difficult challenge and it is not for lazy minds. It needs the full application of the mind; it needs problem solving ability; and it needs mental toughn ess. Most of all, it requires acute attention to detail. It is not for drawing room amateurs. We Indians are good when it comes to defining the broad picture. But we fall apart when it comes to detailed planning and tactics which lead to successful implementation. This is a flaw which attaches both to our public and private sectors. Hence our products and governance are both shoddy.

1. There is consensus, at least on paper, on

(*a*) economic reforms

(*b*) socio-economic reforms

(*c*) growth

(*d*) economical growth

2. One of the main reasons that the reforms are not implemented is that there is no

(*a*) people just do the talking

(*b*) fixed agenda

(*c*) consensus on this

(*d*) true reformer at the top

3. We continue to waste our energies in debating

(*a*) "the who" when we ought to focus on "the how"

(*b*) "the what" when we ought to focus on "the how"

(*c*) "the what" when we ought to focus on "the why"

(*d*) "the why" when we ought to focus on "the how"

4. At what instance do we Indian falter?
  - (*a*) Planning
  - (*b*) tactics
  - (*c*) power
  - (*d*) planning and tactics

5. The procedure of reforms requires
  - (*a*) application, problem solving skills and attitude.
  - (*b*) application, analytical skills and attitude.
  - (*c*) application, technical skills and good mind.
  - (*d*) application, writing skills and attitude.

PASSAGE - 10

Bass Fishing is becoming just as popular as a day out at the zoo or a picnic in the local park. Family day outings are now involving bass fishing. At this present moment in time Bass fishing is supposedly to be the number one freshwater sport in the USA and anyone who participates in this very self fulfilling sport will proudly tell you why. Approximate figures show that the bass fishing industry is between 65 to 70% higher than most other forms of fresh water fishing.

Over two decades — Bass Fishing has scaled to monetary heights reaching over the million dollar barrier which has now over these years become an industry worth 4.8 Billion dollars. Bass Fishing is on the increase in numbers where the demand is phenomenal among new anglers.

What is it about this freshwater sport — well this is an outdoor activity that is very relaxing as well as rewarding when the fish start to bite. Bass fishing can be a hobby taken to a pro level status where tournaments are entered to show off the anglers fishing skills.

Remember what ever sport you engage yourself in — practice makes perfect and that goes for bass fishing also. So the more time you spend on the water — the more knowledge intake on the do's and dont's.

When angling for bass it is a good idea to have an expert in this field to guide and give you instructions on your first couple of attempts — at least till you get to know the ropes. An experienced bass fisherman can educate you on the techniques, fishing tackle and lure and in some cases enlightens you on how the fish thinks. Believe it or not — it has proved to be successful for many bass fishing enthusiasts.

If competing in tournaments is your goal then remember to learn all the tricks of the trade. Bass Fishing can be very competitive — you need to be in the know to reach pro level. Depending on your dedication and passion towards the sport then why not consider making a career out of bass fishing by teaching other avid anglers what you know.

Fishing for bass is for every one of all ages — women worldwide are taking to the waters as well as the kiddies.

It is important that children should never be left unattended or unsupervised at any time. This is an outdoor sport which is enjoyed by people the whole world over and why not when the rewards are so great when the catch is bigger than you anticipated.

If this sport is to become a serious part of your life where you want to take it to the next level then you need more information under your hat. You need to know the best location, best bass lure/bait and what fishing equipment of use.

By going that step further and checking out Bass Fishing sites online will give your more intimate details on the skills needed for a sport that is spreading like an epidemic the whole world over.

1. Bass fishing is supposedly to be the
   (*a*) a number one water sport in the USA
   (*b*) number one freshwater sport in the Washington
   (*c*) number one sport in the USA
   (*d*) number one freshwater sport in the USA

2. Bass fishing is also known as
   (*a*) self fulfilling sport
   (*b*) new form of fishing
   (*c*) mind blowing sport
   (*d*) self sport

3. It is true for every sport that
   (*a*) you make came for your country

   (*b*) practice makes perfect
   (*c*) it is difficult in the beginning only
   (*d*) you need a coach

4. Bass Fishing has become
   (*a*) Million Dollar Industry
   (*b*) New revenue earning industry
   (*c*) Billion Dollar Industry
   (*d*) One of the major sports in the world

5. The procedure of reforms requires
   (*a*) application, problem solving skills and attitude.
   (*b*) application, analytical skills and attitude.
   (*c*) application, technical skills and good mind.
   (*d*) application, writing skills and attitude.

PASSAGE - 11

The clash between Anderson's family and the FBI is the latest example of the Bush Administration's post-9/11 push to crack down on leaks of sensitive information. A CIA official was fired last week because the agency says she leaked information to the press about secret CIA prisons for alleged terrorists; at the same time, the FBI is continuing its probe into who released details about an undercover domestic eavesdropping program run by the National Security Agency. Last month the National Archives halted an effort by the U.S. intelligence community to make thousands of declassified documents secret once again. To Tom Blanton, head of the G.W.U. —affiliated National Security Archive, which monitors government secrecy, the FBI's request to scrub Anderson's files "looks like another front in the government-wide effort to squash dissent".

For its part, the FBI says the law is clear. "Nobody is protected from having in their possession a classified document," says Persichini. When asked if the Anderson family could be criminally prosecuted for possession of the files they inherited, Persichini replied, "At this point, we haven't gone down that route". The Anderson family is relishing the tug-of-war with the powerful agency. "It almost seems like the good old days", Kevin Anderson says "I wish Dad were around to enjoy it".

1. A CIA official was fired last week because
   (a) he leaked sensitive information to the press
   (b) he leaked sensitive information to the government
   (c) she leaked sensitive information to the world
   (d) he leaked sensitive information to the foes.

2. An example of Bush Administration's push to crack down on leaks of sensitive information
   (a) The clash between Jeff's family and government
   (b) The clash between Jeff's family and the FBI
   (c) The clash between Anderson's family and the FBI
   (d) The clash between Anderson's family and the government

3. The FBI is still probing who released information
   (a) about an undercover program run by the NSA
   (b) about an undercover document of the NSA
   (c) about an undercover program run by the NASA
   (d) about undercover domestic eavesdropping program run by FBI

4. "Nobody is protected form having in their possession a classified document", is the law by
   (a) NSA, USA
   (b) FBI, USA
   (c) NSA, UK
   (d) FBI, UK

5. Last month efforts were made to
   (a) make thousands of classified documents secret
   (b) make thousands of declassified documents secret
   (c) make thousands of classified documents public
   (d) make thousands of declassified documents public

PASSAGE - 12

When Jazz was born in the early 20th century, its musicians became the first African-American role models to make white people want to act black. They changed the language with words like "hip", "dig", "joint" and "cool". They had a style that was oh so glamorous. Lester Young's pork-pie hat, Billie Holiday's gardenia, Dizzy Gillespie's laugh and his trumpet bell pointing north. Miles Davis's dark and wispy beauty, Duke Ellington's elegance.

Chet Baker was called, with a straight face, "the great white hope". The fact that he could play Jazz as well as it has ever been played had little to do with it. When he was in his 20s, before his teeth were knocked out by a drug dealer, people compared Chet's allure to James Dean's.

When another Jazz icon, Charlie Parker, died at the age of 35, the graffiti "Bird Lives" began to appear everywhere. But the Kind of immortality he assumed was as much because of his cool outlaw image as his musical creativity. That's the image Clint Eastwood featured in Bird the movie. The outlaw has always had a kind of decadent glamour for American audiences.

1. The early 20th century saw the birth of
   (*a*) African American role models
   (*b*) Jazz, the white musician
   (*c*) Jazz, the music
   (*d*) Jazz, the black musician

2. Chet Baker was called
   (*a*) a straight face
   (*b*) the great white hope
   (*c*) the great black hope
   (*d*) the straight white hope

3. What did the musicians do to the language?
   (*a*) They played it with words like "hip", "dig", etc.
   (*b*) They appended it with words like "joint", "dance", etc.
   (*c*) They appended it with words like "hip", "dig", etc.
   (*d*) They used only the words like "hip", "dig" etc.

4. What happened to Chet Baker when he was just adult?
   (*a*) his teeth were knocked out by a drug addict
   (*b*) his eyes were knocked out by a drug dealer
   (*c*) his teeth were knocked out by a truck dealer
   (*d*) his teeth were knocked out by a drug dealer

5. People compared Chet's
   (*a*) temptation to James Dean's
   (*b*) image to James Dean's
   (*c*) stature to James Dean's
   (*d*) life to James Dean's

PASSAGE - 13

Aamir Khan is known to be a perfectionist and not without reason — there is not other Bollywood actor who has done justice to such a wide plethora of roles with an equal ease. Aamir's known to get into the skin of the characters he plays. So, whether it is as the Gen X rebel from his latest flick Rang De Basanti or as the lovable tapori in Rangeela or as the man who took on the might of the British empire in both 1857 A Rising or Lagan ..... he has always managed to get the viewers hooked.

In the glam world of Bollywood where 'formula products' rule, Aamir has always taken risks and managed to pull them off.

But, it is not just the silver screen which this Khan rules. He has tried his hand at TV too and, as usual, with great success. Not only from films, his dialogues from advertisements too have become the talk of the town.

1. Aamir Khan is known as perfectionist because
   (a) he has acted in good patriotic movies
   (b) he has acted in a number films
   (c) he had done a wide variety of roles
   (d) he has acted with directors of all ages

2. What has Aamir done different in Bollywood than other actors?
   (a) has always done his homework
   (b) has always taken risks
   (c) has a number of hits
   (d) has tried his hand at TV too

3. What does the sentence "Aamir's known to get into the skin of the characters he plays" signify?
   (a) Aamir's reel and real lifer are same.
   (b) Aamir's reel and real lifer are different.
   (c) Aamir's is a perfectionist.
   (d) Aamir's lives the character he plays.

4. Apart from his acting, what else has become the talk of the town?
   (a) his dialogues in movies
   (b) his hairstyles
   (c) his dialogues form advertisements too
   (d) his heroines

5. Which is the latest movie by Aamir Khan referred to in the paragraph above?
   (a) Fanna
   (b) Rang de Basanti
   (c) Lagaan
   (d) Rangeela

PASSAGE - 14

Easier to spot is the 1793 courthouse. Hurricanes damaged it several times, but it remains one of Philipsburg's architectural gems, others are the Methodist Church at number 90 [although a replica of the original 1851 building] and the pasanggrahan, the 1995 government guest house that became St. Maarten's first hotel. On the other side of the road, colourful Guavaberry House sells tasty liqueurs and other products made form the local guavaberry.

Most of the stylish restaurants make cocktails featuring this exotic guavaberry liqueur, which has been produced here for centuries. And although the sophisticated shops, glitzy casinos and elegant hotels may give the place an upbeat aura of glamour, St. Maarten hasn't renounced its origins. So don't be all too surprised when a hen and her chicks run out in front of you as you cross Front Street the island may be chick, but it still has retained all of its Caribbean charm.

Like the famous song about a certain city, you might think St. Martin/St. Maarten was a case of the "so good, they named it twice" syndrome. In fact, there's a practical reason why this sophisticated Caribbean island has two, albeit very similar, names — it's shared by two different government [and is often claimed to be the smallest land mass on earth to be so divided]. The north is French, while the southern half belongs to the Netherlands Antilles. Each part even has its own capital city; Philipsburg on Great Bay is Dutch, while Marigot on the west coast is its French counterpart.

1. The place referred to as Philipsburg's architectural gems is
   (*a*) The restaurant
   (*b*) A Church
   (*c*) The government guesthouse
   (*d*) An Island

2. What has been produced here for centuries?
   (*a*) sophisticated shops
   (*b*) guavaberry liqueur
   (*c*) elegant hotels
   (*d*) restaurants

3. Which of the following add to the glamour?
   (*a*) stylish restaurants, glitzy casinos and elegant hotels
   (*b*) sophisticated shops, stylish restaurants and elegant hotels
   (*c*) glitzy casinos, elegant hotels and guavaberry liqueur
   (*d*) glitzy casinos, sophisticated shops, and elegant hotels

4. St. Maarten can still boost of
   (*a*) guavaberry liqueur
   (*b*) its origins
   (*c*) its perfection
   (*d*) its greenery

5. What does Guavaberry House do?
   (*a*) It sells tasty liqueurs and other products
   (*b*) It buys tasty liqueurs
   (*c*) It sells tasty liqueurs only
   (*d*) It produces tasty liqueurs

PASSAGE - 15

In cobra country a mongoose was born one day who didn't want to fight cobras or anything else. The word spread from mongoose to mongoose that there was a mongoose who didn't want to fight cobras. If he didn't want to fight anything else, it was his own business, but it was the duty of every mongoose to kill cobras or be killed by cobras.

"Why?" asked the peacelike mongoose, and the word went round that the strange new mongoose was not only pro-cobra and anti- mongoose but intellectually curious and against the ideals and traditions of mongoosism.

"He is crazy," cried the young's mongoose's father.

"He's sick," said his mother.

"He is a coward", shouted his brothers.

"He's a mongoosexual", whisspread his sisters.

Strangers who had never laid eyes on the peacelike mongoose remembered that they had seen him crawling on his stomach, or trying cobra hoods, or plotting the violent overthrow of Mongoodia.

Finally the rumour spread that the mongoose had venom in his sting, like a cobra, and he was tried, convicted by a show of paws, and condemned to banishment.

1. What did the new mongoose say that made him against the ideals and traditions of mongoosism?
    (a) He didn't want to fight cobras
    (b) He was intellectual
    (c) He didn't want to get killed by cobras
    (d) He didn't want to be like his family

2. What was the duty of every mongoose was
    (a) live and let others live too
    (b) kill or get killed by cobras
    (c) get killed by cobras
    (d) kill or get killed by mongooses

3. The mongoose was described by his family members as
    (a) crazy, mongoosexual, coward, different and sick
    (b) crazy and sick
    (c) mongoosexual and coward
    (d) crazy, mongoosexual, coward and sick

4. What is the moral of the story?
    (a) one should not try to be intellectual
    (b) Never go against one's family
    (c) if the enemy doesn't get you your own folks may
    (d) Duties should always be kept

5. What happened to the new mongoose finally?
    (a) He was killed by Cobra
    (b) He was killed by his family members
    (c) He was killed by himself
    (d) He was killed by his own people

PASSAGE - 16

Dusk was falling last Tuesday when news of the attack on America first reached this war-ruined city, Kabul. In the dusty twilight, Afghans held radios to their ears, listening to static-filled accounts on the Voice of America and the BBC Pashto- and Persia-language services. Because the country's Taliban rulers forbid television, Afghans could see no pictures of he destruction that had people everywhere else glued to their sets. The immensity of the World

Trade Center had to be described. When Afghans asked me about the Twin Towers, I compared them to Afghanistan's giant Bamiyan Buddha statues, a symbol of national heritage that the Taliban blasted to dust six months ago.

The immensity of America's agony, however, required no explanation. More than 20 years of war have heightened Afghans's empathy for the suffering of others. Though their rulers remain inscrutable, Afghans's emotions are familiar. "The attack on the U.S. was very bad. It killed innocent people, ordinary citizens", Zalmai Khan, a housepainter, said sadly. "Why must so many people die?" another man cried. "It doesn't matter who they are; they all have a mother and a father". Many said they believe that Osama Bin Laden, whom the Taliban treats as an honored guest, is a liability and should be expelled from Afghanistan. "It's a good idea", said a Kabul pharmacist, nodding resolutely. "Problem finished". But the Taliban has little intention of giving up bin Laden. "He was friend in a time of need. It would be very much cowardly to leave him at this stage in his life." Foreign Minister Wakil Ahmad Muttawakil told me. And so Kabul is bracing to pay the price for that hospitality. "Will America send rockets and bombs to hit Afghanistan?" some residents asked anxiously.

1. The people of Kabul could not see pictures of the destruction that others could because
   (a) Watching was forbidden
   (b) TV was forbidden
   (c) Showing such things was forbidden
   (d) American did not wanted it

2. The immensity of the World Trade Center was described as the blast of
   (a) lives of hundreds of people
   (b) Afghanistan's giant Taliban rule
   (c) Twin Towers
   (d) Bamiyan Buddha statues

3. What had heightened Afghans' empathy for the suffering of others?
   (a) More than two decades of war in Afghanistan
   (b) More crazy and sick people in Kabul
   (c) America's policy against the Afghans
   (d) More than 20 years of war in America

4. What was the general reactions of the people of Afghans?
   (a) They were happy that USA has learnt a lesson
   (b) They disliked the attack
   (c) They wanted to know the actual culprit of attacks
   (d) They felt it was destiny

5. What did people of Kabul feared most?
   (a) Will America start war against Osama
   (b) Will Osama return to Afghanistan
   (c) Will Taliban rule come again
   (d) Will America start another war

PASSAGE - 17

It's not exactly Mandal allover again, but is the fire spreading again? Circa 2006 and the protests against reservations in premier institutes have spilled over from the cyber world into the streets. Medical students are the ones who have picked up the gauntlet. And despite a promise by the HRD minister Arjun Singh that he will address the issue, the protests continue. The medical students are waiting for May 11, when the government will address the topic, post elections.

But, by braving tear gas and water cannons, the students have shown that the government will have to hear them out. And the venue, post Rang De Basanti and Jessica Lall, remains the same-India Gate.

1. The fire is spreading all over again because of the
   (*a*) Mandal issue
   (*b*) Reservations in medical colleges
   (*c*) Movies like Rang de Basanti
   (*d*) Reservations in premier institutes

2. Which of the following have spilled over from the cyber world into the streets?
   (*a*) protests against Mandal in premier institutes
   (*b*) protests against reservations in schools
   (*c*) protests against reservations in premier institutes
   (*d*) protests against reservations in all sectors.

3. The medical students are waiting for May 11 to
   (*a*) Arjun Singh to join the protests
   (*b*) See what is reservation is all about
   (*c*) Continue agitation
   (*d*) See what government have to say about

4. What is common in Jessica Lall case and the movie Rang De Basanti?
   (*a*) Both are true
   (*b*) the venue
   (*c*) the agitation
   (*d*) both are of current era

5. By braving tear gas and water cannons, the students have shown the government
   (*a*) that they will not be quiet
   (*b*) will have to watch them
   (*c*) should not ignore them
   (*d*) will have to rethink about reservations

PASSAGE - 18

After so many years of war, Kabul, formerly a cosmopolitan capital, has become a city of grinding poverty, distrust and fear under the watchful eyes of the Taliban and its heavy-handed religious police. Residents have learnt to live alongside an array of the Taliban's so-called foreign guests, including Arabs, Chechens, Kurds, Uzbeks and Pakistanis — all believed to be in Afghanistan for secret military training. In the 1980s, Washington fueled Afghan resistance to the Soviet invasion by passing billions of dollars of covert aid to mujahedin fighters. Once the Soviets pulled out, the mujahedin turned on one another, and country descended into civil war. When the Taliban a band of warrior students — swept into Kabul five years ago, it imposed a ruthless Islamic rule. It brought peace to the city, but the world was outraged by its practices, including public executions and a ban on work for women and schooling for girls. Music, TV and photographs were prohibited, and men were forced to grow beards.

Among those evacuated last week were relatives of two American aid workers on trial here, accused of preaching Christianity. After traveling 10,000 miles to a country where few dare to venture, the parents had to leave their daughters behind to an uncertain fate. Waiting to board a U.N. plane for Islamabad, Pakistan, Deborah Oddy, mother of Heather Mercer, 24, wore a black headscarf and sobbed uncontrollably. Since the Soviet invasion in 1979, this country has seen more than its share of tears. Now the frightened residents of Kabul are worried that this latest incident will bring on even more.

1. What has contributed to Kabul's poverty?
   (*a*) It's own government policies
   (*b*) Taliban rule
   (*c*) Endless war for so many years
   (*d*) Presence of Osama

2. Which guests do people have learnt to live with?
   (*a*) People coming for military training
   (*b*) Foreigners of all countries
   (*c*) Indians and Pakistanis only
   (*d*) Pakistanis

3. Taliban was formed by
   (*a*) Osama Bin Laden
   (*b*) USA
   (*c*) A group of warrior students
   (*d*) USA and Pakistanis

4. How did US fueled Afghan resistance to the Soviet invasion?
   (*a*) By sending mujahedin fighters
   (*b*) By giving monetary support to Afghan fighters
   (*c*) By creating mujahedin fighters
   (*d*) By giving army support to Afghan fighters

5. Why were people angry with Taliban though it brought peace to the country?
   (*a*) because it demanded money
   (*b*) because of its governance
   (*c*) it got involved in malpractices
   (*d*) because it killed humans

PASSAGE - 19

Sometimes everything goes wrong in life. I came across a joint family in Sainik Farms comprising a father and mother, around 60 years of age, two married sons, and an unmarried daughter of around 25. Domestic friction had caused the older son's wife to leave him for her maayka. The younger son's marriage too was falling apart. And this had caused their unmarried sisters to declare that since marriages end in disaster, she would prefer to stay single all her life...

The atmosphere in this home had become so poisonous that even the senior businessman and his wife had started bickering for the first time in their lives. This man told me mournfully that he and his whole family fought like cats and dogs and he often wished he wasn't alive. Also because all his family members were quarrelling with one another in combinations that changed every single day.

1. What made the younger sister think marriages end in disaster?
   (*a*) The outcome of marriage of brothers
   (*b*) The daily quarrel in the home
   (*c*) The marriage of her younger brother
   (*d*) The quarrel between his mother and father

2. What made the writer say "Sometimes everything goes wrong in life".
   (*a*) His interaction with politician
   (*b*) His interaction with many people
   (*c*) His interaction with a nuclear family
   (*d*) His interaction with a joint family

3. What had caused the older son's wife to leave him?
   (*a*) Fight with the older son
   (*b*) the trauma and mental pain
   (*c*) the bad behaviour of her family
   (*d*) day to day problems in the house

4. The atmosphere in the house forced the writer to say that
   (*a*) it had become poisonous
   (*b*) senior businessman and his wife had started fighting
   (*c*) sister felt marriages are bad
   (*d*) the man was mourning

5. What is significance of "fought like cats and dogs"
   (*a*) fought like domestic animals
   (*b*) fought like enemies
   (*c*) fought like street animals
   (*d*) fought every time

PASSAGE - 20

We have heard of brother-sister duos, sister duos or brother duos creating ripples in the international sports arena. But rarely have we heard of an Indian husband wife 'duo' making it big in the world of sports. Samaresh Jung, who was selected as the best athlete in the Commonwealth Games at Melbourne, after winning five golds, a silver and a bronze in shooting, and his wife Anuja Jung, who clinched one gold and one silver in shooting, fall in this category. They have won laurels for India with their achievements.

Samaresh wields a pistol and Anuja is an air rifle shooter. We met them in their house in Khyber Pass. Samaresh belongs to a family where everybody is in love with weapons and it is no wonder that he took to shooting like a duck takes to water.

1. What was so unique about the paragraph described above?
   (*a*) Brother-sisters fame in sports
   (*b*) Husband-wife fame in sports
   (*c*) Sister duos fame in sports
   (*d*) Indian's fame in sports

2. What is significance of "duck takes to water".
   (*a*) naturally
   (*b*) swimming
   (*c*) without any efforts
   (*d*) home

3. Where did they won laurels for India?
   (*a*) in Khyber pass
   (*b*) in India
   (*c*) in their state
   (*d*) in Australia

4. Who was selected as the best athlete?
   (*a*) Anuja
   (*b*) Neither Samaresh nor Anuja
   (*c*) Samaresh
   (*d*) Samaresh and Anuja

5. How many gold did Samaresh Jung won?
   (*a*) 10   (*b*) 5
   (*c*) None   (*d*) 1

PASSAGE - 21

How would you fell if the nation's biggest superstar is your fan? Well, there's bound to be no end to your joy and that's exactly what's been happening to India's new cricket wonder boy Mahinder Singh Dhoni when he realized Amitabh Bachchan, who has been his childhood idol, turned out to be his die-hard fan. The two of them met on a film's set in Mumbai. Dhoni was shooting in Mumbai's Film city for a commercial, while the big B was also shooting in the same place. When big B learnt to Dhoni presence, he sent in a word to the sporting superstar asking him if they could meet. "At first Dhoni couldn't believe his luck. He thought someone was pulling a fast one on him, but when he realized the truth, he sent a message saying it wouldn't be polite for Mr. Bachchan to come and see him— in stead, after his shoot he himself would come and meet him. And, of course, Dhoni finished his shoot and rushed to the nearby set to meet his idol, "says a unit member Talk of mutual admiration societies".

1. What is Dhoni referred to in the paragraph above?
   (*a*) Wonderful Boy
   (*b*) Wonderful person
   (*c*) Wonder Boy
   (*d*) Wonder Man

2. How did Dhoni refer to Amitabh Bachchan?
   (*a*) Superstar
   (*b*) Childhood star

    (*c*) Mega Star
    (*d*) Childhood idol

3. When Bachchan learnt Dhoni's presence what did he do?
    (*a*) he continued his shooting
    (*b*) he asked for a meeting with him
    (*c*) he asked Dhoni to meet him
    (*d*) he went to meet him

4. Who are the mutual admiration societies referred above?

    (*a*) Cricket and Film
    (*b*) Filmstar and Cricket Star
    (*c*) Commercial shoot and Film Shoot
    (*d*) Amitabh and Dhoni

5. Upon hearing Bachchan's message what happened?
    (*a*) Dhoni rushed to him
    (*b*) Dhoni though someone was playing prank
    (*c*) He called him up
    (*d*) Dhoni thought it was a joke

ANSWERS

PASSAGE-1

1	2	3	4	5
(*c*)	(*d*)	(*d*)	(*a*)	(*c*)

PASSAGE-2

1	2	3	4	5
(*d*)	(*b*)	(*a*)	(*c*)	(*d*)

PASSAGE-3

1	2	3	4	5
(*c*)	(*d*)	(*b*)	(*a*)	(*a*)

PASSAGE-4

1	2	3	4	5
(*d*)	(*a*)	(*d*)	(*b*)	(*a*)

PASSAGE-5

1	2	3	4	5
(*c*)	(*a*)	(*b*)	(*d*)	(*d*)

PASSAGE-6

1	2	3	4	5
(*b*)	(*d*)	(*c*)	(*d*)	(*a*)

PASSAGE-7

1	2	3	4	5
(*d*)	(*a*)	(*b*)	(*d*)	(*c*)

PASSAGE-8

1	2	3	4	5
(*b*)	(*d*)	(*c*)	(*d*)	(*a*)

PASSAGE-9

1	2	3	4	5
(*a*)	(*d*)	(*b*)	(*d*)	(*a*)

PASSAGE-10

1	2	3	4	5
(*d*)	(*d*)	(*c*)	(*c*)	(*a*)

PASSAGE-11

1	2	3	4	5
(*c*)	(*c*)	(*a*)	(*b*)	(*b*)

PASSAGE-12

1	2	3	4	5
(c)	(b)	(c)	(d)	(a)

PASSAGE-13

1	2	3	4	5
(c)	(b)	(c)	(c)	(b)

PASSAGE-14

1	2	3	4	5
(d)	(b)	(d)	(b)	(a)

PASSAGE-15

1	2	3	4	5
(a)	(b)	(d)	(c)	(d)

PASSAGE-16

1	2	3	4	5
(b)	(b)	(a)	(b)	(d)

PASSAGE-17

1	2	3	4	5
(c)	(c)	(d)	(b)	(d)

PASSAGE-18

1	2	3	4	5
(b)	(a)	(c)	(b)	(c)

PASSAGE-19

1	2	3	4	5
(a)	(d)	(d)	(a)	(b)

PASSAGE-20

1	2	3	4	5
(b)	(a)	(d)	(c)	(b)

PASSAGE-21

1	2	3	4	5
(c)	(d)	(b)	(c)	(b)

PLAYING UPON WORDS

CLOZE TEST

PASSAGE - 1

Two defeats on the trot have not affected the mood in the England camp and the visitors (1) — confident of bouncing back in the seven – match series, left-arm spinner Ian Blackwell said. "The mood in the camp is (2) — good. We should have won the last two games (3) — we had performed a little better. But we still have a good chance to win the series," the 27-year-old said. "We are 2-0 down but it's a seven-match series. There's still a long way to go," Blackwell said. "We will assess our performance (4) — the last two games, at how people gave the wickets away, and the way we bowled at certain people. It's something we have to (5) —."

1. (*a*) is   (*b*) are
    (*c*) was   (*d*) were

2. (*a*) lovely   (*b*) mainly
    (*c*) for   (*d*) very

3. (*a*) if   (*b*) when
    (*c*) which   (*d*) who

4. (*a*) over   (*b*) above
    (*c*) inside   (*d*) in

5. (*a*) do   (*b*) ignore
    (*c*) rectify   (*d*) see

PASSAGE - 2

The image of the music has come a long way since the mid-20th century, when its (1) — energy was used to illustrate movies about the evil energy of drugs, alcohol, and violence. Duke Ellington, for example, (2) — the soundtrack of The Man With The Golden Arm, and Gerry Mulligan played for I Want To Live. And now we end up (3) — The Terminal, a family movie about the glamour of jazz with just about no jazz music in it. That's progress. You get (4) — of the decadence and all of the glamour of jazz-without even having to listen to it. This could be described as (5) —.

1. (*a*) main   (*b*) good
    (*c*) positive   (*d*) new

2. (*a*) make   (*b*) made
    (*c*) hear   (*d*) saw

3. (*a*) and   (*b*) were
    (*c*) with   (*d*) in

4. (*a*) neither   (*b*) no
    (*c*) zero   (*d*) none

5. (*a*) inheritance
    (*b*) exploitation
    (*c*) bad
    (*d*) imagination

PASSAGE - 3

"The stars (1) — visit the Casino Royale," adds Niranjan Motwani helpfully. He is the owner of four (2) — shops, including G.N. jewelers, which is close to the Casino Royale in the Maho Beach area. "Melanie Griffith has visited one of my shops, and in the casino we've spotted celebrities (3) — Brad Pitt, John Travolta, Denzel Washington, Robert de Niro and Beyonce." But the stars don't have a monopoly on glamour on the island. "Some women customers are dressed so extravagantly that (4) — of people gather outside my shop to (5) — them," Motwani smiles.

1. (a) oftenly   (b) go
   (c) will   (d) often

2. (a) stylish   (b) high
   (c) main   (d) new

3. (a) e.g.   (b) like
   (c) which are   (d) as

4. (a) crowd   (b) person
   (c) people   (d) bunch

5. (a) buy   (b) like
   (c) watch   (d) visualize

PASSAGE - 4

Noida has (1) — scored over Gurgaon and (2) — satellite townships. With the singing of a memorandum of understanding with Noida Authority on Tuesday, Delhi Metro will begin work on NCR's (3) — line, which will link Dwarka to CP and will reach Noida City Center covering almost 50-Km. So how long will it (4) — to reach Noida from Dwarka Sector 22? 105 minutes on an interesting line, which will be at grade to begin with, then elevated, (5) — by an underground stretch and will cross the river over a bridge. It will then stop over at commonwealth Games village to finally reach Noida Sector 15.

1. (a) lastly   (b) endly
   (c) finally   (d) mainly

2. (a) similar   (b) all
   (c) nearby   (d) other

3. (a) furthest   (b) fastest
   (c) longest   (d) strongest

4. (a) taken   (b) take
   (c) drive   (d) talk

5. (a) within   (b) after
   (c) in   (d) followed

PASSAGE - 5

Three decades (1) — be a long time in politics and that's how long the Left (2) — been in power in West Bengal. It will again win hands down, bucking anti-incumbency.

Three are several theories for the Left's domination: the success of land reforms, Left's organizational muscle and disarray in (3) — ranks. Ask CPM MP Sudhangshu Seal and he trots out standard reasons: "Seventy (4) — of the people in West Bengal (5) — in rural areas.

1. (a) would   (b) may
   (c) can   (d) shall

2. (a) has   (b) have
   (c) has been   (d) have been

3. (a) people   (b) center
   (c) man   (d) opposition

4. (a) men   (b) per cent
   (c) women   (d) person

5. (a) leave   (b) die
   (c) live   (d) stay

PASSAGE - 6

There is no loss of nerve in the Bush administration over resistance to the Indo-US nuclear (1) — from some American lawmakers and there remains a commitment at the highest levels of the government to take the deal (2) —, a senior US administration official said on Monday.

Asking that opposition to the deal (3) — Senators and Congressmen be seen in perspective in a system where (4) — forces are at work, the official, who spoke on background, suggested it was premature to pronounce the demise of the deal considering the president's commitment to building closer (5) — with India.

1. (a) agreement (b) deal
   (c) application (d) talk

2. (a) enforced (b) done
   (c) checked (d) forward

3. (a) from (b) for
   (c) with (d) of

4. (a) difficult (b) hard
   (c) complex (d) tough

5. (a) bond (b) relation
   (c) love (d) ties

PASSAGE - 7

Proving prehistoric man's ingenuity and ability (1) — withstand and inflict excruciating pain, (2) — have found that dental drilling dates back 9,000 years.

Primitive dentists drilled (3) — perfect holes into live but undoubtedly unhappy patients between 5–500BC and 7,000 BC , an (4) — in Nature reports. Researchers carbon dated (5) — nine skulls with 11 drill holes found in a Pakistan graveyard.

1. (a) in (b) for
   (c) to (d) of

2. (a) doctors (b) scientists
   (c) intruders (d) researchers

3. (a) normally (b) nearly
   (c) partly (d) fully

4. (a) page (b) column
   (c) adjective (d) article

5. (a) at last (b) at all
   (c) at least (d) on

PASSAGE - 8

Some might call it an auction to die for, as the Chinese observe their traditional Qing Ming (1) — honoring the dead A man in his late 20s in Jiaxing, city near shanghai, has attempted to sell (2) — soul on Taobao, China's top online auction site, attracting (3) — from some 58 soul-searching buyers before the posting was pulled. "We reviewed Taobao's policies and realized we had no (4) — policy on the selling of soul," said Porter Erisman, spokesman for Taobao's parent, Alibaba.com. "The posting (5) — taken down last Friday." Erisman said Taobao wasn't opposed to the idea of soul selling online, but wanted more proof that the seller could provide the goods.

1. (a) holiday (b) tradition
   (c) festival (d) culture

2. (*a*) her   (*b*) his
    (*c*) own   (*d*) its

3. (*a*) offer   (*b*) deal
    (*c*) bids   (*d*) reward

4. (*a*) fix   (*b*) main
    (*c*) written   (*d*) specific

5. (*a*) were   (*b*) had
    (*c*) is   (*d*) was

PASSAGE - 9

The New Testament (1) — that Jesus walked on water, but a Florida university professor (2) — there could be a less miraculous explanation – he walked on a floating piece of ice.

Professor Doron Nof also theorized in the early 1990s that Moses's parting of the Red Sea (3) — solid science behind it.

Nof, a professor of oceanography at Florida State University, said on Tuesday that his study (4) — an unusual combination of water and atmospheric conditions in what is now northern Israel (5) — led to ice formation on the sea of Galilee.

1. (*a*) said   (*b*) warned
    (*c*) saw   (*d*) says

2. (*a*) believes   (*b*) believed
    (*c*) think   (*d*) believe

3. (*a*) has   (*b*) has been
    (*c*) had   (*d*) had been

4. (*a*) saw   (*b*) found
    (*c*) invented   (*d*) find

5. (*a*) could have   (*b*) can
    (*c*) should   (*d*) could had

PASSAGE - 10

Premature babies can (1) — pain and are not just (2) — a reflex reaction to a stimulus, a (3) — of doctors and scientists said on Tuesday.

Using brain scans of babies (4) — as early as 24 weeks after conception they found that during routing procedures such as obtaining a blood (5) — from a heel they feel pain.

1. (*a*) speak   (*b*) imagine
    (*c*) listen   (*d*) feel

2. (*a*) displaying   (*b*) reflecting
    (*c*) watching   (*d*) taking

3. (*a*) pool   (*b*) bunch
    (*c*) hub   (*d*) team

4. (*a*) born   (*b*) heard
    (*c*) seen   (*d*) looked

5. (*a*) drop   (*b*) sample
    (*c*) group   (*d*) test

PASSAGE - 11

Fossils (1) — in southern Utah are (2) — a new species of birdlike dinosaur that resembled a seven-foot-tall brightly coloured turkey (3) — could run up to 25mph, scientists said Tuesday.

Fossils of the meateater's hand-like claw and foot were found in the Grand Staircase-Escalante National Monument near the Arizona border, (4) — paleontologists reason to believe some dinosaurs known as raptors roamed from Canada to northern New Mexico about 75 million years (5) —

1. (*a*) invented (*b*) discovered
   (*c*) created   (*d*) originated

2. (*a*) of   (*b*) inside
   (*c*) from   (*d*) for

3. (*a*) together   (*b*) and
   (*c*) as well as (*d*) with

4. (*a*) displaying (*b*) citing
   (*c*) giving   (*d*) watching

5. (*a*) ago   (*b*) behind
   (*c*) earlier   (*d*) previously

PASSAGE - 12

Known to comprehend the pulse of (1) — audience, Ekta Kapoor, producer and (2) — of Balaji Telefilms Ltd, is a name to reckon with in the television world today. And with her programmes (3) — managing to move TRP rating (4) —, anyone thinking of venturing into the channel launching business today (5) — want collaboration with her company!

1. (*a*) his   (*b*) her
   (*c*) its   (*d*) our

2. (*a*) musician   (*b*) writer
   (*c*) owner   (*d*) lyricist

3. (*a*) mainly   (*b*) casually
   (*c*) oftently   (*d*) always

4. (*a*) top   (*b*) up
   (*c*) upwards   (*d*) further

5. (*a*) would   (*b*) may
   (*c*) can   (*d*) shall

PASSAGE - 13

India accounts for over (1) — quarter of maternal deaths worldwide. And (2) — the country, Rajasthan has one of the (3) — maternal mortality rates [MMR] of 670 per lakh live births, as compared to national (4) — of between 420540. Incidentally, the (5) — has one of the highest infant mortality rates too

1. (*a*) an   (*b*) one
   (*c*) the   (*d*) full

2. (*a*) within   (*b*) with
   (*c*) of   (*d*) inside

3. (*a*) furthest   (*b*) high
   (*c*) highest   (*d*) higher

4. (*a*) sum   (*b*) average
   (*c*) total   (*d*) ratio

5. (*a*) city   (*b*) country
   (*c*) state   (*d*) town

PASSAGE - 14

Global terrorist Dawood Ibrahim has been aware that an Interpol (1) — against him was on its way and intelligence reports have (2) — his growing restlessness as he hunts for save houses in Pakistan.

The general secretariat of Interpol at Lyon, France, forwarded contents of the new notice to all 184-member countries on Thursday (3) — them to freeze the D-company CEO's assets, (4) — a travel ban and arms embargo as "Dawood (5) — the subject of UN's anti-terrorism sanctions"

1. (*a*) policy   (*b*) notice
   (*c*) police   (*d*) news

2. (*a*) told   (*b*) said
   (*c*) shown   (*d*) indicated

3.   (*a*) seeking   (*b*) looking
    (*c*) asking   (*d*) displaying

4.   (*a*) mark   (*b*) place
    (*c*) request   (*d*) put

5.   (*a*) is   (*b*) of
    (*c*) are   (*d*) in

PASSAGE - 15

A political movement is on in Nepal. Students and city's residents were out in full (1) — on Saturday defying curfew, shoot-at-sight orders, and even bullets that killed one person and injured three women.

It was the day (2) — the two-day bandh was to translate into a rally in the heart of the city. For Nepal's hereditary ruler, Gyanendra, the countdown may have just (3) —. It would be futile to name one place as the nerve center of defiance since most of the arterial roads (4) — full of thousands of protesters (5) — slogans and waiting to spill over to the city's ring road nervously manned by Royal Nepal Army and police.

1.   (*a*) swing   (*b*) force
    (*c*) fear   (*d*) fore

2.   (*a*) which   (*b*) in
    (*c*) when   (*d*) within

3.   (*a*) begun   (*b*) begin
    (*c*) beginning (*d*) began

4.   (*a*) was   (*b*) is
    (*c*) were   (*d*) are

5.   (*a*) fighting   (*b*) crying
    (*c*) talking   (*d*) shouting

PASSAGE - 16

Inspired to create a mobile-tracking solution (1) — his 16-year-old son lost his cellphone, P. Sekhar, chairman of Micro Technologies, began work on a program to (2) — phones. The code – downloadable at Rs 200-300 a year on most handsets from Micro's website – allows the owner to track the exact location (3) — his phone and the number of the new SIM card that (4) — inserted. As of now, the only action a subscriber can take is to frantically call the service (5) — and block his card.

1.   (*a*) of   (*b*) for
    (*c*) while   (*d*) after

2.   (*a*) look   (*b*) guide
    (*c*) track   (*d*) buy

3.   (*a*) inside   (*b*) for
    (*c*) in   (*d*) of

4.   (*a*) had been (*b*) were
    (*c*) was   (*d*) has been

5.   (*a*) owner   (*b*) provider
    (*c*) subcriber (*d*) giver

PASSAGE - 17

It's perhaps (1) — the best of times to be lustful about gold. The price of gold on Tuesday pierced a 25-year high in the (2) — market, and in sympathy, touched an all-time high of Rs 8,900/10gm in the (3) — market.

Avadhesh Agrawal of Goyal Jewellers in Chandni Chowk, who is also president of Delhi Bullion & Jewellers' Association, said that (4) — has tapered off as prices have gone up. Kamal Gupta of PP Jewellers said that (5) — marriage requirements, there's hardly anyone buying gold.

1. (*a*) no   (*b*) neither
   (*c*) not   (*d*) for

2. (*a*) food   (*b*) crude
   (*c*) world   (*d*) international

3. (*a*) domestic   (*b*) our
   (*c*) main   (*d*) country's

4. (*a*) demand   (*b*) supply
   (*c*) demands   (*d*) supplies

5. (*a*) covering   (*b*) hiding
   (*c*) leaving   (*d*) barring

PASSAGE - 18

It (1) — to be a season of strikes. After last week's strike at the State Bank of India, contract workers at Hero Honda's Gurgaon plant have struck work. The strike, which began on Monday (2) — as Supreme Court ruled that daily wage workers with government had no right to regular jobs brought production to a halt.

While talks were under way (3) — the company's management, contractors, contract worker representatives and government officials the latest "direct action" was being seen as yet another sign of organized labour's militancy (4) — with increase in Left's leverage (5) — the Center.

1. (*a*) looks   (*b*) is looking
   (*c*) seems   (*d*) sees

2. (*a*) though   (*b*) even
   (*c*) with   (*d*) as well

3. (*a*) between   (*b*) inside
   (*c*) with   (*d*) on

4. (*a*) look   (*b*) coinciding
   (*c*) coincide   (*d*) looking

5. (*a*) for   (*b*) and
   (*c*) with   (*d*) in

PASSAGE - 19

Gurgaon was also the site of an aggressive strike by (1) — of Honda Motorcycles and Scooters, which generated headlines because of the brutal (2) — it (3) — from the local administration. The footage of cops (4) — berserk after a brutal (5) — on their superiors led to turmoil in Parliament and angry protests from Left

1. (*a*) labourers   (*b*) crowd
   (*c*) people   (*d*) workers

2. (*a*) show   (*b*) reason
   (*c*) response   (*d*) look

3. (*a*) shown   (*b*) attracted
   (*c*) given   (*d*) publicized

4. (*a*) going   (*b*) getting
   (*c*) working   (*d*) looking

5. (*a*) kick   (*b*) word
   (*c*) assault   (*d*) death

PASSAGE - 20

Growth of the biotech sector in Asia – Pacific (1) — outpaced its performance in other parts of the world, with (2) — unprecedenting.46% increase in revenues.

Globally, the revenues of publicly-trading biotechnology companies (3) —- $60 billion for the first time

(4) — the sector's 30-year history, the Ernst & Young Global Biotech Report 2006 (5) —.

1. (*a*) region   (*b*) country
   (*c*) area   (*d*) part

2. (*a*) some   (*b*) a
   (*c*) an   (*d*) the

3. (*a*) recovered   (*b*) increased
   (*c*) surpassed   (*d*) decreased

4. (*a*) with   (*b*) in
   (*c*) for   (*d*) inside

5. (*a*) says   (*b*) heard
   (*c*) written   (*d*) said

ANSWERS

PASSAGE-1

1	2	3	4	5
(*b*)	(*d*)	(*a*)	(*a*)	(*c*)

PASSAGE-2

1	2	3	4	5
(*c*)	(*b*)	(*c*)	(*d*)	(*b*)

PASSAGE-3

1	2	3	4	5
(*d*)	(*a*)	(*b*)	(*a*)	(*c*)

PASSAGE-4

1	2	3	4	5
(*c*)	(*d*)	(*c*)	(*b*)	(*d*)

PASSAGE-5

1	2	3	4	5
(*c*)	(*a*)	(*d*)	(*b*)	(*c*)

PASSAGE-6

1	2	3	4	5
(*c*)	(*b*)	(*a*)	(*c*)	(*d*)

PASSAGE-7

1	2	3	4	5
(*c*)	(*d*)	(*b*)	(*d*)	(*c*)

PASSAGE-8

1	2	3	4	5
(*c*)	(*b*)	(*c*)	(*d*)	(*d*)

PASSAGE-9

1	2	3	4	5
(*d*)	(*a*)	(*c*)	(*b*)	(*a*)

PASSAGE-10

1	2	3	4	5
(*d*)	(*a*)	(*d*)	(*a*)	(*b*)

PASSAGE-11

1	2	3	4	5
(*b*)	(*c*)	(*b*)	(*c*)	(*a*)

PASSAGE-12

1	2	3	4	5
(*b*)	(*c*)	(*d*)	(*c*)	(*a*)

PASSAGE-13

1	2	3	4	5
(*b*)	(*a*)	(*c*)	(*b*)	(*c*)

PASSAGE-14

1	2	3	4	5
(*b*)	(*d*)	(*c*)	(*b*)	(*a*)

PASSAGE-15

1	2	3	4	5
(b)	(c)	(a)	(c)	(d)

PASSAGE-16

1	2	3	4	5
(d)	(c)	(d)	(d)	(b)

PASSAGE-17

1	2	3	4	5
(c)	(d)	(a)	(a)	(d)

PASSAGE-18

1	2	3	4	5
(c)	(b)	(a)	(b)	(c)

PASSAGE-19

1	2	3	4	5
(d)	(c)	(b)	(a)	(c)

PASSAGE-20

1	2	3	4	5
(a)	(c)	(c)	(b)	(d)

SENTENCE IMPROVEMENT

Directions: *In these questions, a part of the sentence is bold. Below are given alternatives to the bold part at (a), (b) and (c) which may improve the sentence. Choose the correct alternative. In case no improvement is needed, your answer is (d).*

1. For most people who exercise **at the** morning, there is no getting around the question: Eat and run? Or run and eat later?
   - (a) in the
   - (b) in
   - (c) at the time of
   - (d) No Improvement

2. Are ad agencies even attempting to peer into the keyhole of this indulgence sanctum to garner consumer insights **ahead of** the curve?
   - (a) above
   - (b) over
   - (c) within
   - (d) No Improvement

3. Too many people rush into the world of credit and don't stop to think about how **their actions could affect their** credit score and ability to qualify for credit in the future.
   - (a) their actions may affect their
   - (b) their actions might affect their
   - (c) their actions will affect their
   - (d) No Improvement

4. According to the report, **number of deal with** vaccines were energized by concerns around avian flu, SARS, and biodefense products, while looming patent expirations led to more deals in generics.
   - (a) number of deals in
   - (b) number of deal in
   - (c) number of deals with
   - (d) No Improvement

5. This is how the Bombay High Court responded to the state government's purported **moral stand which** dance bars were causing grave harm to society.

 (*a*) moral stand in
 (*b*) moral stand at
 (*c*) moral stand that
 (*d*) No Improvement

6. If you have a high credit limit, use **at least a** third of it.

 (*a*) atleast a
 (*b*) at last a
 (*c*) utmost a
 (*d*) No Improvement

7. Fitness experts will say that **first eating provides** fuel for a proper workout.

 (*a*) eating in the beginning provides
 (*b*) first eat provides
 (*c*) eating first provides
 (*d*) No Improvement

8. One study that examined the claim directly in 1995 found that a group of people did **burned much calories from fat on days** when they exercised on an empty stomach than on days when they had a small breakfast first.

 (*a*) burn more calories from fat on days
 (*b*) burn more calorie from fat on days
 (*c*) burnt more calories from fat on days
 (*d*) No Improvement

9. Carefree children spent their afternoons **to run about barefoot**, their clothes dusty, and telltale twigs of the neighbour's mango tree in their hair.

 (*a*) running barefoot in the sun
 (*b*) run about barefoot in the sun
 (*c*) running about barefoot in the sun
 (*d*) No Improvement

10. A year ago, a 13-year-old girl attempted suicide because her mother **refuses to pay his** mobile bills.

 (*a*) refuses to pay her
 (*b*) refused to pay her
 (*c*) refused to pay his
 (*d*) No Improvement

11. Discreet salience **is extremely important** to create that 'irresistible-yet-unattainable' image for brands that want to take India seriously

 (*a*) was extremely important
 (*b*) is mainly important
 (*c*) was important extremely
 (*d*) No Improvement

12. This, over a designer outfit that he wanted for a friend's party and **that his sensitive** parents refused him.

 (*a*) which his sensitive
 (*b*) which his insensitive
 (*c*) that his insensitive
 (*d*) No Improvement

13. Goa was full of non-Goa property hunters **rushing about buying up the place** like tomorrow was an expired lease.

(*a*) rushing in buying up the place

(*b*) rushed about buying up the place

(*c*) rushing about to buy up the place

(*d*) No Improvement

14. Property hunting is a **tired and hungry** making business.

(*a*) is a tiresome and hungry

(*b*) is a tiring and hungry

(*c*) is a tiring and waste

(*d*) No Improvement

15. Cultural differences aside, **till luxury need speaks** in a manner that befits.

(*a*) luxury still needs to speak

(*b*) luxury still need to speak

(*c*) luxury till need to speak

(*d*) No Improvement

16. Indian food – the culinary avatar of the subcontinent's social history presented on a platter – **is without doubt the best food** in the world.

(*a*) is undoubtly the greatest food

(*b*) is without doubt greatest food

(*c*) is best food without doubt

(*d*) No Improvement

17. It must retain the language of poetry. **It needed to create** stories, and not statements.

(*a*) It needed creating

(*b*) It needs creating

(*c*) It needs to create

(*d*) No Improvement

18. In 2005, Asia-Pacific has become the first region **to reach aggregate profiting** in biotech.

(*a*) to reach aggregated profitability

(*b*) to reach aggregate profitability

(*c*) to reach aggregate of profit

(*d*) No Improvement

19. India is deviating to embrace the West. If Western luxury brands deviate a little, **albeit selectively**, they will find rich Indian arms open far and wide.

(*a*) though selectively

(*b*) however selectively

(*c*) albeit selectedly

(*d*) No Improvement

20. China and India continued to attract attention and deals, motivated by the desire to increase access to these **largest and growing** drug markets and by the need to lower the costs of drug development.

(*a*) larger and growing

(*b*) large and growing

(*c*) larger and grown

(*d*) No Improvement

21. Luxury brands are **still above of the** clover curve here, with their elite (small) audiences.

(*a*) still ahead of the

(*b*) still in the

(*c*) still far of the

(*d*) No Improvement

22. Agencies **hence needed to be** sure of returns before investing, say ad men.

(a) hence needs to be
(b) so needs to be
(c) hence need to be
(d) No Improvement

23. India is still a nascent market and that's the spirit everyone's **looking at it**.
(a) looking for it
(b) looking in it
(c) looking with it
(d) No Improvement

24. Questioning the state's move to allow women to serve liquor but not dance in bars **of the ground that** dancing aroused physical lust
(a) on the grounds that
(b) of the grounds that
(c) over the grounds that
(d) No Improvement

25. For England the positives from their crushing series lose come in the shape of James Anderson and Kevin Pietersen, **both of which** have made significant strides up the rankings
(a) both of which
(b) both of whom
(c) both of who
(d) No Improvement

26. International campaigns can work well for luxury here, **but context cannot be** ignored.
(a) so context cannot be
(b) but context cannot
(c) but context couldn't
(d) No Improvement

27. For one, the Indian luxury context, **while evolved rapidly**, still has its own meaning, and its own implications.
(a) while evolved rapid
(b) which evolving rapidly
(c) while evolving rapidly
(d) No Improvement

28. But too much of availability can compromise a luxury brand or **made it lose** its lustre.
(a) make her lose
(b) make him lose
(c) make it lose
(d) No Improvement

29. Still, it's under-the-upper **layers themselves who** are aspiring for slivers of luxury
(a) layers themselves which
(b) layer itself who
(c) layers themself which
(d) No Improvement

30. It is like saying Hindi movies, with skimpily dressed dancers, would **effect public** order
(a) effect your
(b) affect public
(c) affected public
(d) No Improvement

31. The court held that a few women being involved in prostitution was no **justice to deny other** bar girls the right to livelihood
(a) justification to declare other
(b) justification to deny other
(c) justice to let other
(d) No Improvement

32. All-rounder Irfan Pathan has also made some progress **over the** player rankings.
(a) above the

(b) at the
(c) up the
(d) No Improvement

33. Former PM V.P. Singh on Sunday **joined hands** with suspended SP Lok Sabha member Raj Babbar to float a new political outfit.
(a) folded hands
(b) walked hand in hand
(c) shaked hands
(d) No Improvement

34. Pakistan's former PMs Benazir Bhutto and Nawaz Sharif will meet in London on Monday **to ask** a strategy to return home from exile.
(a) to chalk out
(b) to negotiate
(c) to create
(d) No Improvement

35. It's a family potboiler, medical thriller and political drama **all in one** – except that it's all too real and all too grim.
(a) all 3 in one
(b) all coupled into one
(c) all rolled into one
(d) No Improvement

36. India's efforts to get international support for its civil nuclear energy programme got **a go ahead on** Sunday as Germany indicated it would not come in the way of the India-US nuclear deal.
(a) a life in
(b) a boost on
(c) a boost at
(d) No Improvement

37. Is it time for old bungalows to **bite the dust**?
(a) go down
(b) get down
(c) come down
(d) No Improvement

38. The bungalows was an outward manifestation of a certain **way in life**, and with that era gone
(a) way for life
(b) way of life
(c) way at life
(d) No Improvement

39. The builder Mittals will reportedly **raise their money**-raking high-rise behind it.
(a) highten their money
(b) rise their money
(c) raise there money
(d) No Improvement

40. The impatient present has usually demolished **more of the** past before we wake up to the irretrievable loss.
(a) much of
(b) much of their
(c) much of the
(d) No Improvement

41. Preservation is a romantic notion; demolition **quiet** more practical reasons.
(a) has many,
(b) had many,
(c) have many,
(d) No Improvement

42. You must get back to your **charming self** and impress the audience with your social skills.

(*a*) own self
(*b*) main self
(*c*) own uniqueness
(*d*) No Improvement

43. Stay focused on your goals and don't **get disturbed by** non-materialistic possessions.
(*a*) get involved by
(*b*) get betrayed by
(*c*) get distracted by
(*d*) No Improvement

44. You may appear more optimistic than your detractors **may want it to be**.
(*a*) want you to be
(*b*) wish yourself to be
(*c*) seek you be
(*d*) No Improvement

45. There are a number of mineral springs in the Czech territory, which **has been used** for medicinal purposes since the early 15th century.
(*a*) have been used
(*b*) had been used
(*c*) has being used
(*d*) No Improvement

46. The picturesque mountains **offer**s excellent bungee jumping spots.
(*a*) shows
(*b*) provides
(*c*) offer
(*d*) No Improvement

47. Begin your **meal with** traditional faves like potato soup, beef soup with liver dumplings or dill soup made from sour milk.
(*a*) meals with

(*b*) meal in
(*c*) meals of
(*d*) No Improvement

48. You can also **go to the** National Museum building and the famous Prague State Opera.
(*a*) went to
(*b*) visit the
(*c*) saw
(*d*) No Improvement

49. If they close the Gulf for a **length of time** to shipping, then certainly we could look at $150, probably higher.
(*a*) larger amount of time
(*b*) larger duration of time
(*c*) larger amount of hours
(*d*) No Improvement

50. **More of them** are owned by the state and even the privately-owned ones are open to the public.
(*a*) Most of which
(*b*) Most of them
(*c*) Most of all
(*d*) No Improvement

51. Constructed in the ninth century by the Prince Booivoj, the castle has transformed **oneself** from a wooden fortress surrounded by earthen bulwarks to the imposing form it has today.
(*a*) himself
(*b*) herself
(*c*) itself
(*d*) No Improvement

52. Apart from frequent art exhibitions, **their are also** permanent collections devoted

to archaeology, anthropology, mineralogy, natural history and numismatics.
(*a*) there is also
(*b*) there are also
(*c*) their are also
(*d*) No Improvement

53. You can visit the Czech Museum of Fine Arts, **at a** permanent exhibition on Czech Kubism.
(*a*) with a
(*b*) for a
(*c*) in a
(*d*) No Improvement

54. Tensions **above** Iran come at a time of strong demand for energy.
(*a*) under
(*b*) inside
(*c*) over
(*d*) No Improvement

55. Because its shores line the narrow Straits of Hormuz, Iran **could quickly hit** both military and commercial shipping
(*a*) will quickly hit
(*b*) shall quickly hit
(*c*) will be quick hitting
(*d*) No Improvement

56. US **can launch** strikes at uranium enrichment facilities in Iran.
(*a*) might launch
(*b*) could launch
(*c*) might launched
(*d*) No Improvement

57. Trust your instincts and **see** all hurdles.
(*a*) get freedom from
(*b*) visualize

(*c*) overcome
(*d*) No Improvement

58. You may lose the war, but with clam, poise and serenity you will win the big battle **that may be following**.
(*a*) that may follows
(*b*) that may follow
(*c*) that might be following
(*d*) No Improvement

59. **There is times** when your best efforts could prove fruitless because of wrong timing.
(*a*) There are time
(*b*) There are times
(*c*) There is time
(*d*) No Improvement

60. You'll be a little more romantic and may want to **go away** from the hustle-bustle around you.
(*a*) get away
(*b*) have get away
(*c*) got away
(*d*) No Improvement

61. All you want are a few more hugs of affection, which will not be too difficult **to come**.
(*a*) to come by
(*b*) to came
(*c*) to come in
(*d*) No Improvement

62. People **around you** could get too sensitive, but try to respect them for that perhaps it will help you during pay-back time.
(*a*) by you
(*b*) about you
(*c*) near you
(*d*) No Improvement

63. Success **is a made up of** good fortune and hard work.
(*a*) is
(*b*) is a
(*c*) is a blend of
(*d*) No Improvement

64. The flower style and placement can completely change **the feel of** a room.
(*a*) the feeling of
(*b*) the feeling for
(*c*) an feel of
(*d*) No Improvement

65. The material (of artificial flower), style of arrangement and location should **complementing each other**.
(*a*) complement one another
(*b*) complement each other
(*c*) complement other
(*d*) No Improvement

66. Houses with **more of** carvings in their interiors, can go for gerberas.
(*a*) many
(*b*) lots of
(*c*) lot of
(*d*) No Improvement

67. For an artistic look, have lots of cherry blossoms **put together** in a vase.
(*a*) together
(*b*) jumbled together
(*c*) made together
(*d*) No Improvement

68. If you **have heavy carving** furniture, go for an arrangement in a container with an antique touch.

(*a*) have heavy carved
(*b*) had heavy carved
(*c*) had heavy carving
(*d*) No Improvement

69. For a traditional party, such as Diwali or Holi, traditional marigold and jasmine are **a best option**.
(*a*) the better option
(*b*) the best option
(*c*) the best options
(*d*) No Improvement

70. Don't expose to direct sun or keep them **under fan and near an AC**.
(*a*) under fan or near an AC
(*b*) beside fan or near an AC
(*c*) under fan or under an AC
(*d*) No Improvement

71. Use of disprin and aspirin **help the** buds to bloom faster.
(*a*) helped the
(*b*) helps in the
(*c*) helps the
(*d*) No Improvement

72. If you prefer the lived-in comfy look, clear glass flower vases **make for** cheerful addition.
(*a*) makes for
(*b*) make for a
(*c*) makes for a
(*d*) No Improvement

73. Cut the stem of the flower every other day. This helps it to consume water and last for a **longer duration of time**.
(*a*) longer span of time
(*b*) longer period of time
(*c*) larger period of time
(*d*) No Improvement

74. The ability to trust others, and understand the needs of others, is **directly relates** to touching.
(*a*) directly relating
(*b*) directly related
(*c*) direct relation
(*d*) No Improvement

75. Touch and positive attitudes **has been proven** to go together.
(*a*) have been proven
(*b*) have been proved
(*c*) have been prove
(*d*) No Improvement

76. New Delhi **was watching the** political thriller unfold in the hilly kingdom with apparent nervousness.
(*a*) was watching the
(*b*) is watching the
(*c*) was watching a
(*d*) No Improvement

77. Anti-monarch agitators cheer **on top of a** bus in Kathmandu on Tuesday.
(*a*) above a
(*b*) at the top of a
(*c*) above the
(*d*) No Improvement

78. Indian Railway Catering and Tourism Corporation an autonomous body under the railways ministry, **has drawing up** a plan to open 2000 such stalls which would serve standard" food.
(*a*) has drawed up
(*b*) have drawn up
(*c*) has drawn up
(*d*) No Improvement

79. The stalls are **to come** up at ''A'' and ''B'' grade station.
(*a*) likely to be coming
(*b*) likely to come
(*c*) like to come
(*d*) No Improvement

80. To avoid controversies, IRCTC also **plans to continue** samosa-chai stalls which currently dot stations.
(*a*) plan to continue
(*b*) plan's to continue
(*c*) plan to continuing
(*d*) No Improvement

81. Airbus has been quietly pitching the standing-room only option to Asian carriers, though **none had agreed** to it yet
(*a*) none have been agreed
(*b*) none have being agreed
(*c*) none have agreed
(*d*) No Improvement

82. High fuel costs, for example, are **making it difficult for** carriers to turn a profit.
(*a*) making difficult for
(*b*) making difficulty for
(*c*) making it as difficult as
(*d*) No Improvement

83. The new seat technology alone, **when used in** add more places for passengers, can add millions in additional annual revenue.
(*a*) used to
(*b*) when used to
(*c*) when using to
(*d*) No Improvement

84. While you may never win the lottery, **able to** get cash for paper assets is a sure bet.
  (*a*) being able to
  (*b*) getting able to
  (*c*) in being able to
  (*d*) No Improvement

85. At Chattarpur Enclave, **the first thing** that hits you is a massive under construction illegal building where work has been stopped.
  (*a*) a first thing
  (*b*) one of the first thing
  (*c*) the first best thing
  (*d*) No Improvement

86. Multi-storeyed housing units would be constructed through public private partnership **at the land** occupied by slum-dwellers.
  (*a*) in the land
  (*b*) on the land
  (*c*) over the land
  (*d*) No Improvement

87. In view of the **few availability of** land, the ministry has decided to take up rehabilitation work on a self sustaining basis.
  (*a*) little availability of
  (*b*) some availability of
  (*c*) scarce availability of
  (*d*) No Improvement

88. A new notification by the urban development ministry now **makes land available to school** only through auction.
  (*a*) makes land available to schools
  (*b*) making land available to schools
  (*c*) making land available to school
  (*d*) No Improvement

89. One of the first **lesson that a** young MNC manager learns is that "God is in the details."
  (*a*) lesson which a
  (*b*) lessons that a
  (*c*) lessons which a
  (*d*) No Improvement

90. Likewise, investors are more interested in crunching numbers than **they are for** fielding calls from potential sellers.
  (*a*) they are in
  (*b*) they are at
  (*c*) they are in favour of
  (*d*) No Improvement

91. With each passing day your memories **grow deep**, your loving nature will always be cherished.
  (*a*) grew deep
  (*b*) grew deeper
  (*c*) grow deeper
  (*d*) No Improvement

92. It may not beat winning the lottery, **but money** you can take to the bank.
  (*a*) but it's money
  (*b*) so it's money
  (*c*) but it's money that
  (*d*) No Improvement

93. Wisdom, Vision, Ideals & Thought **continue to guide** us every moment in our Journey ahead.

(*a*) continue to guiding
(*b*) continuosly guide
(*c*) continuing at guiding
(*d*) No Improvement

94. Delhi government **are now blaming** DDA for stalling big infrastructure projects in the Capital.
(*a*) is now putting blaming on
(*b*) is now blaming
(*c*) is now blaming the
(*d*) No Improvement

95. Be happy with the status quo and **preserve it by** conciliating others.
(*a*) preserve that by
(*b*) it is preserved
(*c*) preserving it by
(*d*) No Improvement

96. Have graceful movements, liquid eyes, and a gliding walk, **although** overweight.
(*a*) though
(*b*) even if
(*c*) even
(*d*) No Improvement

97. But people resent that most of the poverty funds **are lost for** corruption and administrative expenses.
(*a*) are lost in
(*b*) are lost at
(*c*) is lost in
(*d*) No Improvement

98. It is **very difficult** to store and save almost everything- money, possessions, energy words food, fat.

(*a*) most difficult
(*b*) very much difficult
(*c*) highly difficult
(*d*) No Improvement

99. Now Pause Live TV & watch **with your convenience** & also Record your favorite TV program.
(*a*) at your convenient
(*b*) your convenience
(*c*) at your convenience
(*d*) No Improvement

100. To avoid **last hour rushing**, please immediately deposit VAT and file your Monthly and Quarterly DVAT return.
(*a*) last rush
(*b*) last minute rush
(*c*) last minute rushing
(*d*) No Improvement

101. The voters will respect them and **might even** vote for them.
(*a*) would even
(*b*) should even
(*c*) will even
(*d*) No Improvement

102. All along the 27-km-long Ring Road that surrounds Kathmandu, agitators were **seen walking towards to** Ratna Park in huge numbers.
(*a*) seen walk towards
(*b*) seen walking towards
(*c*) seeing walking towards
(*d*) No Improvement

103. This marks the first time an integrated 32-page full-colour paper is being produced in India.

(*a*) has been
(*b*) was being
(*c*) is being
(*d*) No Improvement

104. Thus, the only alternative **to live in** darkness is to have private power.
(*a*) to living in
(*b*) for living in
(*c*) with living in
(*d*) No Improvement

105. The problem with private power is that our state electricity boards are bankrupt, and no sensible supplier **will buy** electricity to a bankrupt customer.
(*a*) would have bought
(*b*) will sell
(*c*) may buy
(*d*) No Improvement

106. India has rejected any notion of sanctions or **use of a force** against Iran.
(*a*) use of force
(*b*) use of the force
(*c*) use of a forces
(*d*) No Improvement

107. One of the **most compelling** is the seller-financed mortgage.
(*a*) compellest
(*b*) highest compelling
(*c*) largest compelling
(*d*) No Improvement

108. Almost of our politicians and businessmen suffer from this disability.
(*a*) Most of
(*b*) Almost all of

(*c*) Mostly all
(*d*) No Improvement

109. However, putting up a power plant **costs a money**.
(*a*) costs the money
(*b*) costs money
(*c*) are costing money
(*d*) No Improvement

110. You might not be able to buy that dream home, quit your job, or sail around the world - **if you knew** someone
(*a*) if you know
(*b*) unless you know
(*c*) unless you knew
(*d*) No Improvement

111. This is a **laudable objective** and few will contest it.
(*a*) laud objective
(*b*) laudable objectives
(*c*) laud objectives
(*d*) No Improvement

112. Everyone knows that our government **don't have** money. But the global private sector does.
(*a*) do not have
(*b*) doesn't have
(*c*) doesn't has
(*d*) No Improvement

113. It is not **much to have** a broad strategy; success depends on penetrating the details of an issue.
(*a*) more to have
(*b*) enough of having
(*c*) enough to have
(*d*) No Improvement

114. One has to be mentally tough **in choosing the** unpalatable alternatives.
(*a*) in choosing between
(*b*) in choosing a
(*c*) in choosing
(*d*) No Improvement

115. While the odds of winning the lottery are a long shot, virtually everyone has spent **at most a** few minutes daydreaming about how they would spend their newfound riches.
(*a*) at last a
(*b*) at least a
(*c*) at least some
(*d*) No Improvement

116. In fact, there **are over four dozen** different types of notes that interest investors.
(*a*) is over four dozen
(*b*) is above four dozen
(*c*) are four dozen more
(*d*) No Improvement

117. We're always **on the look** for people who want to sell notes
(*a*) on the lookin
(*b*) on the looks
(*c*) on the lookout
(*d*) No Improvement

118. If you are just **starting out on** building your credit, you want to be smart about building good credit from the beginning.
(*a*) starting in on
(*b*) started out on
(*c*) starting out in
(*d*) No Improvement

119. You will establish a good payment history **very fastly** this way.
(*a*) very quickly
(*b*) quickly enough
(*c*) fastly enough
(*d*) No Improvement

120. This late payment **will shown up** on your credit report and lower your credit score.
(*a*) will show
(*b*) will showed up
(*c*) will show up
(*d*) No Improvement

ANSWERS

1	2	3	4	5	6	7	8	9	10
(*a*)	(*d*)	(*c*)	(*a*)	(*c*)	(*d*)	(*c*)	(*a*)	(*c*)	(*c*)
11	12	13	14	15	16	17	18	19	20
(*d*)	(*c*)	(*d*)	(*b*)	(*a*)	(*d*)	(*c*)	(*c*)	(*d*)	(*b*)
21	22	23	24	25	26	27	28	29	30
(*c*)	(*c*)	(*d*)	(*a*)	(*c*)	(*d*)	(*c*)	(*c*)	(*c*)	(*c*)
31	32	33	34	35	36	37	38	39	40
(*b*)	(*c*)	(*c*)	(*a*)	(*c*)	(*b*)	(*d*)	(*b*)	(*d*)	(*c*)
41	42	43	44	45	46	47	48	49	50
(*a*)	(*d*)	(*c*)	(*a*)	(*d*)	(*c*)	(*a*)	(*b*)	(*d*)	(*b*)

51	52	53	54	55	56	57	58	59	60
(c)	(b)	(a)	(c)	(d)	(a)	(c)	(b)	(b)	(a)
61	62	63	64	65	66	67	68	69	70
(a)	(c)	(c)	(d)	(b)	(b)	(d)	(a)	(b)	(a)
71	72	73	74	75	76	77	78	79	80
(c)	(d)	(b)	(b)	(a)	(a)	(d)	(c)	(b)	(c)
81	82	83	84	85	86	87	88	89	90
(c)	(d)	(b)	(a)	(d)	(b)	(c)	(a)	(b)	(a)
91	92	93	94	95	96	97	98	99	100
(c)	(a)	(a)	(b)	(d)	(b)	(a)	(d)	(c)	(b)
101	102	103	104	105	106	107	108	109	110
(d)	(b)	(c)	(a)	(b)	(a)	(d)	(a)	(b)	(c)
111	112	113	114	115	116	117	118	119	120
(d)	(b)	(c)	(a)	(b)	(d)	(c)	(d)	(a)	(c)

JUMBLED SENTENCES

Directions: *In these questions, the first and the last sentences of the passage are numbered (1) and (6). The rest of the passage is split into four parts and named P, Q, R and S. These four parts are not given in their proper order. Read the sentence and findout which of the four combinations is correct. Then choose the correct answer.*

1. This double helping of European culture, mixed with heady African influences, give the island a charm which helped to attract the jet set here in the 1970s, along with its beautiful white-sand beaches, stunning landscape and Caribbean climate.

   (P) All in all, the island was a perfect getaway for celebrities and movie stars fleeing the spotlight.

   (Q) After a few hours or days here, a water taxi takes them to St. Bart's.

   (R) Though many VIPs have now moved on to neighbouring St. Bart's.

   (S) They still arrive at St. Maarten's Princess Juliana Airport, however, because their private jets cannot land on the other island.

   (a) PQRS   (b) PQSR
   (c) PRQS   (d) PRSQ

2. Among those evacuated last week were relatives of two American aid workers on trial here, accused of preaching Christianity.

(P) After traveling 10,000 miles to a country where few dare to venture, the parents had to leave their daughters behind to an uncertain fate.

(Q) Waiting to board a U.N. plane for Islamabad, Pakistan, Deborah Oddy, mother of Heather Mercer, 24, wore a black headscarf and sobbed uncontrollably.

(R) Since the Soviet invasion in 1979, this country has seen more than its share of tears.

(S) Now the frightened residents of Kabul are worried that this latest incident will bring on even more.

(a) PQRS   (b) PQSR
(c) QRPS   (d) PRQS

3. Feroz Khan was the original hot-blooded filmi hero, the dapper bad boy whom women loved to hate.

(P) His behaviour at Taj Mahal's premiere in Pakistan, where he made anti-Pak statements and shouted at an anchor caps a long and illustrious career.

(Q) Cowboy shoes and bandanas, brawls and a foot forever in his mouth, you can love him or hate him, but there's no way you can ignore him.

(R) At a time when his class-mates would come to school in staidly conventional cars and buses, Khan's on a whim, would come riding on horseback.

(S) Khan's fascination with steeds dates back to his school days.

(a) QPSR   (b) PQSR
(c) QPRS   (d) PSQR

4. During his heyday, Khan's parties in Juhu could be heard miles away.

(P) Not only were they lustily loud, apparently more abuses, and often scuffles were exchanged in one evening of festivity than gifts.

(Q) During one of Fardeen's baby showers, Feroz decided to have him dipped him in champagne

(R) Once, he vented his frustration by hoisting the camera into the sea.

(S) Often, he got so frustrated because he just couldn't get a shot right.

(a) PQSR   (b) QPSR
(c) PQRS   (d) PSRQ

5. The situation between actress Priyanka Chopra and her secretary Prakash Jaju has worsened.

(P) Now, Jaju is threatening to get a stay on all her films till he gets his dues from her.

(Q) If Rakeshji had not signed her or would have told her to first clear my dues, I would have got my money long back.

(R) So, when she saw that even after holding onto all my money, she could still get a film like Krrish, she obviously didn't feel the need to return it at all.

(S) According to Jaju he'd also had a word with Rakesh Roshan about this.

(*a*) PRQS   (*b*) PSRQ
(*c*) PQSR   (*d*) PSQR

6. An electric rice cooker, a standard appliance in kitchens around the world.

((P) An electric rice cooker can be purchased at various retail stores.

(Q) It is typically used for the preparation of plain or lightly seasoned rice

(R) In Asian countries, it is a self-contained electrical appliance with small to large capacity where rice and liquid are placed in a container to cook rice.

(S) But more elaborate recipes are possible using an electric rice cooker.

(*a*) RPSQ   (*b*) RPQS
(*c*) RQPS   (*d*) PSRQ

7. Back in December of 2005, Survey USA tracked views on immigration in all 50 states.

((P) In Alabama, 56 per cent agreed, Arkansas 53 per cent, Mississippi 53 per cent, South Carolina 53 per cent.

(Q) Meanwhile, only 33 per cent in New Mexico agreed that immigrants take away American jobs. In Arizona it was 42 per cent, Colorado 44 per cent, Nevada 44 per cent and California 30 percent.

(R) In West Virginia, 60 per cent of respondents agreed, "immigrants take jobs away from Americans."

(S) The picture was the same throughout most of the South.

(*a*) RPSQ   (*b*) RSPQ
(*c*) RQPS   (*d*) PSRQ

8. Ahmed Khalil was shot at point-blank range after being accosted by men in police uniforms, according to his neighbours in the al-Dura area of Baghdad.

(P) Ali Hili, the co-ordinator of a group of exiled Iraqi gay men who monitor homophobic attacks inside Iraq, said the fatwa had instigated a "witch-hunt of lesbian and gay Iraqis.

(Q) "He was summarily executed, apparently by fundamentalist elements in the Iraqi police."

(R) "Young Ahmed was a victim of poverty," he said.

(S) This included violent beatings, kidnappings and assassinations.

(*a*) RPSQ   (*b*) RSPQ
(*c*) RQPS   (*d*) PSRQ

9. It's still the Easter season. Catholics have fifty days to ponder the great mystery at the heart of our faith - ten more than the more famous forty days of Lent.

   (P) The new documentary, "Saint of 9/11", is a revelation primarily because it fills in the rest of Judge's astonishing life of service: to the poor and homeless, the victims of terrorism and of AIDS, the warring Irish and the courageous fire-fighters of New York City.

   (Q) And the life and work of Mychal Judge, brought before us primarily because of the sacrifice of his death, is a new chapter in the Easter miracle.

   (R) And the core of that mystery is how such great life can come out of such terrible death.

   (S) This mystery is, indeed, as Jesuit priest Christopher Devron explains here, inexhaustible.

   (*a*) RPQS   (*b*) RSQP
   (*c*) PQRS   (*d*) PSRQ

10. Don't think that those who say that the war was "about oil," literally think that we decided to invade Iraq in order to secure supplies and lower the price of crude.

   (P) I think most people look at the regime in Iraq and have a hard time distinguishing it from others around the world. Libya, Sudan, North Korea, Syria - all dictatorships, all enemies of the United States, all suspected of WMD's, all with potential connections to Al Qaeda - yet we pick Iraq?

   (Q) So in this sense, we did not go to war in Iraq in an attempt to get cheap oil right off the bat.

   (R) No one expected that the full invasion of an oil rich country in the heart of the Arab world was going to causes prices to drop, at least not right away.

   (S) But are you arguing that oil played no part in our decision to go to war?

   (*a*) RPQS   (*b*) QSPR
   (*c*) RQSP   (*d*) PRSQ

11. Now that the CPM led Left front in Kerala has received a massive mandate to rule the State for the next five years, they should reflect on the long term future of Kerala.

   (P) The Congress party has to blame none except itself for its ignominious defeat at the polls.

   (Q) The internecine quarrels in the party, clubbed with its alliance with DIC (K) has irretrievably damaged the party's reputation in the state.

(R) The LDF in the past has been experimenting with an economic model that is led by the state and the public sector.

(S) This has led to the all round decline of Kerala.

(*a*) PQSR   (*b*) SPQR

(*c*) RPQS   (*d*) PQRS

12. If we went to war to "transform the middle east" then we went to war over oil.

(P) The only importance the Middle East ever had, and will ever have, as far as the U.S. is concerned, are its massive oil reserves.

(Q) We're trying to bring democracy to the region because we believe democracy equals stability, and stability equals cheap and free flowing supplies of oil.

(R) You don't hear neocons talking about transforming Africa or intervening militarily to oust dictators in nations with no vital natural resources.

(S) However, you hear endless talk about transforming the Middle East.

(*a*) PRSQ   (*b*) RSPQ

(*c*) SQRP   (*d*) PSQR

13. The dreaded neocons supported intervention in Bosnia and Somalia, and I see no oil there.

(P) Many neocons support intervening in Darfur. Ditto. Of course, some weight must be given to a region with so much leverage over the essential substance for the world economy.

(Q) But before 9/11, we have no evidence that Bush was seriously planning on war against Saddam.

(R) Al Gore was more vocally anti-Saddam than Bush was, and favoured more defense spending.

(S) I stick to my point. This was about national security. Oil is a part of that, but it was never the primary mover behind the Iraq war.

(*a*) RPQS   (*b*) RSQP

(*c*) PQRS   (*d*) PSRQ

14. "On television, Colbert is often funny. But on his own show he appeals to a self-selected audience that reminds him often of his greatness.

(P) He had a chance to tell the president and much of important (and self-important) Washington things it would have been good for them to hear.

(Q) In this sense, he was a man for our times. He also wasn't funny," - Richard Cohen, alienating many liberal readers, Washington Post today.

(R) In Washington he was playing to a different crowd, and he failed dismally in the funny person's most solemn obligation: to use absurdity or contrast or hyperbole to elucidate — to make people see things a little bit differently.

(S) But he was, like much of the blogosphere itself, telling like-minded people what they already know and alienating all the others.

   (*a*) RPSQ   (*b*) RSPQ
   (*c*) RQPS   (*d*) PSRQ

15. It's alleged that Hitchens has a drinking problem.

(P) I'm a journalist, and I just spent a week laboring over a relatively straightforward 1,200-word essay (on wine, coincidentally.)

(Q) If so, perhaps you'd be kind enough to pass on specifics regarding his daily intake, so I can emulate.

(R) But I'm obviously not drinking the right stuff.

(S) Though I don't always agree with him, I have nothing but admiration for someone who can knock out a weekly Slate column, an erudite review for the Atlantic each month, a longer, bimonthly piece for Vanity Fair and a book a year.

   (*a*) RPQS   (*b*) QSPR
   (*c*) RQSP   (*d*) PRSQ

16. Consider immigration reform.

(P) The Senate compromise bill that flickered to life last month and then just as suddenly died is the kind of measure that ought to be easily revived.

(Q) After balking at the idea a few weeks ago, even Democratic Leader Harry Reid has come around

(R) He hinted that he might now consider amendments to the measure.

(S) It appeared to have more than 60 votes during its brief half-life.

   (*a*) PRSQ   (*b*) RSPQ
   (*c*) SQRP   (*d*) PSQR

17. Still, that doesn't mean it will happen. A lot has been written in the last 48 hours about how Monday's rallies won't force

(P) Washington's hand.

(Q) This week's rallies could moderate that view with some Democrats, but the logic of waiting could — and almost certainly will — be applied to every elective piece of legislation Congress will consider this year.

(R) House version of the immigration bill after the fall elections. Even if the Democrats don't take back the House, they argue, the party will have picked up more seats in the chamber that produced the restrictive bill, so why act now?

(S) I'm not sure that's right, but I am certain that going into the weekend, Democratic party leaders had begun to say in private that they will have more leverage to alter the more conservative

(*a*) RPSQ (*b*) RSPQ
(*c*) RQPS (*d*) PSRQ

18. If you like watching a car rust, you'll love entitlement reform.

(P) But many people reacted to it differently.

(Q) This is because they teamed up just a few years ago to add a largely unfunded drug benefit to the program.

(R) Even the news this week that the Medicare program will go broke in 2018 — two years sooner than expected — was barely worth a blip in the papers.

(S) Of course, it's a little awkward for Congress and the White House to react too dramatically to this news.

(*a*) RPQS (*b*) RSQP
(*c*) PQRS (*d*) PSRQ

19. Still, when it comes to fiscal matters, Washington operates according to what one former Clinton official recently called "just-in-time politics."

(P) This approach has worked well enough in the past to see us through; it may not serve our interests in world powered by a fast-changing, far more competitive, globalized economy.

(Q) But a deeply divided Washington, which has not enacted a major reform of any government program in a decade, is gradually losing the knowledge and experience of how to forge compromises that make big reforms possible.

(R) That means the lawmakers will get around to making a fix only in the nick of time.

(S) Which means that when a crisis — be it fiscal, demographic or constitutional — finally descends on us, we will be drawing on weak muscles and a thin skill set to address the problem.

(*a*) RPQS (*b*) QSPR
(*c*) RQSP (*d*) PRSQ

20. Finally, if you've been wondering what happened to that effort by moderate Republicans this spring to find a middle ground between the Bush officials who secretly created an extra-legal wiretapping operation after 9/11 and Democrats who were so angry about it, wonder no more.

(P) Which means nothing is really happening. And since neither party — including Democrats — will take the political risk of cutting off a program designed to catch terrorists, it continues unregulated.

(Q) Pennsylvania Sen. Arlen Specter's plan to ask a

special panel of judges to review the law isn't going anywhere.

(R) And Ohio Sen. Mike DeWine's proposal to create a special subcommittee to review the Administration's work in this super-secret area every 45 days isn't selling well either.

(S) A hearing of the Senate Judiciary Committee last week made it pretty clear that none of the various compromise proposals have sufficient votes to pass, even out of the committee.

   (*a*) PRSQ   (*b*) RSPQ
   (*c*) SQRP   (*d*) PSQR

21. If former World Bank chief James Wolfensohn's appointment by the international community to help lay the economic foundations of Palestinian statehood was an expression of optimism in the prospects for peace following Israel's withdrawal from Gaza last year, then his resignation last Sunday should sound an alarm.

(P) He said the current U.S.-Israeli financial blockade of the Hamas-led Palestinian Authority looks set to destroy the administrative institutions on which a two-state solution would be based.

(Q) Moreover, he suggested, it is sure to plunge Palestinian society deeper into the vortex of poverty.

(R) Trained as a banker rather than a diplomat, former World Bank chief Wolfensohn didn't mince words about his reasons for stepping down.

(S) This would make it more fertile ground for just the brand of Islamist extremism that the U.S. is trying to defeat.

   (*a*) RPQS   (*b*) QSPR
   (*c*) RQSP   (*d*) PRSQ

22. The new Israeli government seated on Thursday has made clear that it plans to redraw the borders between Israel and the Palestinians on its own terms.

(P) But Wolfensohn is warning that the current siege of the West Bank and Gaza makes it increasingly unlikely that what will emerge on the Palestinian side of Israel's new border wall will be a viable state at all.

(Q) Once the U.S. and European Union forbade him from working with the new Hamas-led Palestinian government, Wolfensohn's job became untenable.

(R) Israeli papers report that Wolfensohn's decision also came in response to the U.S. — at the behest of Israeli officials — blocking a plan by Britain, the E.U. and the

Arab League to have salaries of PA employees paid directly into their bank accounts, bypassing the Hamas administration.

(S) U.S. Treasury officials have warned that any banks processing such transactions would face sanctions from Washington, and none dared risk being shut out of the international finance system.

(*a*) RPSQ   (*b*) RSPQ
(*c*) PQRS   (*d*) PSRQ

23. The problem is that Abbas, and his party, Fatah, may fare even more poorly in an election called under such circumstances than that brought Hamas to power.

(P) And if Hamas is returned for a second time, the stalemate would simply deepen.

(Q) But that would not only make a mockery of the Bush administration's stated commitment to democracy in the Arab world.

(R) It would likely set off a Palestinian civil war that would have negative implications for Israel as well as other U.S. interests and allies throughout the region.

(S) The alternative might be to back Abbas seizing control over all the levers of government without new elections.

(*a*) PRSQ   (*b*) RSPQ
(*c*) SQRP   (*d*) PSQR

24. I asked a bunch of people if these were the 100 people who were most important in their lives this year—and not one of them said yes.

(P) I don't know what kind of research Time's editors are doing, but may be they should get out of the building more.

(Q) Especially during the hours they have to edit me.

(R) But no matter how many times I suggest we focus the Time 100 on the people who actually affect us—the buyer at Wal-Mart, the office IT person, the two guys who sing the Applebee's Shrimp Sensations song—no one listens to me.

(S) And if there's one thing the past few years have taught me, it's that when something needs to be altered, the best thing to do is tear it down and replace it with a shoddily built alternative.

(*a*) RPQS   (*b*) RSQP
(*c*) PQRS   (*d*) PSRQ

25. The first thing I noticed when putting together the Joel 100™ was the same thing you noticed when riffling through this issue: namely, that 100 is way too many. I don't know how I found 130 for my wedding.

(P) Only one of the Time 100 has anything to do with food, and none of them directly involve anything else.

(Q) By No. 65 on my list, I was thinking about how much my wife's waxer means to me.

(R) O.K., by 35. I also noticed some very significant differences between the Time 100 and the Joel 100™.

(a) RPQS   (b) QSPR
(c) RQSP   (d) PRSQ

26. I decided to steal from my favourite part of the Time 100, where someone like Tom Cruise writes about director J.J. Abrams.

(P) So I got people who mean an awful lot to me to write about other people who mean an awful lot to me.

(Q) When I asked my wife Cassandra to write about my mother, for instance, she said, "Oh, God."

(R) As with the Time 100, the people approached to do this writing universally considered it a great honor and were very excited.

(S) I felt slightly bad about doing this—not because it's hokey and emotionally manipulative but because I'm probably accidentally stealing Mitch Albom's next book.

(a) RPSQ   (b) RSPQ
(c) RQPS   (d) PSRQ

27. One of the four people with the distinction of making the Time 100 and the Joel 100™ was George W. Bush.

(P) The President made the Joel 100™ because he lowered my taxes, just like Scott Jeffers, my accountant, who also made the list.

(Q) Gorker did the Bush entry in three sentences. If the Time art department had its way, he would be the magazine's main political writer.

(R) Luckily, I remembered that my friend Mike Gorker from high school is now a G.O.P. member.

(S) The problem was, being a Jew who works in the media and lives in Los Angeles, I didn't know any Republicans to write the Bush entry.

(a) RPQS   (b) RSQP
(c) PQRS   (d) PSRQ

28. Recognizing the need to provide a smooth transition for users of the Microsoft® Java Virtual Machine (MSJVM), Sun Microsystems and Microsoft have agreed to extend Microsoft's license to use Sun's Java source code and compatibility test suites.

(P) This extension allows Microsoft to support the MSJVM until December 31,

2007, providing customers with the ability to transition from the MSJVM on a schedule and plan that is most effective for them.

(Q) The MSJVM will reach its end of life on December 31, 2007.

(R) Customers are encouraged to take proactive measures to stay informed about obsolete software and move away from the MSJVM in a timely fashion.

(S) The MSJVM is no longer available for distribution from Microsoft and there will be no enhancements to the MSJVM.

(a) PRSQ   (b) RSPQ
(c) SQRP   (d) PQRS

29. The CBI today conducted simultaneous raids at 24 places across six states and union territories against former Haryana Chief Minister Om Prakash Chautala for allegedly amassing property worth over Rs 1400 crore.

(P) The list of properties allegedly belonging to Chautala or his family members including three plots in Gurgaon Phase V worth Rs 150 crore, a hotel and a restaurant in upmarket

(Q) The raids were carried out after the CBI registered a case against Chautala, his family members and other 'unknown persons' accusing him of amassing assets disproportionate to his known sources of income during the period from July 1999 to March 2005, official sources said.

(R) Karol Bagh worth Rs 150 crore, a shopping mall in Karol Bagh worth Rs 180 crore, a plot on Ring Road worth Rs 120 crore and a plot again in Karol Bagh worth Rs 55 crore, the CBI's FIR alleged.

(S) The searches were conducted at Sirsa, Dabwali, Tejakhera (Haryana), Bhunter (H(P), Udham Singh Nagar (Uttaranchal), Gurgaon (Haryana), Jaipur, Chandigarh and Delhi.

(a) RPQS   (b) QSPR
(c) RQSP   (d) PRSQ

30. During the searches, the CBI also recovered arms licences for 17 weapons from a farmhouse in Mehrauli and the agency would verify them before registering yet another case under the arms act against the Chautalas, CBI sources said.

(P) The former Haryana Chief Minister had in the past maintained that whatever properties he and his sons owned had been disclosed in their income tax returns.

(Q) He had said whatever properties CBI finds as their's during the raids, it could keep them with it.

(R) Mr Chautala and his son Ajay Chautala are at present in the United States and the latter is likely to return home shortly in the wake today's CBI raids.

(S) The CBI had stumbled upon the various assets allegedly belonging to Chautalas during the searches conducted by the investigating agency on April 7, 2005.

(a) RPQS   (b) QSPR
(c) RQSP   (d) PRSQ

31. The CBI had then informed the Haryana Government for necessary action since it did not have jurisdiction to act on this information suo-moto.

(P) Certain other immovable assets have also been unearthed during the searches," he said adding "the phenomenal extent of properties seemingly accumulated by the accused persons would require extensive and in-depth investigations by CBI."

(Q) "The locations selected for searches today were intended mainly to collect evidence.

(R) "During the searches, CBI has found evidence of possession of extensive movable assets and also documents regarding immovable assets.

(S) Subsequently, a disproportionate assets case was registered on April 3, 2006 after a notification was issued by the Centre.

(a) PRSQ   (b) RSPQ
(c) SQRP   (d) PSQR

32. Delhi Police Sub-Inspector Pranav Kumar is basking in the spotlight. And loving every minute of it.

(P) Kumar has passed the Union Public Service Commission's national examination, which sees the nation's best and brightest compete for a place in the elite civil services.

(Q) You have managed your time excellently. You can be a source of inspiration for your colleagues."

(R) The 31-year-old Kumar is answering journalists' questions with a smile, and accepting Delhi Police Commissioner Dr. K.K. Paul's glowing words: "Well done. You have done an exceptional job.

(S) And he has done so while carrying out his duties as a police officer.

(a) RPSQ   (b) RSPQ
(c) RQPS   (d) PSRQ

33. Motor vehicle tax or 'road tax' is collected from buyers directly by the manufacturers or dealers.

(P) It is a vast sum of money — for an upper-end private car, it can run into a lakh. Collected on 'life basis,' the tax is for 10 years or a 'fitness' period of 15 years.

(Q) After that the car has to be re-registered, and more tax paid. For commercial vehicles, it is higher.

(R) This tax is supposed to be based on the ex-factory manufacturing cost, plus excise duty, sales tax/VAT.

(S) Manufacturers are, however, charging buyers on the basis of ex-showroom cost, which is higher.

(*a*) RPQS   (*b*) RSQP

(*c*) PQRS   (*d*) PSRQ

34. Terming the Supreme Court's judgment rejecting the plea for stopping construction work on the Narmada Dam as "shocking", Narmada Bachao Andolan leader Medha Patkar on Tuesday vowed to continue her campaign against the "injustice" meted out to the people displaced due to the dam.

(P) "If this is the response by the system, we will have no alternative but to take it by the horns," she said adding, she wanted to show that NBA activists were undeterred by any "pressure."

(Q) The NBA leader, along with a number of activists, including writer Arundhati Roy , organised a sit-in before the Supreme Court to mark her protest against the decision.

(R) She also slammed some media organisations for being "puppets in the hands of industrialists" and publishing news reports "without verifying facts."

(S) She accused the Centre of "making a mockery of its role with regard to the rehabilitation of the project affected families, especially Adivasis.

(*a*) RPQS   (*b*) QSPR

(*c*) RQSP   (*d*) PRSQ

35. Big and small employers alike created some 2.1 million jobs in the US in the last year alone, averaging nearly 200,000 new jobs per month since December, according to the Department of Labour.

(P) At that kind of breakneck pace, the Bureau of Labour Statistics (BL(S) expects total employment across the country to grow by 13%, from 145.6 million jobs to 164.5 million, over the next 10 years.

(Q) Through a variety of sources—from labour

statistics to payroll executives—we've com-piled a list of 10 of the hottest industries for job growth in the years ahead.

(R) "Almost all the job growth is fromed small and mid-sized companies," says Allan Schweyer, president of the Human Capital Institute, an employment researcher group based in Washington, D.C.

(S) So where will those 18 million-plus new jobs be?

(*a*) PRSQ   (*b*) RSPQ
(*c*) SQRP   (*d*) PSQR

36. In fact, while the long-term gains in the labour market are spread out among a wide variety of fields—from restaurants to retailers, hospitals to accounting firms—some industries are simply heating up faster than others.

(P) That's because both the labour market and the labour force are changing, accor-ding to payroll, staffing and human resource executives.

(Q) By comparison, the number of 16- to 24-year-olds will grow by just 2.9%, while 35- to 44-year-olds are expected to decline.

(R) Take baby-boomers, for instance. While the U.S. population as a whole is expected to grow by over 23 million within the next

decade, the cohort aged 55 to 64 will increase by a third, or about 10.4 million people—more than any other age group.

(S) Over the next 10 years or so, gradual shifts in the makeup of the population—the single most important factor in determining the size and composition of the labor force, according to the BLS—will not only effect who's working, but also where and why.

(*a*) RPQS   (*b*) RSQP
(*c*) PQRS   (*d*) PSRQ

37. More jobs mean a higher demand for staffing firms, says Sperion's Rik Elliott.

(P) That's expected to make the employment services sector one of the economy's biggest job engines in the years ahead.

(Q) A greater need for placement agencies and temporary service firms—much of it coming from the expanding healthcare industry, which tends to hire more temporary and contract employees — is also fueling the surge in growth of online job sites.

(R) By 2014, the professional and business services industry will have added 4.5 million new jobs to the economy, with two-thirds stemming from a growing need to manage, maintain and service those jobs and others.

(S) According to Online Recruitment magazine, there are now more than 1,600 job sites operating in offices spread across North America—all looking for employment, recruitment, and placement specialists, along with administrators, managers and IT staff.

(*a*) RPQS   (*b*) QSPR
(*c*) RQSP   (*d*) PRSQ

38. At work or at home, we rely on an ever-expanding network of information technology.

(P) That's why the job sector devoted to making it all work is expected to grow by 40% within the next decade.

(Q) Within this broad employment sector, the jobs most in demand will be network systems and data communications analysts, and computer software engineers for both applications and systems software.

(R) "We're now seeing that second wave of growth," says SurePayroll's Alter.

(S) "Small businesses have a big need to use technology, but not necessarily the folks on their staff to handle that."

(*a*) PRSQ   (*b*) RSPQ

(*c*) SQRP   (*d*) PSQR

39. A friend of mine and her husband would fit well into the Double-Income-No-Kids category for now.

(P) My friend, Anita, is adamant that, in the first two years after their child is born, she will not work.

(Q) They have decided that they will have their first child sometime towards the end of next year (2007).

(R) But, not every couple stays a DINK forever. These two are a case in point.

(S) After that, she will not pursue a nine-to-five work schedule (for a few years at least) but will look out for assignments on a consul-tancy/ freelance basis.

(*a*) RPSQ   (*b*) RSPQ
(*c*) RQPS   (*d*) PSRQ

40. Bill Gates, co-founder and chairman of the world's largest software company, Microsoft Corporation, is also the world's richest man.

(P) His personal wealth has been estimated at $50 billion (Rs 225,000 crore).

(Q) Chairman Gates has always interesting things to say and we present some memorable Gatesian observations: "I wish I wasn't (the world's richest man). There's nothing good that comes out of that. You get more visibility as a result of it."

(R) Amazing for a man who does not have a college degree, having dropped out of Harvard to establish Microsoft.

(S) Interestingly, he has been ranked the world's second most influential management guru just behind the legendary Michael Porter and just ahead of our very own C.K. Prahalad.

(a) PRSQ   (b) RSPQ
(c) SQRP   (d) PSQR

41. The Board of Control for Cricket in India on Tuesday sought to gag players from speaking about Sourav Ganguly and the issue of player burnout by warning vice-captain Virender Sehwag from speaking on these subjects to the media.

(P) "Sehwag has been warned verbally from speaking to the media on the burnout and Ganguly issue.

(Q) If you have apprehensions of a burnout, take rest and do not give your opinion on Ganguly, Sehwag was bluntly told by the Board.

(R) Players cannot speak on Board policies and selection matters," Shah declared.

(S) Days after the dashing opener had said that Ganguly was "missed" by the team and that the issue

of player burnout had been taken up with the Board, he was verbally warned by BCCI secretary Niranjan Shah.

(a) RPQS   (b) QSPR
(c) RQSP   (d) PRSQ

42. Upset over the delay in the implementation of various schemes, the Standing Committee on Agriculture of Parliament at its two-day meeting which concluded last evening summoned the Union Finance Secretary, Expenditure, and the Secretary, Planning, to seek an explanation regarding the delay in the clearance of various schemes.

(P) The schemes relate to dry-land farming, insurance for farmers and their crops, the buffalo improvement programme and poultry.

(Q) Likewise, other schemes such as insurance for farmers and their crops are still stuck in the Planning Department.

(R) However, it has not moved beyond the office tables of babus in Delhi yet. Dry-land farming is an important scheme for several states which have meagre resources for irrigation.

(S) The dry-land farming scheme was announced in the Budget last year.

(*a*) RPQS   (*b*) RSQP
(*c*) PQRS   (*d*) PSRQ

43. Obviously, the summoning of the Finance Secretary, Expenditure, and the Secretary, Planning, was a path-breaking step taken by the Standing Committee, which normally calls the Secretary of Agriculture, Animal Husbandry and others concerned to ask about the implementation of various schemes.

(P) Sources said that both Secretaries were grilled at the meeting.

(Q) They were asked to explain the delay in the clearance of the schemes which were announced last year.

(R) Both the Secretary, Planning, and the Secretary, Expenditure, turned up at the meeting with their supporting staff. Even the Commerce Secretary was called.

(S) The sources said that though the allocation of funds was made in the Budget for various schemes, their implementation lin-gered on for years because of the indifferent attitude of the bureaucracy at the approval and clearance stages.

(*a*) RPSQ   (*b*) PQSR
(*c*) RQPS   (*d*) PSRQ

44. Punjab Chief Minister Amarinder Singh today declared that his party would fight the Assembly poll on the offensive mode while flaying the decision of SAD chief Parkash Singh Badal for boycotting the historic dedication ceremony of the Minar-e-Mutka on the occasion of the 301 years of the martyrdom of 40 Muktas (liberated ones).

(P) Addressing a mammoth shrandhanjali samaroh after the ceremony here today, the CM today asked the people of Punjab to seek an explanation from the former Chief Minister about the latter's absence on one of the most sacred occasions in Sikh history and accused him of adopting 'double standards' for claiming himself to be the protagonist of the Sikh Panth.

(Q) He also charged Mr Badal and the SGPC with embezzlement of Rs 50 crore released by the then Prime Minister Atal Bihari Vajpayee for the construction of Khalsa Heritage Complex at Sri Anandpur Sahib on the occasion of 300th anniversary of Khalsa Panth.

(R) Captain Singh said the Akalis had only spent Rs 43 crore while the balance Rs 7 crore was still un-accounted.

(S) He said that the total cost

of the project was Rs 221 crore and it was likely to be completed by April 2007.

(*a*) PRSQ   (*b*) PQRS
(*c*) SQRP   (*d*) PRQS

45. The statement of the Punjab Chief Minister, Capt Amarinder Singh, questioning the logic behind the CBI raids on the residences two top IAS officers in the Forest Hill case, has been dubbed as sitting in judgement on the orders of the Punjab and Haryana High Court.

(P) A PIL filed by advocate Ujjal Singh Sahni has also questioned the controversial clean-chit issued by the Chief Minister, Capt Amarinder Singh, to his blue-eyed bureaucrats.

(Q) A few days back, teams of the CBI had raided the residences of the officers in connection with the probe into the Forest Hill Golf and Country Club case.

(R) Mr Sahni has alleged that the CBI was dragging its feet in the matter and pointed out that the agency was given six months' period to complete the probe but had not been able to do so despite the passage of over one and a half years.

(S) The PIL also prays that directions be issued to the CBI to submit a status report on the progress made by it so far.

(*a*) RPSQ   (*b*) RSPQ
(*c*) RQPS   (*d*) PSRQ

46. A Dalit widow, her unmarried daughter and other members of family have been compelled to take shelter in an Army bunker for the past five months after their house was razed by unscrupulous persons on the Defence Drain, 3 km from Khem Karan.

(P) This is just peanuts of what normally happens to Dalit members of the border belt who were mercilessly beaten up to take possession of the land which they had been cultivating for the past four decades.

(Q) Majha Ex-Servicemen Human Rights Front president Col G.S. Sandhu (Retd), who produced the affected family before mediapersons here yesterday alleged that influential persons of the ruling Congress party were involved in the alleged crime .

(R) The civilians, who are not used to Army life are seen sweating profusely in the 'living bunker', which can't accommodate more than eight persons.

(S) He alleged Dalit widow Harbans Kaur, her unmarried daughter and son had to shift to the Army bunker when their three-room set and a cattle shed were razed.

(*a*) RPQS   (*b*) QSPR
(*c*) RQSP   (*d*) PRSQ

47. Two Canada-based NRIs Sanjiv Alhuwalia and Bharpur Singh, who are linked with their motherland though thousands of miles away from it and have been running a voluntary organisation, Helping Hands, came to the help of Rajeev Sharan and gave about Rs 1.50 lakh for his treatment.

(P) Rajeev Sharan, father of two sons, his father, who is bed ridden after he donated his kidney for him, his mother and wife are being given all kinds of help by Mr Alhuwalia and Dr Bharpur Singh.

(Q) A surgery was done on Rajeev Sharan in January 2006 and after getting postoperative care, he has started moving out.

(R) But it will take about a year before he can start his tailoring job again.

(S) After the money reached Sangeet Alhuwalia, brother of Sanjiv Alhuwalia, both Mr Alhuwalia and Mr Man Mohan Singh started making rounds of the PGI, Chandigarh, to get Rajeev

Sharan treated at the earliest.

(*a*) PRSQ   (*b*) RSPQ
(*c*) SQRP   (*d*) PSQR

48. Shiromani Akali Dal (Amritsar) president Simranjit Singh Mann is likely to head the panthic front being constituted by the splinter Akali groups.

(P) Mr Prem Singh Chandumajra of the Shiromani Akali Dal (Longowal) and Mr Ravi Inder Singh of the Shiromani Akali Dal (1920) are also likely to join the front.

(Q) Sources disclosed that while the SAD (A) was represented by Mr Mann, Mr Harjinder Jakhu and Mr Daljeet Singh Cheema, the AISAD was represented by Mr Jaswant Mann and Mr Gurtej Singh.

(R) The first meeting in this process was held at the residence of Mr Mann at Qilla Harnam Singh, Fatehgarh Sahib, today between Mr Mann and All-India Shiromani Akali Dal (AISAD) president Jaswant Singh Mann.

(S) It is learnt that the meeting discussed two possibilities —either merging all the splinter groups into the SAD(A) or constituting a new panthic front to be led by Mr Mann.

(*a*) RPQS   (*b*) QSPR
(*c*) RQSP   (*d*) PRSQ

49. Ms Kamaljit Kaur of Gidderbaha, a mental patient will be reunited with her family after eight years due to the efforts of the All-India Pingalwara Society.

(P) At present she is residing in Bunyan in Chennai where she landed after a mental disorder and is now cured fully.

(Q) During a chance visit to a programme of Bunyan, a Chennai-based NGO for destitute and mentally ill women, last week Dr Inderjit Kaur, chairperson, All-India Pingalwara Society, a home for destitute and old persons, volunteered to reunite her with her family.

(R) Dr Inderjit Kaur has informed the family of Kamaljit which has decided to go to Chennai to bring her home. According to details, Kamaljit by mistake had boarded a train to Chennai in an abnormal mental condition.

(S) There she was taken to Bunyan.

(a) RPQS   (b) RSQP

(c) PQRS   (d) PSRQ

50. The elections to the post of senior vice-president and vice-president of the Municipal Council Sirhind-Fatehgarh Sahib were held unanimously.

(P) Mr Ram Lubhaya Puri was elected senior vice-president and Mr Devinder Bhatt vice-president.

(Q) The name of Mr Puri was proposed, Mr Gulshan Rai Puri and the name of Mr Devinder Bhatt, proposed by Mr Sher Singh and all members supported them.

(R) All 18 members including Dr Harbans Lal, Chief Parliamentary Secretary attended the meeting.

(S) According to Mr Charanjit Singh, Executive Officer of the council the meeting was presided over by officiating SDM, Ms Hargunjeet Kaur and all 17 councillors and Dr Harbans Lal MLA attended the meeting.

(a) RPSQ   (b) RSPQ

(c) RQPS   (d) PSRQ

51. Development at the expense of social justice has far-reaching consequences.

(P) The Naxalite phenomenon is only one of them.

(Q) Medha Patkar has warned that a bigger movement, not confined to the Narmada ousters, is inevitable.

(R) In some tribal areas, the slogan already is: No displacement without prior rehabilitation.

(S) It is equitable as well as necessary that people ousted from a place to make room for a project are fully rehabilitated before they are disturbed.

(*a*) PQRS   (*b*) PRQS
(*c*) QPRS   (*d*) PQSR

52. Conventional wisdom in our country says that boys should weigh eight pounds at birth and girls seven and a half pounds.

(P) A helpful aunt may volunteer the information that lean children are a tradition in the family.

(Q) Another might say you cannot apply the same yardstick to children of hefty Sikh households as well as to wiry Kerala boatmen's families.

(R) If there is a wise grandmother at home, she would advise the young parents not to get too worried if the actual weight was less, by citing some old proverb to the effect that the children of the well-off grow not in the womb but the cradle.

(S) If a young woman fails to deliver to this specification, she has much explaining to do.

(*a*) QRPS   (*b*) QRSP
(*c*) QPRS   (*d*) RQSP

53. With the advance of technology, vast amounts of research data can now be conveniently stored and accessed at will and at a low cost.

(P) Each can be transformed through innovative use of technology.

(Q) The three pillars of education are lectures, laboratories and libraries.

(R) Any information can be made available for reference on one CD ROM or free on demand through the internet.

(S) Face to face lectures can be replaced in some cases by distance learning tools such as transmitting live video of lectures using multimedia computers and digital transmission using high bandwidth data networks.

(*a*) RPQS   (*b*) RQPS
(*c*) RPSQ   (*d*) RQSP

54. But while the severe heat has made life miserable for middle-class Indians, it is the poor and the homeless who are as usual having to bear the burnt of nature's fury.

(P) It is not harsh weather alone that has contributed to the death toll but poverty that stands in the way of millions in this country from finding shelter from the heat and food and water to tide over dehydration.

(Q) Construction workers, agricultural labourers and rickshaw pullers are having to continue working in the searing heat to earn their daily wages.

(R) Most of the casualties of the heat wave are from Uttar Pradesh and Orissa and almost all those who died are from the under-privileged sections of society.

(S) Many of those who died were homeless.

(a) SRPQ   (b) SRQP
(c) SPRQ   (d) SQRP

55. Young women raising families these days are not necessarily whole-time mothers. They go to work in offices and they do not want to be on maternity leave longer than absolutely necessary.

(P) Many reasons compel them to wean their babies at the earliest.

(Q) They are sensitive about smelling milky in their workplace and are keen to regain their svelte figure.

(R) The milk tin becomes the surrogate mother. All over the world a powerful baby food industry has grown up.

(S) So the responsibility for feeding the baby gets transferred from breast to bottle.

(a) PQRS   (b) PRQS
(c) QPRS   (d) PQSR

56. The Memorandum of Understanding (MoU) inked between Indian Space Research Organisation (ISRO) chief G. Madhavan Nair and National Aeronautics and Space Administration (NASA) administrator Michael Griffin in Bangalore on Tuesday spells a new phase in the Indian space programme.

(P) The spacecraft will also carry three scientific instruments from the European Space Agency (ESA) and one from the Bulgarian Space Laboratory, besides five Indian instruments.

(Q) Chandrayaan-1, an unmanned maiden Indian mission to the moon, will carry two NASA payloads which will look for minerals and ice on the lunar surface.

(R) The prestigious moon mission is set to be launched in 2008 and will map the lunar surface using an array of sensors.

(S) What is significant is that the US instruments were selected on the basis of merit from nearly 16 international proposals ISRO received.

(a) QRSP   (b) QRPS
(c) QPRS   (d) RQSP

57. The petroleum ministry on Wednesday made out a strong case for increasing the fuel prices by up to Rs 10.43 a litre in petrol and Rs 114.45 per cylinder of cooking gas to save oil companies from a massive financial loss with the Left parties opposing the move.

(P) They instead suggested cut in duties and CNG pricing policy to mitigate the surging international oil prices.

(Q) The oil ministry said without the price hike, oil companies would suffer a revenue loss of Rs 73,512 crore (Rs 735.12 billion) in 2006-07 fiscal.

(R) In a presentation to Left leaders including Sitaram Yechury of CPM and Gurudas Dasgupta, the oil ministry said prices of petrol need to raised by Rs 9.33 per litre, diesel by Rs 10.43 per litre, kerosene by Rs 17.16 per litre and LPG by Rs 114.45 per cylinder if prices are to be brought in parity with imported costs.

(S) Sources said Left leaders wanted customs duty to be halved and a specific excise duty levied on products

(a) PQRS   (b) PRQS
(c) QPRS   (d) PQSR

58. Sachin Tendulkar, who is currently recovering from a shoulder injury, had a light batting session with a cricket ball at the Mumbai Cricket Association Ground at the Bandra Kurla Complex in Mumbai on Wednesday.

(P) On Tuesday, he had a light workout with coach Greg Chappell and physio John Gloster.

(Q) Meanwhile, Team India's bio-mechanist Ian Frazer watched closely as the master batsmen played at the deliveries.

(R) Tendulkar batted for around 25 minutes and hit deliveries thrown to him by trainer Gregory King.

(S) This was Tendulkar's second day of practice since undergoing shoulder surgery in March.

(a) RPQS   (b) RQPS
(c) RPSQ   (d) RQSP

59. Irfan Pathan on Wednesday said if he had reached the top of all-rounders' rankings it was because he never bothered to be there.

(P) "I am the number three all-rounder in the world now.

(Q) So, I am going to continue that way, I don't want to think about the rankings."

(R) If it has happened, it's because I never thought about it," the Indian pace spearhead said.

(S) "I don't believe in rankings and that has helped me perform well.

(a) SRPQ   (b) SRQP
(c) SPRQ   (d) SQRP

60. Early in her reign, Tamil Nadu Chief Minister J Jayalalithaa sacked almost 200,000 state government employees at one go.

(P) Added to that was her attempt to shift a Christian college in Chennai to make space for a government office.

(Q) They were later reinstated but their public humiliation was not forgotten.

(R) Tamil Nadu's Anti-Conversion Act, which targeted Christian evangelists and missionaries, was later repealed.

(S) But the Christians never forgave Jayalalithaa.

(*a*) QRSP   (*b*) QRPS
(*c*) QPRS   (*d*) RQSP

61. Seven batsmen and four bowlers. For a long time, that has been India's most successful combination in One-dayers, with Rahul Dravid reluctantly doubling up as wicket-keeper.

(P) The formula allowed India to bat deep, hope to chase any total and generally cover up for its (till then) toothless and bland attack.

(Q) Sourav Ganguly attained a reputation, if not immorta-lity, by sticking to it through lots of thick and thin.

(R) The basic problem, though, was Dravid's long face during that phase.

(S) He didn't like standing behind the stumps and he believed, quite rightly too, that he had mastered the art of keeping the score card happy and busy; he was anyway not a natural 'keeper and that meant there was always a catch or two dropping by to everybody's chagrin.

(*a*) PQRS   (*b*) PRQS
(*c*) QPRS   (*d*) PQSR

62. Seventeen years ago, in the dust and din of Karachi, Sachin Tendulkar took his first, tentative steps into the world of international cricket.

(P) He doesn't know himself. He is not fit for the One-day series in West Indies next month; he is, however, very keen to make it for the subsequent Test matches.

(Q) Tomorrow, at the crack of dawn or a little earlier, he will turn 33 and gingerly enter the final stretch of his amazing career; rather ironically, at this point too, he is surrounded by similar questions and doubts.

(R) Has the future overtaken him? Will tomorrow ever be as explosive or sublime as yesterday?

(S) He was barely 16 then, and like any gawky teenager, was full of questions and a few doubts.

(*a*) SRQP (*b*) SRPQ
(*c*) SPRQ (*d*) SQRP

63. Pretty soon, Greg Chappell will complete a year at the helm of the Indian cricket team.

(P) True, he hasn't transformed India into a champion side yet; but he has at least ingrained the ethos of a winner in some of the players.

(Q) Somewhere along the way, he might just allow himself a wry smile.

(R) When he goes home, to take a much-needed break from all this hype and hoopla, he will surely sit back and reflect over all the long days and short nights spent here.

(S) The tougher part, though, is going to begin now.

(*a*) RPQS (*b*) RQPS
(*c*) RPSQ (*d*) RQSP

64. Harbhajan Singh had a crucial role to play in the impressive performances of Monty Panesar in his debut series against India, the England left-arm spinner said.

(P) The first Sikh to play cricket for England, Panesar now hopes to improve his skills by watching another maestro, Muttiah Muralitharan in action.

(Q) Players like that have the added variation but they also have great experience of how to bowl to different batsmen, how to adjust field settings and how to adjust different game-plans," Panesar said on the eve of the first Test against the visiting Sri Lankans at Lord's.

(R) "He is a bowler I really admire because he has so many variations and always keeps the batsman guessing," Panesar, selected for the Test as first choice spinner Ashley Giles was ruled out due to injury, said.

(S) "I got a chance to talk to him (Harbhajan) and watched how he bowled.

(*a*) SRQP (*b*) SRPQ
(*c*) SPRQ (*d*) SQRP

65. From viewing human rights as a political tool by the West to rap countries on the knuckles, India now finds itself in a position of power and authority as it was chosen with perhaps the most votes onto the UN's first Human Rights Council.

(P) India's election by a massive 173 votes to the UN's first Human Rights council was a victory for its position, that human rights cannot be a tool used by the West against the developing world.

(Q) Now Delhi gets to work on a whole new set of rules as part of sweeping UN reform.

(R) The council replaces a

commission where India shared some bitter moments in 1994 when Benazir Bhutto publicly berated it over Kashmir.

(S) "It underscores India's position, role and commitment. For this Human Rights council India will try to play a major role in ensuring that human rights of all people are upheld in all societies," said Anand Sharma, Minister of State External Affairs.

(a) PQRS   (b) PRQS
(c) QPRS   (d) PQSR

66. The Delhi High Court has restrained private schools from conducting interviews of both children and their parents as part of the admissions procedure for nursery classes.

(P) Though the court has asked schools to suggest alternate methods for screening students, it has made its stand fairly clear.

(Q) The order also bars private schools aided by the government from conducting such interviews without the permission of the court.

(R) A Division Bench of acting Chief Justice Vijender Jain and Justice S N Aggarwal gave four weeks to the managements of private schools to end the practice of interviewing parents and children at the time of admissions.

(S) Even though the court order comes at a time when admissions are not on, it's an important victory for parents.

(a) QRSP   (b) QRPS
(c) QPRS   (d) RQSP

67. The Election Commission has said that HRD Minister Arjun Singh violated the code of conduct for his proposal on increasing reservation for OBCs in centrally-funded institutions.

(P) Singh's remarks to the media on reservation on April 5 in the midst of elections in five states had sparked a countrywide debate on the issue.

(Q) In a five-page ruling, the EC said, "In upholding of the model code of conduct, the party and persons in power have.....higher responsibility and they are expected not only to uphold it but should also be perceived to be so doing."

(R) "In the instant case, the Commission has come to the sad conclusion that they cannot be perceived to have done so," it added.

(S) However, it refrained from passing any adverse comment on the minister due to lack of conclusive proof.

(*a*) QRSP   (*b*) QRPS
(*c*) QPRS   (*d*) RQSP

68. The Mandal Commission was officially called Second backward Classes Commission. It derives its name from parliamentarian BP Mandal, who chaired the Commission.

(P) The Mandal Commission was constituted by the Morarji Desai government in 1978 to consider action politics for backward classes, aimed at redressing caste discrimination.

(Q) The Commission Report was submitted in Dec 1980.

(R) It sought reservation for 27 per cent of all services and public sector undertakings under the central government and 27 per cent of all admissions to institutions of higher education for Other Backward Classes (OBCs).

(S) The percentage was over and above the existing 22.5 per cent reservation for SCs/STs.

(*a*) SRQP   (*b*) SRPQ
(*c*) SPRQ   (*d*) SQRP

69. As the reservation debate rages, the Maharashtra Government has made its first move by extending reservations to all professional colleges in the state.

(P) Now the Maharashtra Cabinet has approved reservation of 50 per cent seats in all unaided professional colleges as well.

(Q) Earlier, reservations for SC, ST and OBC candidates were restricted to government and state-aided colleges only.

(R) "Everyone in the Cabinet was of the opinion that the current facility of reservation given to OBCs should not be taken away from them," said Maharashtra Deputy Chief Minister R R Patil.

(S) The state government will now present the proposal to Governor SM Krishna as an ordinance to make it a law.

(*a*) PQRS   (*b*) PRQS
(*c*) QPRS   (*d*) PQSR

70. After targeting bigger towns, the deadline police have now struck Pune.

(P) The pubs were abuzz a few weeks back, growing livelier with the night. The pub owners say the timing is not a factor and that they are being harassed for bribes.

(Q) In the metros, the police argument for closing down pubs early is safety and crime control.

(R) "We have to follow the norms. We found that these hotels were running sometimes till 3 in the morning. We had to take this action," said DCP (Crime) Chandrakant Daithankar.

(S) In just two days, the Pune police cancelled licenses of eight lounges and bars for a fortnight because they were operating beyond the 12.30 deadline.

(a) SRQP   (b) SRPQ

(c) SPRQ   (d) SQRP

71. The Patna University teachers, who struck work for four months in 2000, want to compensate the academic loss now, six years after their agitation.

(P) But what is the point in compensating the loss six years after the strike, when the affected students have already passed out?

(Q) They have decided to engage classes during the summer vacation, scheduled from May 27 to June 29, to offset the loss of 70 days during their strike.

(R) Confirming this, Vice-Chancellor Dr. S. Ehteshamuddin told Deccan Herald on Sunday that the Patna University Teachers' Association (PUTA) had taken a decision to this effect and the PU officials had agreed to the proposal.

(S) The PUTA offer follows the state government's decision regarding the payment of arrears salary to the teachers for the strike period after adjusting their earned leave, or the leave which they were supposed to earn in future.

(a) QRSP   (b) QRPS

(c) QPRS   (d) RQSP

72. The new pact is another sign of the increasingly close ties that have been developing between India and the US, set in motion during the visit of US President George Bush to India in March, when the civilian nuclear deal between the two countries was signed.

(P) The US and several other western nations imposed sanctions on ISRO, after India's nuclear tests in 1998.

(Q) This delayed many ISRO programmes including the launch of the GSLV.

(R) It is a major feather on the cap of ISRO and recognition of its growing reputation in the field of space research and ventures.

(S) What is also significant is Dr Griffin's apology for the past years of sanctions and offer of his "good offices" to lift sanctions still being imposed on some Indian space units.

(a) RPQS   (b) RQPS

(c) RPSQ   (d) RQSP

73. Summer has only just begun but soaring temperatures across North India have already claimed the lives of about 34 people.

(P) The temperature in Amritsar was 45 degrees centigrade, 7 degrees above normal and even a hill station like Shimla, where people flock to escape the heat and sweat of the plains, is sizzling this summer at 29 degrees, 7 degrees above normal.

(Q) Delhi experienced a maximum temperature of 44.4 degrees centigrade on Monday, prompting authorities to call on schools to close a week early for summer vacation because of the blistering heat.

(R) Temperatures are far higher than what is normal for this time of the year.

(S) The Met department's forecast promises no respite for another few days.

(a) SRPQ   (b) SPQR
(c) SPRQ   (d) SQRP

74. President Bush is in a very tough dilemma.

(P) Getting the UN to impose sanctions against Iran may be a softer substitute acceptable to him for the present but there are obstacles on that route too.

(Q) If he does not, he loses whatever face he has still left.

(R) If he goes to war with Iran, as he wants to, he will land himself in a mess bigger than the one he created in Iraq.

(S) The draft resolution tabled at the Security Council by France and Britain, who are acting as surrogates to US, did not mention sanctions immediately but reserved that kind of punishment within the scope of "further measures".

(a) RPQS   (b) RQPS
(c) RPSQ   (d) RQSP

75. It was a fine Sunday afternoon. We had been to a restaurant to take a break away from the monotonous daily chores of life. It was a rare occasion - all the members of the family, from 'six' to 'sixty' sitting together for the much advertised 'classic lunch' in a 'classic hotel'.

(P) Thirty minutes had gone by since our orders were placed and we were still waiting.

(Q) Looking at these men in action, my mother-in-law, a woman of few words, heaved a big sigh and said, "Perhaps it is we who are the Waiters!" What a statement!

(R) Men in white uniforms kept bustling from one table to another.

(S) Everyone recognised the words of wisdom that came from our beloved senior citizen. The casual remark of my mother-in-law made me think. Yes, we are waiters in every phase of life, in one-way or the other.

(*a*) PQRS   (*b*) PRQS
(*c*) QPRS   (*d*) PQSR

76. Student-teacher interactions can be facilitated through internet chat rooms.

(P) Thus, every district can have a micro branch of an institution, permitting local students to attend and participate in classroom activities outside the main campus.

(Q) This can be a low-cost equivalent for those who do not have the space, people or materials needed to maintain a real laboratory.

(R) Virtual labs can be created through the use of computer simulation.

(S) These chat rooms will soon provide voice and video capabilities rather than just text.

(*a*) SRQP   (*b*) SRPQ
(*c*) SPRQ   (*d*) SQRP

77. It was a glamorous evening in one of Delhi's most exclusive venues. As the music played, the rich and fashionable gossiped and waiters moved through the crowd with silver trays of drinks and canapes.

(P) After the presentation, I asked Mr Khosla what kind of people he hoped would buy the bone china, platinum-stemmed wine glasses and other luxury catalogue items.

(Q) Standing in a cascade of glitter, he launched his latest venture, Elvy - described as India's first lifestyle catalogue.

(R) Before dinner was served, the main lights dimmed and the master of ceremonies announced the star of the show, businessman Lovy Khosla.

(S) "Aspiring Indians", he said, "the new emerging middle class". He admitted the divide at the moment between rich and poor was huge - but eventually, he said, everyone in India would prosper.

(*a*) RPQS   (*b*) RQPS
(*c*) RPSQ   (*d*) RQSP

78. Back in 1991, we took the Kowloon Canton Railway to cross-over to Shenzhen, China.

(P) The series of hi-tech factories were producing all manner of goods from footwear to fashion clothes for the world.

(Q) We could well have been on the tube in London. The train smoothly cut through New Territories, and breezed into Hong Kong's last station, Lo Wu.

(R) The train ride came as a pleasant surprise. It was spotlessly clean with not too many passengers.

(S) After Custom clearance at Shenzhen, we stopped at McDonald's to grab a burger and a coke, before we went to the Special Economic Zone (SEZ), to check out production sourcing possibilities.

(a) RPQS (b) RQPS
(c) RPSQ (d) RQSP

79. An interesting outcome of this economic prosperity is the workers' choice in jobs.

(P) To avoid a crisis in labour supply, factories have upped salary packages throwing in liberal money, holidays, and a gamut of freebies for workers and family.

(Q) Jobs are moving away from manufacturing to the service sector.

(R) Even though factory wages currently average $ 100 pm, the service sector pays more.

(S) Youngsters have been quick to take to the convenience and glamour of working in malls, cinema halls, fashion clothing stories, and restaurants.

(a) QRSP (b) QRPS
(c) QPRS (d) RQSP

80. Although Indians like to place Mahatma Gandhi, unapproachably, on a high moral pedestal, Nehru is still with us, not least, as Ramchandra Guha points out in his essay, "An Indian Fall" in Prospect of December 2005, because of the dynasty he left behind.

(P) However, we may remember that on Motilal's persuasion, Nehru became Mahatma Gandhi's presidential anointee at the Lahore Congress.

(Q) Thus, Nehru was certainly complicit in founding the myth of the "first and only family" which later helped Indira become PM.

(R) He himself appointed Indira president of the Congress Party during his tenure and sent Vijayalakshmi Pandit to lead the Indian delegation to the United Nations.

(S) In Guha's reading, this happened despite Nehru, and since his epigone have in fact worked to undo the democratic institutions established by him, the "dynasty" should more rightly be named after Indira Gandhi and not Nehru-Gandhi.

(a) SRQP (b) SRPQ
(c) SPRQ (d) SQRP

81. When a baby is born, the first question asked is "Is it a boy or a girl?" And the second is "What is the weight?" The sociologist M.N. Srinivas used to be so exasperated by this obsession with birth weight that he would say: "They don't ask whether the child is well made and healthy and bright. They only want to know how much it weighs, as if it is a lump of mutton and not a human being."

(P) They are subjected to a good deal of cheek-squeezing and bum-patting.

(Q) Chubby children are much admired.

(R) The ultimate in accolade is to say that he or she looks like a young Sumo wrestler.

(S) If a bonny and a bony child are next to each other you can guess who will be picked up more often.

(a) PQRS   (b) PRQS
(c) QPRS   (d) PQSR

82. Americans make wonderful friends. They are engaging, curious, adventurous, inventive, creative and much more.

(P) They are always looking at their watches and thinking of the next appointment.

(Q) Decision on momentous events are taken without deep reflection.

(R) The pace and pressure of working is chronically hectic.

(S) They love to be loved, and are surprised when they are not.

(a) RPQS   (b) RQPS
(c) RPSQ   (d) RQSP

83. Great powers have to learn the virtues and uses of restraint. Keeping their cool. Not being trigger happy.

(P) He died last year aged 101. Lived and worked in Princeton.

(Q) Barbara Tuchman is always worth reading on Vietnam.

(R) Senator Fulbright wrote a book called The Arrogance of Power. It is a good read.

(S) But let me quote George F. Kennan, perhaps the greatest foreign policy pundit the American foreign service has produced.

(a) QRSP   (b) QRPS
(c) QPRS   (d) RQSP

84. It is true that the situation in Nepal would not have come to such a pass if the King had listened to New Delhi which had tried its best to persuade him to give up power.

(P) After all, he finally yielded to India's pressure.

(Q) The Nepalese, who put their eggs in the Indian basket, are disillusioned.

(R) This is the reason why New Delhi has not emerged unscathed and has been seen to be on the side of the King.

(S) But it is also true that the

King would have bowed out if New Delhi had been firm earlier.

(*a*) SRQP   (*b*) SRPQ
(*c*) SPRQ   (*d*) SQRP

85. How the Alliance brings the Maoists into the mainstream of democracy, is now the real challenge before Nepal.

(P) Both the Alliance and the Maoists have been on the opposite sides except when they were jointly fighting against the King.

(Q) Although the Maoists have rejected parliamentary democracy, people still believe that a rapprochement would come about because a Constituent Assembly is being convened.

(R) People want both of them to join hands to establish a democratic polity.

(S) In fact, the Maoists raised the red flag in 1999, only after they felt that the Alliance's peaceful, parliamentary way would not bring about a socialist revolution.

(*a*) RPQS   (*b*) RQPS
(*c*) RPSQ   (*d*) RQSP

86. The strife-ridden battleground of Indian politics has entered a phase of curious and paradoxical stalemate: the government is ceding space but there is no one to occupy it. In a sense, the government is losing the battle with itself. There is no one else to lose it against.

(P) But sequence must not overlap with consequence.

(Q) This fits in with a standard operating law of Indian politics: no one wins an election but someone loses it.

(R) We are still in the sequence stage.

(S) A wit might add that power is such a con that it takes no time at all to attach itself to sequence.

(*a*) QRSP   (*b*) QRPS
(*c*) QPRS   (*d*) RQSP

87. Dr Manmohan Singh, the most successful bureaucrat in history, has found the perfect solution to this problem.

(P) It is axiomatic that nothing gets done. But that, presumably, is the point.

(Q) Tell him about any problem, from Kashmir to a shortage of knitting needles, and a committee is born out of the conversation.

(R) He has converted governance into hundreds of committees.

(S) The point of existence is survival, not service.

(*a*) RPQS   (*b*) RQPS
(*c*) RPSQ   (*d*) RQSP

88. The temptations of Delhi are magnetic. Let me leave those who prefer Delhi to India with a sobering thought.

(P) The British announced the change of their capital from Calcutta to Delhi in 1911, but effectively moved in 1931.

(Q) Shahjehan moved halfway through his reign; and his heir, Aurangzeb could barely hold what he had inherited, as he himself realised on his deathbed.

(R) The Mughal empire never really survived the shift from Agra to Delhi.

(S) Does the Mughal empire seem too remote?

(*a*) RPQS   (*b*) RQPS
(*c*) RPSQ   (*d*) RQSP

89. There is something about Union home minister Shivraj Patil that makes it appear that each time he speaks, the words are being dragged out of him.

(P) Unfortunately, the attitude plays on the officials as well, with the government machinery under the home minister now appearing uncertain as to whether it should be "seized" of the situation, or whether it should follow the natty Mr Patil's lead in insinuating that there is actually no situation at all to be seized about.

(Q) His is an amazingly successful impersonation of the reluctant maiden, which would have been fine had

he not been the home minister of India.

(R) No one can fault Mr Patil on his appearance, with every crease and strand of hair in place.

(S) But the "there is nothing wrong, and if there is, it is being taken care of" attitude does not inspire confidence, particularly as he manages to completely play down the importance of the situation in the process, and reduces government reaction to a non-assertive response.

(*a*) QRPS   (*b*) QRSP
(*c*) QPRS   (*d*) RQSP

90. Pramod Mahajan is dead, and while one is sorry about the manner in which he died, it is somehow difficult to understand the completely hysterical media reaction.

(P) A weeping media — he was a good source — virtually canonised the BJP leader and imbued in him many a virtue that was not very visible when he was alive.

(Q) Pramod was a dashing personality, but an ordinary leader who had won only one election out of the three or four he had contested, useful for sections of the BJP, a good fund-raiser, with contacts in the corporate world.

(R) The media hysteria does raise one question — if this was the coverage Pramod Mahajan got, 20 of the 24 hours on television channels, 20 of the 30 pages in newspapers (or some such figures), then what would we have done if Gandhi had been killed today?

(S) Surely, not much more space would have been made available for him that has been made available for this very ordinary MP, whose contribution to the party might be worth a mention, but whose contribution to the nation remains under a big question mark that even the frenzied media response has not been able to turn into a halo.

(a) SRQP   (b) SRPQ

(c) PQRS   (d) SQRP

91. We have a serious security problem, both internal and external, and sadly, we fail to realise the gravity of the situation.

(P) We can give sermons and lectures on the militants' goal of creating communal disturbances and disrupting the peace process, but can all this divert us from the reality that 35 innocent villagers were butchered by militants in Jammu and Kashmir.

(Q) So the massacre at Doda was clearly meant as a message for the government.

(R) The J&K chief minister, Ghulam Nabi Azad, won a "spectacular" victory a few days ago, and he comes from Doda.

(S) We all know that the J&K peace talks will continue.

(a) PQRS   (b) PRQS

(c) QPRS   (d) PQSR

92. We have another tragic loss of life: this time in Afghanistan, as the Taliban abduct and murder an Indian citizen.

(P) We will ofcourse not be intimidated by this act of murder.

(Q) The sheer brutality of the act indicates their desperation.

(R) But we must also realise that we have 2,000 Indians working in Afghanistan, and their security has to be guaranteed by the host government.

(S) I do not know what security forces the Afghan government has in place, but we should seriously consider sending in more of our security contingents for the safety of our citizens.

(a) QRSP   (b) QRPS

(c) QPRS   (d) RQSP

93. The state Assembly elections will come to an "end" within the next few days and all eyes will be on Tamil Nadu and J. Jayalalithaa, but for me the situation to watch is the hectic horse trading (political trading) going on in Assam before the votes are counted.

(P) It is obvious that the Congress Party is not reflecting the "confidence" of the opinion polls.

(Q) The security issue cannot be compromised by striking deals and negotiating with rogue elements, and it would be a disaster to deal with militant minority groups.

(R) I think it is time for all the parties (Congress, BJP, Left, AG(P) to consider in what direction we are heading, as I genuinely think that the state will spin out of control, and we will need a protracted period of President's Rule to preserve national security and interests.

(S) I rate this area today as our weakest link with the maximum potential for violence

(a) PQRS   (b) PRQS
(c) QPRS   (d) PQSR

94. The economy continues to do well and the stock market defies all predictions as it continues to soar to new heights.

(P) Clearly, the gap between the haves and the have-nots is increasing, as for electoral gains, political parties concentrate on religion, class and minority appeasement, instead of development and economic growth.

(Q) We have oil prices beyond $75, and this means very high inflation for us and increased cost of money and interest rates and all these factors cannot be wished away.

(R) The situation in Iran is far from happy.

(S) All this may not impact our immediate GDP projections, but something to me looks very wrong, as there is a complete imbalance between the evolving political situation which is full of caste and class conflicts, and the economic situation where the upper and the middle classes prosper and make windfall profits.

(a) QRSP   (b) QRPS
(c) QPRS   (d) RQSP

95. They never practise what they preach is perhaps the most appropriate way of describing the majority of our political parties and politicians.

(P) They can go to any extent to ensure popular support.

(Q) At least this is certainly the

public perception.

(R) But no one should grudge this, so long as national and community interests are not compromised.

(S) Indians have experienced exploitation on the basis of religion and caste for short-sighted political gains.

(*a*) QRSP   (*b*) QRPS

(*c*) QPRS   (*d*) RQSP

96. No one would have any reservation about initiatives that help the cause of education, particularly in providing equality of opportunity to the weaker sections.

(P) No one, however, should be allowed to exploit these for political purposes.

(Q) The much-hyped Common Minimum Programme, CMP, of the Central government is very clear in its intention to politicise the issue of minorities, particularly in education.

(R) These need not be taken on sectarian or religious considerations. Constitutional provisions made for the minorities have to be respected in letter and spirit.

(S) It all began with the minorities and their education and the much-publicised "detoxification" and "desaffronisation" campaign.

(*a*) RPQS   (*b*) RQPS

(*c*) RPSQ   (*d*) RQSP

97. The perils of pursuing religion- and caste-based politics can be understood only as a continuation to what happened to the country because of the inappropriate handling of communalism.

(P) No one can ignore it was the president of the Indian National Congress, Maulana Azad, who, while chairing the session in Nagpur in September 1923, declared: "I will give up Swaraj but not Hindu-Muslim unity, for if Swaraj is delayed it will be a loss for India, but if Hindu-Muslim unity is lost, it will be a loss for the whole mankind."

(Q) India must learn from its history, particularly its recent past.

(R) Can it be denied that Partition was a consequence of the communal divide created by politicians?

(S) Is it not a fact that political expediency outweighed national needs and the Indian leadership agreed to Partition instead of creating conditions of communal harmony even at the cost of a delayed independence?

(*a*) QRSP   (*b*) QRPS

(*c*) QPRS   (*d*) RQSP

98. There are instances of attempts to offer religion-based reservations in jobs and in institutions.

(P) They just cannot remain unconcerned

(Q) No party or person need ever compromise certain aspects, particularly respect to the Constitution and its spirit for political gains.

(R) Those who can think beyond the next election and party lines, have to take the initiative and let the country know the disastrous results of exploitation of religions.

(S) All such pranks serve no purpose and create a climate of distrust within society.

(*a*) SRQP   (*b*) SRPQ

(*c*) SPRQ   (*d*) SQRP

99. This is not the first time that the Gujarat government has gone back on its obligation to resettle those who have been ousted from their homes because of the Narmada dam.

(P) There are many awards and judgments on this point.

(Q) Medha Patkar case was that increasing the height by nearly 13 metres, from 110 metres to 122.9 metres, had been sanctioned despite the fact that the families.

(R) Gujarat has the responsibility of rehabilitating even those who Madhya Pradesh and Maharashtra, the two beneficiaries, cannot settle.

(S) As recently as March 5, 2005, the Supreme Court had said unequivocally that "submergence would not be allowed to take place until complete settlement and rehabilitation of oustees is done."

(*a*) RPQS   (*b*) RQPS

(*c*) RPSQ   (*d*) RQSP

100. Our son David was engaged in social work for the mentally challenged, finding some useful activity for each of his wards.

(P) His welfare organisation used to distribute milk to poor children of the locality.

(Q) The boy did it with assiduity and concentration. Another of David's patients had been given an even odder occupation.

(R) David had trained one of his wards to wave a newspaper over the cans of milk to keep the flies away.

(S) Their establishment had an antediluvian refrigerator whose thermostat was unserviceable and irreplaceable.

(*a*) PRQS   (*b*) RQSP

(*c*) QPSR   (*d*) QRSP

101. India's election to the United Nations Human Rights Council is an opportunity for the country to play a decisive and responsible role in the world body.

(P) India secured 173 votes - the largest - in a secret ballot to choose 13 members from Asia.

(Q) Other members elected from Asia include China, Japan and Pakistan.

(R) Discredited for failing to live up to its mandate of acting against some of the worst human rights violations, the Commission on Human Rights was wound up some months ago.

(S) The Human Rights Council replaces the controversial UN Commission on Human Rights.

(*a*) PQSR   (*b*) PRQS

(*c*) QPRS   (*d*) PQSR

102. There are lessons that the new council needs to learn from the experience of its predecessor.

(P) The Human Rights Commission started off well.

(Q) It gave the world the 1948 Universal Declaration of Human Rights and a body of international laws that outlawed genocide, racism and torture.

(R) But politicisation of the body stood in the way of its performance in subsequent years, rendering it impotent and unable to deal with some of the worst crises.

(S) Critics of the new council

have pointed out that some of the worst violators of human rights are on board, making the body ineffective even before it can start work.

(*a*) RPQS   (*b*) RQPS

(*c*) RPSQ   (*d*) RQSP

103. The massive mandate India has received from the international community places it in a special position of responsibility.

(P) This is an opportunity for India to show the world that it is a responsible leader, dedicated to enhancing the welfare of the world community and not just committed to furthering its own power interests.

(Q) It should act, whether the violation is by a friend or a rival.

(R) India must ensure that it does not allow politics to determine whether it will speak up when rights are violated.

(S) Its term is for a year only; it must therefore discharge its responsibilities energetically.

(*a*) QRSP   (*b*) QRPS

(*c*) QPRS   (*d*) RQSP

104. The Securities and Exchange Board of India's (Sebi) decision to allow listed companies to privately place shares to qualified institutional buyers (QIBs) is an appropriate step which will increase the supply of shares in the domestic market and thereby enhance its depth.

(P) In recent years the corporate world has been seeing an increasing number of companies through issue of shares (GDRs, ADRs or convertible bonds).

(Q) Since share issues abroad can be made without many procedural needs, companies prefer this route.

(R) An issue in the domestic market calls for a number of approvals from regulators and it is a tedious process.

(S) Sebi's new move will now allow listed companies to privately place their shares without any regulatory filing and will save them the hassles of many time-consuming formalities.

(*a*) SRQP   (*b*) SRPQ
(*c*) PQRS   (*d*) SQRP

105. When more shares are issued to QIBs — who are financial institutions, mutual funds and foreign institutional investors, supply of shares will increase (subject to the reselling conditions), liquidity will improve and the market will be able to withstand price fluctuations better.

(P) Retail investors will also benefit because 10 per cent of the shares placed will have to be offered to mutual funds.

(Q) A vibrant capital market is needed for a growing economy like ours where there is a large need for capital for fuelling investments.

(R) In short, Sebi's decision will add more life to the share market and make it more vibrant.

(S) Creating a better investment environment is even more important now because this will make the Indian capital market wider with a larger investor base.

(*a*) RPQS   (*b*) RQPS
(*c*) RPSQ   (*d*) RQSP

106. The local newspapers are full of news about several crises afflicting the ruling Pakistan Muslim League.

(P) Yet despite the jumbo size of the Cabinet, far too many have remained dissatis

(Q) This King's party had forced President Pervez Musharraf to have the largest ever Cabinet that Pakistan has ever had as a result of an effort to make ministers of all those who led even small groups within the ruling party. fied.

(R) After all the size of a Cabinet has to be finite.

(S) There have recently been rather loud grumblings from a certain forward bloc among its dissident groups.

(*a*) PQRS   (*b*) PRQS

(c) QPRS   (d) PQSR

107. Unrest obtains for many reasons. The first is that they are all defectors either from Nawaz Sharif's PML faction or Benazir Bhutto's Pakistan Peoples Party. They expect to be rewarded for the switch, apart from the withdrawal or freezing of cases being proceeded against them by the National Accountability Bureau (NAB).

(P) Much is expected to happen in 2007. The ruling PML and its allies are conscious of their unpopularity.

(Q) Some call it a bit of blackmail. Secondly, they have been kept wondering about the future.

(R) Their survival is at stake. Why? because it depends on what kind of elections would there be?

(S) Should they be truly transparent and unmanaged, few of them can return; their chances of returning to power, through fair vote, are not high.

(a) QRSP   (b) QRPS
(c) QPRS   (d) RQSP

108. However, few take a deal with Nawaz and Benazir seriously. Nawaz is personally inflexible in opposing Musharraf all along the line no matter what term, he is offered.

(P) Most observers believe that no deal is likely simply because of Musharraf's own inflexibility and hubris.

(Q) Those terms do not exclude her becoming the PM.

(R) Benazir also requires conditions to be met before she would extend her cooperation.

(S) That her becoming the PM is a must, though Presidentship can be kept by Musharraf with appropriate assurances.

(a) RPQS   (b) RQPS
(c) RPSQ   (d) RQSP

109. The 12th Assembly polls in Assam resulted in a hung House, but the ruling Congress has emerged as the single largest party and seems set to retain power in the state.

(P) The Congress, which had won 70 of the total 126 seats in 2001, has scored just 52 this time.

(Q) The party, however, is almost sure to get the support of the Bodo People's Progressive Front-Hagrama (BPPF-H), which won in 12 constituencies in western Assam. The ruling party had a pre-poll understanding with the BPPF-H.

(R) "In Assam, no party could remain in power for two consecutive terms since 1972.

(S) But it is for our success in delivering good governance in the past five years that people have once again mandated us to rule the state for another term," Chief Minister told media persons.

   (*a*) RPSQ   (*b*) RQSP
   (*c*) PQRS   (*d*) SQPR

110. The plain fact is – and to invoke "plain fact" is of course itself a classic English intellectual trope – that Britain has one of the richest intellectual cultures in Europe today.

(P) There are probably more genuine, substantial, creative debates about ideas, policies and books – and reaching a wider public – in Britain than there are in France, the homeland of less intellectuals.

(Q) Nowhere else outside the US has such an array of thinktanks. Every month seems to bring a new literary festival.

(R) Britain has the best universities in Europe, and some British academics still manage to escape the ghastly, Soviet-style clutches of the government-imposed Research Assessment Exercise, for sufficient time to share their knowledge with a wider public.

(S) Britain has the BBC Radio to help them do that. There're commercial book publishers and first-rate intellectual journals.

   (*a*) QRSP   (*b*) QRPS
   (*c*) QPRS   (*d*) PQRS

111. As the date of my retirement approached I began to look forward to the long, lazy days ahead.

(P) "Resistance!" he exclaimed, "My wife calls out to me at ten every morning, 'It's time you got out of my way.

(Q) I've got to get things into order so you'd better be out of the house.' So here I am, exiled each morning to the welcoming arms of the RSI."

(R) I had asked one of these senior citizens whether his daily programme met with resistance from his wife.

(S) The RSI defence services club was full of old codgers who chatted happily to anyone they could buttonhole, from the time the bar opened till the abdhar announced, "Last orders, please".

   (*a*) SRPQ   (*b*) SRQP
   (*c*) SPRQ   (*d*) SQRP

112. By topping Union Public Service Commission's Civil-Services-Examination-2005, Mona Pruthi of Faridabad (Haryana) has done Indian women proud in our male-dominated society.

(P) Publication of such data will put an onus on political rulers to give justice to real talent rather than lobbying in placement of IAS officers.

(Q) The society where killing of females - foeticide and infanticide - is common even in so-called high society.

(R) Seven girls out of the top 20 IAS aspirants with first two positions going to girls suggest that girls are no less than boys in wisdom, and can do wonders if provided with an opportunity.

(S) To encourage future IAS aspirants and for knowledge of public, the union government should publish complete data about IAS officers who topped respective Civil-Services-Examinations till date in different years.

(a) QRPS   (b) QRSP

(c) QPRS   (d) RQSP

113. Once again there is news about the proposed Ring Roads - Satellite Town Ring Road and Intermediate Ring Road.

(P) Property owners around these roads will be happy expecting huge increase in price.

(Q) Contractors vie for big profits and not to speak of corruption as a bye product.

(R) This proposal will mean different things to different people. Those who lose their land will be sad and distressed.

(S) As usual, the innocent road users dream for a better transportation.

(a) RPQS   (b) RQPS

(c) RPSQ   (d) RQSP

114. In the Pramod-Pravin Mahajan episode, there is a lesson for all of us — that we should never let negative emotions like anger and jealousy get the better of us.

(P) At their height, they spell nothing but doom and render repentance impossible.

(Q) Only by keeping our cool and exercising restraint when it is needed most, can we spare ourselves a tragedy of such magnitude.

(R) Can we ever put back the clock and undo the damage done? These two destructive emotions leave such a shattering impact on our lives that nothing is ever the same again.

(S) These highly volatile emotions can turn our world upside down in an instant, and wreck relationships beyond repair.

(a) SRQP   (b) SRPQ

(*c*) SPRQ (*d*) SQRP

115. The proposal for the 4000 MW, coal based, super thermal power project at Tadadi (North Karnataka) makes neither any economic sense, nor any sense viewed from the environmental angle.

(P) The NTPC – Power Grid Corporation tie-up has already shown the almost perfect route to solving the supply side of the problem.

(Q) Between them, they are in a position to generate (in pit-head super thermal power stations along the Eastern coal belt) and supply as much power as you want in any corner of the country at the cheapest possible rates.

(R) All they want is that you arrange to pay them on time.

(S) But, because the KPTCL is not in a position to do that, and the government refuses to release it from its clutches to enable it to organise itself to do that, in pursuance of its cross-subsidy policy in the name of socialism, the government is having to come up with all these hare-brained schemes.

(*a*) RPQS (*b*) PQRS
(*c*) RPSQ (*d*) RQSP

116. Why does BJP get angry when Sonia renounces the opportunity to become Prime Minister?

(P) She instigated, they alleged, the attempt to have disqualified Rajya Sabha M.P. Jaya Bachchan on the 'office of profit' ground.

(Q) They were unhappy quite understandably, following her victory in the 1999 and 2004 elections.

(R) Or why do they sound frustrated and display a rage that is both amusing and pitiable when she resigns.

(S) They are miserable when she renounces – we can understand why – her Lok Sabha seat and all other positions held without batting an eyelid following the 'office of profit' controversy?

(*a*) QRSP (*b*) QRPS
(*c*) QPRS (*d*) RQSP

117. After the 1999 election victory, her confidence in taking on Vajpayee and Advani in the Parliament and her attack of the protagonist of Hindu revivalism, Murli Manohar Joshi, for his dangerous attempt to saffronise education must have rattled the BJP quite a bit.

(P) More recently, one had believed that Mr.Advani would quit both the posts he held — Leader of opposition and President of BJP following the insults and humiliation heaped on him by the Sangh parivar for his observations on Jinnah.

(Q) Instead, he tries desperately to recover his lost space within BJP by setting out an yet another Yatra. He even indicated about his Prime Ministerial ambition.

(R) She had also declared in Parliament addressing Murli Manohar Joshi that he was being put on notice that he could not substitute a national agenda with the hidden agenda of Hindu fundamentalist lessons in history textbooks.

(S) Vajpayee's repeated declaration that he had five decades of political struggle behind him drew rather sharp parliamentary retort from Sonia.

(a) SRPQ   (b) SRQP
(c) SPRQ   (d) SQRP

118. Judges are not mere 'service providers'. No mercenary interpretation of their high office will do any good to us

(P) The judges of the lower courts and of the tribunals would be called 'Sir', or by its equivalent in the regional language.

(Q) The Bar Council of India has resolved to bid good-bye to the colonial practice of addressing the judges of the superior courts as 'My Lord' or 'Your Lordship'. Instead,

they would be addressing them, 'Your Honour' or 'Honorable court'.

(R) A supposedly servile remnant of the British Raj is being done away with.

(S) The matter had been in the melting pot for quite sometime and the judges themselves had no opinion on the subject. They had left it to the BCI to decide.

(a) RPQS   (b) RQPS
(c) RPSQ   (d) RQSP

119. Variations in the temperature of hot water springs throw up more on earth's interiors and can even help in predicting earthquakes, writes V K Joshi.

(P) The earthquake though never kills anyone of its own, people die of house collapse or secondary disasters such as quake generated landslides.

(Q) And all the more fatal that it cannot be predicted.

(R) An earthquake is one of the most dreaded natural disasters.

(S) Most of the time humanity is taken by surprise.

(a) QRSP   (b) QRPS
(c) QPRS   (d) RQSP

120. As the name indicates geothermal water is hot water erupting as springs.

(P) It is established that temperature inside the earth

rises by about 1.50 to 20 Centigrade per kilometer.

(Q) Often geothermal water is the meteoric water that has been lying trapped in the interior of the earth since geological past.

(R) It is natural for a layman to ponder why underground water in some areas is heated!

(S) It is an indicator of the health of the earth's interior.

(a) SRQP   (b) SRPQ

(c) SPRQ   (d) SQRP

ANSWERS

1	2	3	4	5	6	7	8	9	10
(b)	(a)	(c)	(a)	(d)	(b)	(b)	(d)	(b)	(c)
11	12	13	14	15	16	17	18	19	20
(d)	(a)	(c)	(a)	(b)	(d)	(d)	(b)	(a)	(c)
21	22	23	24	25	26	27	28	29	30
(a)	(c)	(d)	(c)	(d)	(d)	(d)	(d)	(b)	(a)
31	32	33	34	35	36	37	38	39	40
(c)	(c)	(c)	(b)	(d)	(d)	(a)	(a)	(c)	(d)
41	42	43	44	45	46	47	48	49	50
(b)	(d)	(b)	(b)	(d)	(a)	(c)	(c)	(c)	(a)
51	52	53	54	55	56	57	58	59	60
(d)	(b)	(b)	(a)	(d)	(a)	(b)	(d)	(a)	(c)
61	62	63	64	65	66	67	68	69	70
(a)	(d)	(b)	(d)	(b)	(a)	(a)	(b)	(c)	(b)
71	72	73	74	75	76	77	78	79	80
(a)	(c)	(a)	(d)	(b)	(c)	(b)	(d)	(a)	(c)
81	82	83	84	85	86	87	88	89	90
(c)	(a)	(d)	(c)	(b)	(c)	(b)	(d)	(b)	(c)
91	92	93	94	95	96	97	98	99	100
(b)	(c)	(a)	(d)	(c)	(a)	(a)	(d)	(c)	(a)
101	102	103	104	105	106	107	108	109	110
(a)	(c)	(d)	(c)	(c)	(c)	(c)	(d)	(c)	(d)
111	112	113	114	115	116	117	118	119	120
(a)	(b)	(a)	(c)	(b)	(d)	(a)	(b)	(d)	(a)

YOUR SPACE

YOUR SPACE